ISBN 978-1-330-02629-8
PIBN 10007188

English
Français
Deutsche
Italiano
Español
Português

www.forgottenbooks.com

Mythology Photography **Fiction**
Fishing Christianity **Art** Cooking
Essays Buddhism Freemasonry
Medicine **Biology** Music **Ancient
Egypt** Evolution Carpentry Physics
Dance Geology **Mathematics** Fitness
Shakespeare **Folklore** Yoga Marketing
Confidence Immortality Biographies
Poetry **Psychology** Witchcraft
Electronics Chemistry History **Law**
Accounting **Philosophy** Anthropology
Alchemy Drama Quantum Mechanics
Atheism Sexual Health **Ancient History**
Entrepreneurship Languages Sport
Paleontology Needlework Islam
Metaphysics Investment Archaeology
Parenting Statistics Criminology
Motivational

961

INDIA AND ITS PROBLEMS

BY

WILLIAM SAMUEL LILLY

OF THE INNER TEMPLE, BARRISTER-AT-LAW
FORMERLY OF THE INDIAN CIVIL SERVICE
HONORARY FELLOW OF PETERHOUSE, CAMBRIDGE

LONDON
SANDS & CO.
12 BURLEIGH STREET, STRAND

SiR ALEXANDER JOHN ARBUTHNOT, K.C.S.I.

Dear Sir Alexander,

In dedicating this book to you, with your kind permission, I desire to acknowledge a great debt of gratitude, accumulated through many years. When I went out to India, you held the important office of Chief Secretary to the Government of Madras, and it was my good fortune to be brought by common friends under your direct notice. Your encouraging kindness greatly assisted me during my brief Indian career, and was especially manifested when I acted as Under Secretary to the Madras Government in the Departments of which you then had immediate charge as a Member of Council. Ill-health compelled me to leave a country in which I was absorbingly interested, and a service to which I was deeply attached. You remained to administer, for a time, the Government of Madras, and then to give the Empire the benefit of your extensive experience and sound statesmanship as a Member of the Viceregal Council. But while our paths in life thus diverged, our friendship continued unbroken and undimmed. My last obligation to it is for many most valuable suggestions with which your perusal, undertaken at my request, of the proof sheets of this book, has led you to favour me. Of course I do not claim the sanction of your high authority for any of the opinions expressed in it upon controverted topics. But I rejoice to know that you think it likely to promote my object in writing it : the diffusion of accurate knowledge regarding the country for which you have laboured so long and so faithfully.

I am,

DEAR SIR ALEXANDER,

Very truly yours,

W. S. LILLY.

ATHENÆUM CLUB,
November 1, 1901.

SUMMARY

PART I.—PHYSICAL CHARACTERISTICS

CHAPTER I

THE HIMĀLAYAS

	PAGE
Vastness and variety of India	3
Object of the present volume	5
Four separate and well-defined regions of India : the Himālayas, Hindustān, the Deccan, and Burmah . . .	5
The Himālayas, not a mere range of mountains, but a mountainous country	6
Comparison between the Himālayas and the Alps . .	7
Vegetable and animal products of the Himālayas . .	10
The Himālayas a rampart for the Indian Empire against invaders from Asia	11
And a vast reservoir for Hindustān	11
The three great rivers of Hindustān issue from them . .	11

CHAPTER II

HINDUSTĀN

	PAGE
By Hindustān is meant the country lying to the north of the Vindhyan range : the wide plains watered by the Himālayan rivers and the region round them . .	13
This country divided into five provinces, besides the recently created frontier province :—	
First, the Punjāb, the country of the five rivers : a vast alluvial plain, specially fertile in the Eastern portions . .	14
Second, Sind, for political purposes included in the Bombay Presidency : an almost rainless district. . .	14

Third, Rājputāna, the country of the Rājputs : fertile where   PAGE
watered by the drainage of the Vindhyan range, and
possessing much undeveloped mineral wealth .   .   14
Fourth, The North-West Provinces and Oudh, occupying
well-nigh the whole of the basins of the Ganges and
the Jumna : a vast expanse of monotonous verdure .   15
Fifth, Bengal, consisting chiefly of the two wide alluvial
valleys of the Ganges and the Brahmaputra .   .   15
Sixth, Assam, including the higher valleys of the Brahmaputra,
and those of the Bārak or Surmā, together with the
mountainous watershed intervening between those two
rivers   15
Products of Hindustān   15

CHAPTER III

THE DECCAN

By the Deccan is meant the triangular peninsula which has the
Vindhya Mountains as its base and Cape Comorin as its
apex.   18
But the Vindhya Mountains must not be dissociated from the
Aravalli range, the southern slopes of which are drained
by the Nerbudda, or from the Sātpur hills in which the
Tāpti rises   18
And as the tableland, constituting the Deccan, has the Vindhya
Mountains for its base, so is it supported on either side
by the Eastern and Western Ghāts, which give the key
to the configuration of the peninsula   .   .   .   19
Chief districts of this division of India :—
First, Central India, made up of the nine Political Agencies,
among which are included the dominions of Scindia
and Holkar, a territory for the most part fertile and
well wooded   20
Second, the country of the Guicowar : an open fertile tract .   21
Third : the Central Provinces, a country of highlands and
valleys, of plateaus and plains, only one-third of the
whole area of which is under cultivation   .   .   21
Fourth : the Nizam's country, considerably elevated, and
generally fertile   22
Fifth : the Bombay Presidency, divided by the Nerbudda into
two portions : the northern a low plain of alluvial
origin, the southern a level coast strip rising into
an upland country   22

Sixth : the Madras Presidency, watered by the Godavery, the
Kistna, and the Cauvery, and presenting three natural
divisions : the long and broad east coast, the shorter
and narrower west coast, and the central tableland
which, however, goes considerably beyond the limits
of Madras 22
Products of Southern India 23

CHAPTER IV

BURMAH

Burmah, a country of hills, forests, streams, and abundant rain-
fall : through its centre flows the Irawadi . . . 24
Four natural divisions of Burmah :—
First, the central valley : watered by the Irawadi and the
Chindwin 25
Second : the province of Arakan, divided from it by the Yoma
range, and running down to the Bay of Bengal :
watered by the Kuladan 25
Third : the mountainous country of the Shans, east of the
Irawadi, running up to the Chinese frontier : watered
by the Salween 26
Fourth : the province of Tenasserim, a long, isolated, southern
coast strip : watered by the Salween, the Attaran, and
the Tavoy 26
Products of Burmah 26
The Andaman and Nicobar Islands may be regarded as the
emerging summits of a submarine range of hills, linking
the Arakan Yoma to the central hill range of Sumatra . 27

PART II.—RACES, LANGUAGES, AND LITERATURE

CHAPTER V

RACES

The Aborigines of India, probably Kolarians . . . 31
Mongolian and Dravidian invaders 32
Aryan invaders, who drive the Mongolians into the Himālayas
and beyond the Ganges, and the Dravidians into the
Deccan 32
Scythian and Mohammedan invaders 33
Present racial constituents of the population of India . . 34

CHAPTER VI

LANGUAGES

	PAGE
Sanskrit nearest to the language of the ancient Aryans . .	36
The Prākrit dialects	37
The modern Aryan languages of India	38
The Dravidian languages	39
The Kolarian dialects	39
The Tibeto-Burman languages	39

CHAPTER VII

LITERATURE

The non-Aryan languages of India contain little of high literary value	41
And the modern Aryan tongues nothing	42
The only Indian literature of much real intrinsic merit, the Sanskrit	42
The Vedic Hymns	42
The *Brāhmanas*	44
The *Purānas*	44
The *Tantras*	45
The *Rāmāyana*	45
The *Mahābhārata*	45
The *Raghu-vansa* and the *Kumārasambhava* . . .	49
The Sanskrit drama	49
The *Upanishads*	49

PART III.—HISTORY

CHAPTER VIII

HINDU INDIA

Scantiness of the materials for a knowledge of Hindu India .	55
Historic value of the *Mahābhārata* (1426 B.C.), and the *Rāmāyana* (about 1000 B.C.)	56
And of the *Laws of Manu* (about 500 B.C.) . . .	57
India in the time of Sākya-Muni (about 550 B.C.) . .	57
Alexander's invasion (327 B.C.)	58
The account of Megasthenes (300 B.C.)	59
Asoka (260-223 B.C.)	59

PAGE

Kanishka (A.D. 10) 61
Buddhist India 61
The accounts of Fa Hian (400), Sung Yun (518), and Hiouen-
Tshang (639-645) 62
The disappearance of Buddhism from India . 64

CHAPTER IX

MOHAMMEDAN MASTERS

The thousand years of Buddhist supremacy in India, followed
by a thousand years of Mohammedan invasion and
conquest 65
First incursion of the Moslems into India (604) . . . 66
Arab invasion of Sind with a regular army under Mohammed
Kāsim (714). 66
His conquests and tragic fate 66
Mohammed of Ghazni's seventeen expeditions into India (1001-
1030) 68
The Somnath legend 69
Merits and defects of Mohammed of Ghazni . . . 70
Mohammed Ghorī (1157-1206) 73
Kūtab-ud-dīn (1206-1210) 73
Alā-ud-dīn (1295-1316) 74
Mohammed Tughlak (1325-1351) 74
Fīruz (1351-1388) 76
Tamerlane's invasion (1398) 76
Bāber, the sixth in descent from him, invades India in 1526,
and winning the first battle of Pānipat, founds the
Moghul Empire 77
The Hindu monarchies of the Deccan 77
In 1556 Akbar, Bāber's grandson, then aged thirteen, wins the
second battle of Pānipat over the Afghans, who had
dethroned his father Humāyon 79
And succeeds as Emperor next year upon Humāyon's death
(1556-1605) 79
The affair of Beiram 79
Akbar's victories, administration, and character . . . 81
Jehānghīr (1605-1627) 89
Shāh Jehān (1628-1658) 92
Aurungzebe (1658-1707) 93
The later Moghuls 96
The third Battle of Pānipat (1761), and the dissolution of the
Moghul Empire 97

CHAPTER X

THE ENGLISH CONQUEST

	PAGE
Difficulty of realising in how short a time the British Empire in India has grown up	98
The East India Company	99
The beginnings of Madras, Bombay, and Calcutta . .	100
Struggles with the Portuguese and Dutch in the seventeenth century	100
And with the French in the eighteenth century . . .	100
Clive (1751-1767)	101
Warren Hastings (1774-1785)	104
Lord Cornwallis (1786-1793)	105
Lord Wellesley (1798-1805)	106
Arthur Wellesley's work in India	106
Lord Hastings (1814-1823)	108
Lord William Bentinck (1828-1835)	109
Lord Auckland (1836-1842)	109
Lord Ellenborough (1842-1844)	109
Lord Hardinge (1844-1848)	109
Lord Dalhousie (1848-1856)	110
Lord Canning (1856-1862)	112
Lord Elgin (1862-1863)	114
Sir John Lawrence (1864-1869)	114
Lord Mayo (1869-1872)	114
Lord Northbrook (1872-1876)	114
Lord Lytton (1876-1880)	114
Lord Ripon (1880-1884)	114
Lord Dufferin (1884-1888)	115

PART IV.—RELIGIONS

CHAPTER XI

HINDUISM

	PAGE
Difficulty of accurately defining Hinduism . . .	119
The *Rig-Veda*, the work of transcendent authority on the beliefs and practices which constitute it	120
The Vedic religion the first phase of the polytheistic idea of the universe still dominating the minds of the great majority of the people of India	120

The gods of the *Vedas* personifications of physical forces and   PAGE
  phenomena : no mention in those books of the features
  of modern Hinduism most repugnant to the European
  mind.   121
The Vedic religion passes into Brahminism—how we have no
  means of determining—as its naturalism is metaphysically construed and sacerdotally developed in the
  Brāhmanas.   121
In *caste* we have the explanation of this second phase of the
  Indo-Aryan religion   122
But while the Brahmins were building up a stupendous system
  of rites, they were busy with the philosophic speculations
  enshrined in the *Upanishads*   122
Buddhism, a development of and a reaction against Brahminism,
  though Sākya-Muni was no conscious revolutionist .   124
Within two or three centuries after the Buddha's death (B.C.
  543) it becomes the fashionable religion of India, but
  practically disappears by the tenth century of our era .   125
During those thousand years a great transformation takes place
  in the Brahminical religion : the *Vedas* give place to the
  Purānas, and the worship of Siva becomes general .   125
Siva.   126
Vishnu   127
Brahmā   128
Characteristics of modern Hinduism   129
Not an ethical religion   130
But a mass of superstitions   131
Benares   135
Resources of the religious sentiment   137

CHAPTER XII

OTHER NON-CHRISTIAN CREEDS

Buddhism perhaps the most interesting to us of all the religions
  of the East.   139
Some account of it.   139
Jainism possibly a survival of it   144
Mohammedanism.   145
Sikhism   149
The religion of the Parsis.   151

CHAPTER XIII

CHRISTIANITY

Widespread desire in England and the United States for the   PAGE
    conversion of India to Christianity. How far is that
    desire likely to be gratified?   154
Christianity in India in primitive and medieval times   .   .   154
Catholic missions in India in the sixteenth century   .   .   155
Present position of the Catholic Church in India   .   .   157
Protestant missionaries first appear in India in the eighteenth
    century   159
Insignificant results as yet achieved by them   .   .   .   160
Causes of their ill success   161
Small prospect that Protestantism, in any of its varieties, will
    make substantial progress in India : the outlook for
    Catholicism not much more hopeful   .   .   .   162
Testimony of the Abbé Dubois   162
Other testimony   163
Sir Alexander Arbuthnot's opinion of the value of the labour of
    the missionaries   169

PART V.—INDIA OF TO-DAY

CHAPTER XIV

THE BRITISH RĀJ

The blessing of peace bestowed on India by the British
    Government   174
Three-eighths of the country under the immediate sway of native
    rulers   174
Some account of them   174
The provinces directly under British rule   .   .   .   176
How governed   176
The Legislative Councils   177
Indian districts and their administration   177
The judicial system   179

PAGE

Causes which mar the administration of justice in India . 181
Indian finance 182
The land-tax 183
Systems of land tenure 185
Other taxes 187
Material progress of India under British rule . . . 187
Excess of exports over imports 188
Indefensible charges on the Indian revenues . . . 189
Blemishes on British rule 190

CHAPTER XV

CASTE

Differing opinions on the merits and demerits of caste . . 194
Origin of the present fourfold system 195
How the exclusiveness of castes is maintained . . . 199
Position of the Brahmins at the apex of Hindu civilisation . ˙200
Vast number of extra castes and sub-castes . . . 201
Caste rules and regulations 201
The vast majority of the Hindus tenaciously cling to caste . 204
But the exigencies of modern life war against its strict obser-
vance 204
Prospects of the caste system 205

CHAPTER XVI

THE HINDU AT HOME

The people of India a dense population of husbandmen . 206
Great antiquity of the social, economical, and religious institu-
tions of an Indian village 206
Importance of the barber 207
Of the astrologer 207
Of the purohit 207
Of the guru 208
The kharta 210
A shrādha 211
Hindu houses 214

CHAPTER XVII

WOMAN IN INDIA

A chief test of a social order, and a sure index to its character,   PAGE
    afforded by the position which it assigns to woman   . 218
The place of woman in modern civilisation unquestionably due
    to Christianity   218
In India the one faith whose ethos has most in common with
    the Christian—Buddhism—the most favourable to woman 221
Though Mohammed's reform did something for woman, her
    condition in Islām one of semi-slavery   .   .   . 221
The position of woman in modern Hinduism indicates how
    vastly that system has degenerated from the ancient
    Vedic religion, where husband and wife were joint rulers
    of the Aryan household   223
Servile state of Hindu wives   223
The lot of Hindu widows harder still   .   .   . 225
Marriage among the Hindus   225
Only in the rarest of cases are Hindu wives companions to
    their husbands   230
A Hindu gentleman desiring a companion of the other sex
    usually seeks her among dancing girls   .   .   . 231
Some account of those women   232

CHAPTER XVIII

SELF-GOVERNMENT IN INDIA

Desire, in certain quarters, to confer on India the blessing of
    self-government   238
What has been done to carry out that desire   .   . 239
Unsatisfactory results thereof   239
Those results foreseen by Sir Henry Maine and other wise
    persons   240
The pretence at representative government in India a fraud . 240
And a folly 241
Indian " Congresses "   242
The Anglicised Hindu   243
The complaint as to the practical exclusion of the natives of
    India from the Covenanted Civil Service examined   . 245
The large effacement under British rule of the native leaders of
    Indian society unquestionably an evil   .   .   . 248
True principle as to the employment of natives of India in the
    public service   249

CHAPTER XIX

THE FINE ARTS IN INDIA

PAGE

Indian music 253
Indian painting 254
Indian architecture 254
Neglect of the magnificent edifices of India by the British
    Government 256
Architectural performances of the Department of Public Works 258
The life of the Hindu people penetrated by the artistic spirit . 258
Indian artisans 260
The trade guilds of India 263
British machinery and Indian art 264

CHAPTER XX

THE FRONTIER QUESTION

Instability of the policy of the Government of India regarding
    the Frontier Question 268
History of that policy 268
The North-West frontier the recognised road for the invaders of
    India for well-nigh three thousand years . . . 270
The advance of Russia towards that frontier . . . 270
Her object 270
" Russophobia " 271
The crucial point 271
A grave mistake 273
The eventual re-opening of the Afghan Question . . 273

CHAPTER XXI

THE CONDITION OF INDIA

Indian debt to British enterprise and British capital, in respect
    of—
    (a) Irrigation works 274
    (b) Metalled roads and railways 280
    (c) Mining, manufacturing, and planting industries . . 280
    (d) Great cities 282

PA'

These things undoubtedly tokens of prosperity .   .   .   2{

But of whose prosperity? Of the prosperity of the people of
    India? The test of a prosperous country is, that the great
    mass of the inhabitants should be able to procure, with
    moderate toil, what is necessary for living *human* lives .   2{

But for millions of the Indian peasantry the difficulty is not to
    live *human* lives—lives up to the level of their low
    standard of comfort—but to live at all   .   .   .   28

Common misconception regarding the riches of India .   .   28

Famine in India chronic   28

Causes of the poverty of the population of India.   .   .   28

Suggested remedies   29

The chief errors which have marred British rule in India due
    to want of insight   30

APPENDIX A

Proclamation creating a new Frontier Province .   .   .   31

APPENDIX B

Balance-sheet of the Indian Empire, 1899-1900 .   .   .

INDEX   .   .   .   .   3.

PART I

PHYSICAL CHARACTERISTICS

CHAPTER I

THE HIMĀLAYAS

THE late Sir Henry Maine thought it not easy to "overrate the ignorance of India which prevails in England on elementary points." My own experience leads me to think likewise. Two of the most patent facts about India are its vastness and its variety. Yet nothing is more common than to hear from people who are called "educated," or "well informed," such a remark as this: "Ah! you have been in India: I wonder whether you met my cousin A. or my friend B. there!" The man to whom the question is addressed may be, say, a Madras Civil Servant, or an employé of the Mysore Government; the friend, or cousin, a soldier doing duty with his regiment on the north-west frontier, or an engineer in the Central Provinces; and the suggested meeting is as likely as one between a Russian official and a Manchester trader, a German colonel and a barber of Seville. That great triangular space on the world's map, stretching from the Himālayas to the ocean, which constitutes the Indian Empire—a length of about 1900 miles, which is also its greatest breadth—

equals in area and population the whole of
Europe except Russia, and is far less homogeneous than Europe, socially, politically, and
religiously. "It is a continent rather than a
country." It is inhabited by one-fifth of the
human race. It comprises peoples and nations
in well-nigh every state of civilisation, from the
abject savagery of certain Vindhyan hill tribes,
some of whom, only a few years ago, still used
flint points for their arrows, to the most com-
plex commercial communities, and the most artificial social organisations. It includes languages,
and religions, and jurisprudence of the most
diverse kinds. "It presents every variety of
climate, from the dry and singularly bracing
cold of the snowy slopes of the Himãlaya, to
the humid tropical heat of the Concan and of
the Coromandel coast. It possesses every variety
of scenery from peaks of ice to reefs of coral;
from treeless, burning plains to thick, tangled
jungle, and almost impenetrable forests." Its
products include almost everything needed for
the service of man. Twelve thousand different
kinds of animals are found in it.

How huge a subject our Indian Empire is,
may, perhaps, be inferred from the fact that
the Statistical Survey of it executed, or rather
edited, for the Government by the late Sir
William Hunter, extends to 128 volumes, aggre-
gating 60,000 pages. What I propose to do in
this little treatise is to put before the general
reader such a bird's-eye view of it as may, at
all events, convey to him some correct concep-

tion of its outlines, and may perhaps lead him
to refer to more ample sources of information.
I shall endeavour to construct my work on the
plan which Lord Bacon recommends for the
compilation of a book of "Institutions" of the
Law. "Principally," he says, "it ought to have
two properties: the one a perspicuous and clear
order or method; and the other an universal
latitude or comprehension, that the student may
have a little prenotion of everything."

And here I will state what my "order or
method" is. In Part I. I shall speak of the
Physical Characteristics of India. In Part II.
I shall give a succinct account of its Races,
Languages, and Literature. Part III. will contain a brief summary of its History. Part IV.
will deal with its Religions. Part V. will present some principal aspects of the India of To-
day, and will discuss a few of the more important
problems now confronting us there, the solution
of which will vastly influence the India of To-
morrow.

First, then, as to the Physical Characteristics
of India, the theme of this Part. India consists
of four separate and well-defined regions: the
Himālayas in the north; the Great River Plains,
which stretch southwards from their base, and
which constitute Hindustān in the proper sense
of the word; the three-sided Tableland which

slopes upwards again from the River Plains, and
which, with the narrow belts of coast between it
and the sea, makes up the southern half of India
—that vast tract of country known as the Deccan,
with the Vindhya Mountains on the north, and
on the east and west with the two chains of
Ghāts running down on either side till they
meet in a point near Cape Comorin; and, lastly,
Burmah, consisting of the valley and delta of
the Irawadi, together with the Yoma ranges, a
coast strip in the Bay of Bengal, and a wild
hill region stretching on the east and south-east
of the Irawadi towards the Chinese and Siamese
frontiers.

I have spoken of the Himālayas—and would the
reader please notice that such, not Himalāyas, is
their name — as a division of India. It is just
possible that he has been accustomed to regard
them as a single mountain range. I myself was
brought up so to think of them. They are really
a mountainous country extending some fifteen
hundred miles in length, and some two hundred in
breadth. I speak of the Himālayas proper. But in
truth the Hindu Kush may rightly be regarded as
merely a continuation of them : and if we take this
view, we must hold them to extend from the Equator
—by their branches into the Malayan Peninsula—
to 45 degrees of North latitude, and over 73
degrees of longitude. Hence the phrase by which
the Arabs designate them, "the stony girdle of
the earth," is amply warranted. But, as Mr
Andrew Wilson points out in his fascinating book,
The Abode of Snow, there is even more meaning

than this, and even more propriety than the Arabs themselves understand, in their phrase, because this great central range can easily be traced from the mountains of Formosa in the China Sea to the Pyrenees, where they sink into the Mediterranean.

We are, however, here concerned only with what are called the Western Himālayas, a series of nearly parallel ranges, lying from south-east to north-west, and enclosed by the Indus, the Brahmaputra, and the great Northern Plain of India, where they terminate abruptly in a precipitous ridge from six to seven thousand feet above the country below. If the reader will refer to the map, he will see that this is "a very simple and intelligible boundary, for the two rivers rise close together in, or in the near neighbourhood of, Lake Mānasarowar: in the first part of their course they flow close behind the great ranges of the Himālayas, and they cut through the mountains at points where there is some reason for considering that new ranges commence."

The word Himālaya is a Sanskrit compound, meaning the Abode of Snow. The Himālayan line of perpetual snow is, of course, much higher than the Alpine. It is, in fact, twice as high: eighteen thousand feet instead of nine thousand. And here it may not be amiss to insert Mr Andrew Wilson's masterly comparison between the great Asiatic range, which can be known only to few of my readers, and the European mountains which are, doubtless, known to many of them.

"The Himālayas as a whole are not so richly apparelled
as the Alps. In Kashmir and some parts of the Sutlej valley,
and of the valleys on the Indian Front, they are rich in the
most glorious vegetation, and present, in that respect, a more
picturesque appearance than any parts of Switzerland can
boast of; but one may travel among the great ranges of
the Asiatic mountains for weeks, and even months, through
the most sterile scenes, without coming on any of these
regions of beauty. There is not here the same close union
of beauty and grandeur, loveliness and sublimity, which is
everywhere to be found over the Alps. There is a terrible
want of level ground and of green meadows enclosed by
trees. Except in Kashmir, and about the east of Ladāk,
there are no lakes. We miss much those Swiss and Italian
expanses of deep blue water, in which white towns and
villages, snowy peaks and dark mountains are so beautifully
mirrored. There is also a great want of perennial waterfalls
of great height and beauty, such as the Staubbach; though
in summer, during the heat of the day, the Himālaya, in
several places, present long, graceful streaks of dust-foam.

"The striking contrasts and the more wonderful scenes
are not crowded together as they are in Switzerland. Both
eye and mind are apt to be wearied among the Himālaya by
the unbroken repetition of similar scenes during continuous
and arduous travel, extending over days and weeks together;
and one sorely misses Goethe's Eckschen, or the beautiful
little corners of nature which satisfy the eye and mind alike.
The picture is not sufficiently filled up in its detail, and the
continuous repetition of the vast outlines is apt to become
oppressive. The very immensity of the Himālaya prevents
us from often beholding at a glance, as among the Alps, the
wonderful contrast of green meadows, darker pines, green
splintered glaciers, dark precipitous cliffs, blue distant hills,
white slopes of snow, and glittering icy summits. There are
points in the Sutlej valley and in Kashmir where something
like this is presented, and in a more overpowering manner
than anywhere in Europe; but months of difficult travel
separates these two regions, and their beauty cannot be said
to characterise the Himālaya generally. But what, even in
Switzerland, would be great mountains, are here dwarfed

into insignificant hills ; and it requires some time for the eye
to understand the immense Himālayan heights and depths.
Some great rock at the foot of some great precipice, which
is pointed out as our camping place for the night, looks at
first as if it were only a few hundred feet off, but after hours
of arduous ascent, it seems almost as far off as ever.

" The human element of the Western mountains is
greatly wanting in those of the East ; for though here and
there a monastery like Kī, or a village like Dankar, may
stand out picturesquely on the top of a hill, yet, for the
most part, the dingy-coloured, flat-roofed Himālayan hamlets
are not easily distinguishable from the rocks amid which
they stand. The scattered châlets and sen-huts of Switzerland are wholly wanting, and the European traveller misses
the sometimes bright and comely faces of the peasantry of
the Alps. I need scarcely say, also, that the more wonderful
scenes of the Abode of Snow are far from being easily accessible, even when we are in the heart of the great mountains.
And it can hardly be said that the cloudland of the Himālaya is so varied and gorgeous as that of the mountains of
Europe, though the sky is of a deeper, more sword-like blue,
and the heavens are much more brilliant at night.

" But when all these admissions in favour of Switzerland
are made, the Himālaya still remain unsurpassed, and even
unapproached, as regards all the wilder and grander features
of mountain scenery. There is nothing in the Alps which
can afford even a faint idea of the savage desolation and
appalling sublimity of many of the Himālayan scenes. Nowhere, also, have the faces of the mountains been so scarred
and riven by the nightly action of frost, and the mid-day
floods from melting snow. In almost every valley we see
places where whole peaks or sides of great mountains have
very recently come shattering down ; and the thoughtful
traveller must feel that no power or knowledge he possesses
can secure him against such a catastrophe, or prevent his
bones being buried, so that there would be little likelihood
of their release until the solid earth dissolves : and, though
rare, there are sudden passages from these scenes of grandeur
and savage desolation to almost tropical luxuriance and more
than tropical beauty of organic nature. Such changes are

startling and delightful, as in the passage from Dras into the upper Sind Valley of Kashmir, while there is nothing finer in the world of vegetation than the great cedars, pines, and sycamores of many of the lower valleys."

I may here note that it was from the Himā-layas that Sir Joseph Hooker introduced into England half a century ago the beautiful species of rhododendron from which have sprung the various hybrid sorts that in some parts of these islands decorate our gardens and our shrub-beries. But in its native home it grows into a great tree, whole forests of which are found throughout the length of the mountains. From them, too, the orchid originally came to us. In return we have given them the potato, which is largely cultivated by the hill tribes, who also raise crops of barley, oats, millet, and various small grains. "The characteristic animals of the Himā-layas include the yak-cow, musk-deer, many kinds of wild sheep and goat, bear, ounce, and fox: the eagle, pheasants of beautiful varieties, partridge, and other birds."

Such are the Himālayas; the most extensive of all mountain ranges, and the highest, culmina-ting as they do in the 29,002 feet of Mount Everest, the loftiest measured peak in the world. And though for the most part they are beyond our frontier—the feudatory kingdom of Kashmir, with an area of 80,900 square miles, is the most important state in them subject to the British Rāj—they rightly claim the notice they have here received. With the offshoots which at their east-ern and western extremities stretch southwards, they form a rampart for the Indian Empire against invaders from Asia. They serve it, on this side, "in the office of a wall." But they also serve as a vast reservoir for Hindustān. I need hardly observe that the great source of the earth's water supply is the sea, whence vapour is raised by solar heat, and is carried and distributed over the land in snow, rain, and dew. And so long as the sun runs his course, the quantity of vapour thus sucked into the atmosphere will ever be the same. Throughout the summer a vast amount is exhaled from the Indian Ocean. This is gathered into clouds which are carried northward, with amazing rapidity, by the monsoon in the month of June. And such of the moisture as does not descend, in the shape of rain, upon the parched plains, and the lower ranges of the Himā-layas, is precipitated in the crystallised form of snowflakes upon the inner heights of those moun-tains.

The drainage of the northern slopes of the Himālayas is collected by two great rivers: the Indus and the Brahmaputra, which, as I have already observed, rise not very far from each other in the neighbourhood of Lake Mānasarowar. The Indus runs for 800 miles through the Himālayas before it enters British territory, first westwards and then southwards. It bursts through the mountains near Iskardo in North-West Kashmīr by a gorge 14,000 feet deep, and then flows through the Punjāb, finally falling into the Indian Ocean after a course of 1800 miles. On the other hand, the Brahmaputra, whose course is

of about the same length, runs in an easterly
direction through the Himālayas for nearly a
thousand miles, entering British territory at
Saduya, in the Assam Valley, whence it descends
to the plain of Eastern Bengal to join, at Goāl-
ānda, the third great river of Hindustān — the
Ganges. A great river, indeed; in some respects
the greatest of Indian streams, sacred in the
highest degree to the Hindus, whose worship of
it is, at all events, intelligible, if we reflect upon
its claims to their gratitude. It issues from an
ice cave at the foot of a Himālayan snow-bed,
and with its most considerable tributary, the
Jumna, which joins it at Allahābād, collects for
1000 miles the drainage from the lower slopes
of the Himālayas, to water the earth and bless
it, and make it very plenteous, in a large portion
of northern India. After a course of 1500 miles,
it merges into the sea through the Bengal Delta,
the largest in the world.

CHAPTER II

A CHAIN of mountains called the Vindhya runs across the peninsula of India from east to west. It extends between the twenty-third and twenty-fifth parallels of latitude, from the desert northwest of Guzarat to the Ganges. The country south of this chain—a triangle of which it forms the base and Cape Comorin the apex — I designate, in accordance with a popular usage, the Deccan. By Hindustān I mean not only the country lying to the north of it, but the wide plains watered by the Himālayan rivers, and the regions around them : the provinces known as the Punjāb, Sind, Rājputāna, Oudh and the North-West Provinces, Bengal and Assam. I shall now touch briefly on the physical characteristics of these lands.

The most striking feature of the Punjāb is indicated by its name. It is the country of the five rivers (*punj āb*) : the country watered by the confluent streams of the Sutlej, the Beas, the Ravi, the Chenāb, and the Jhelum. But the administrative province of the Punjāb at present extends beyond

13

that region. It comprises the whole of British India north of Sind and Rājputāna, and west of the river Jumna, with the exception of the three small strips of Balūchistān subject to British rule, as well as several Himālayan ranges, on one of which the sanatorium of Simla is situated.* Its area is 106,632 miles. Speaking generally, the Punjāb may be described as a vast plain of alluvial formation, fertile where neither sand nor the saline effervescence known as *reh* is present, but especially fertile in the eastern portion where the great cities of Delhi, Amritsar, and Lahore are situated. Its five rivers flow into the Indus, which enters the province at Amb, and which, after receiving them, flows into the Arabian Sea through Sind. The area of that province, which for political purposes is included in the Bombay Presidency, is 48,014 square miles, and its average rainfall is less than ten inches. Sometimes, indeed, no rain falls in it for two or three years. Hence "the Indus is to Sind what the Nile is to Egypt." The State forests lying along its banks extend to 375,329 acres.

On the east of Sind, separated from it by a great desert, is Rājputāna, the country of the Rājputs. It extends to 132,461 square miles, and consists of twenty autonomous native states and the British province of Ajmere - Merwārā. The Aravalli Mountains—the only hills in Rājputāna of much account—intersect it in a line running nearly north-east and north-west. Its more fertile

* While this work was passing through the press, a new frontier province was formed. See Appendix A.

portions are those which are watered by the drainage of the Vindhya range. Its mineral wealth is considerable, but is little developed, and its quarries yield admirable building stone.

The North-West Provinces and Oudh occupy, roughly speaking, the whole of the basins of the Ganges and the Jumna. This is the region to which the Mohammedan chroniclers gave the name of Hindustān. It is highly cultivated ; a vast expanse of monotonous verdure, thanks to the Ganges, with a score of tributary rivers, and to the Jumna, which has almost as many affluents. The extreme edges of the basin, on the north and the south, are skirted by mountainous country. Its area is 111,229 square miles.

The area of the province of Bengal is 193,198 square miles. " It consists chiefly of two broad river valleys. The western of them, the Ganges, brings down the wealth and accumulated waters of Northern India. The eastern valley is the route by which the Brahmaputra ends its tortuous course of 1800 miles. These valleys are luxuriant alluvial plains diversified by spurs and peaks thrown out by the great mountain systems which wall them on the north, east, and south-west." Higher valleys of the Brahmaputra, and those of the Bārak or Surmā, together with the mountainous watershed intervening between these two rivers, form the chief part of the province of Assam, of which the area is 46,341 square miles.

As I have intimated, the river plains of Hindustān are extremely fertile. They yield two crops each year and sometimes three. Wheat is produced chiefly in the North-West Provinces and Oudh. But it is also grown largely in the Punjāb and in the western parts of Bengal. Rice, of course, is very largely cultivated in the great river basins. It is what is called "a wet crop," requiring from 36 to 41 inches of water for its full development. With regard to the other natural products of Hindustān, it must suffice here to quote a portion of the picturesque summary given in the *Imperial Gazetteer*.

"Sugar-cane, oil-seeds, flax, mustard, sesamum, palmachristi, cotton, tobacco, indigo, safflower and other dyes, ginger, coriander, capsicum, cummin, and precious spices, are grown both in the North-Western or Upper Provinces and in the moister valleys and delta of Lower Bengal. A whole pharmacopœia of native medicines, from the well-known aloe and castor-oil, to obscure but valuable febrifuges, is derived from shrubs, herbs, and roots. Resins, gums, varnishes, indiarubber, perfume-oils, and a hundred articles of commerce or luxury, are obtained from the fields and the forests. Vegetables, both indigenous and imported from Europe, largely enter into the food of the people. The melon and huge yellow pumpkin spread themselves over the thatched roofs; fields of potato, *brinjal*, and yams are attached to the homesteads. The tea-plant is reared on the hilly ranges that skirt the plains both in the North-West and in Assam; the opium poppy about half-way down the Ganges, around Benares, and in Behar; the silkworm mulberry still farther down in Lower Bengal; while the jute fibre is essentially a crop of the delta, and would exhaust any soil not fertilised by river floods. Even the jungles yield the costly lac and the *tasar* silk cocoons. The mahuā, also a gift of the jungle, produces the fleshy flowers which form a staple article of food among the hill tribes, and when distilled supply a cheap spirit. The *sāl, sissu, tūn,* and many other indigenous trees yield excellent timber. Flowering creepers, of gigantic size and gorgeous colours, festoon the jungle; while each tank * bears its own beautiful crop of the lotus and water-lily. Nearly every vegetable product which feeds and clothes a people, or enables it to trade with foreign countries, abounds."

* The following explanation, which I take from Mr B. H. Baden-Powell's admirable work, *The Land Systems of British India*, may not be superfluous for some of my readers. "A 'tank' does not mean a rectangular masonry-lined reservoir—that sort of tank is no doubt common, but mostly for bathing or in connection with a sacred place or temple. The irrigation tank is, in fact, a suitable soil-depression, storing up the rain and drainage water, and varying in size from a pond filling the upper part of a small valley, to a vast lake covering hundreds of acres. The tank is closed in by an embankment of earth or masonry, or both. . . . An escape is afforded in case the water threatens to overtop the embankment. In some cases the tank represents a lake which is never dry: in others, the whole of the water is run off, or dries up early in the season, and the bed, enriched with slime, and moistened by the previous soaking of the water, is ploughed up and cultivated."

CHAPTER III

THE DECCAN

By the Deccan, as was stated in the last Chapter, we mean the triangular peninsula which has the Vindhya Mountains as its base, and Cape Comorin as its apex. It includes the Governments of Madras and Bombay, the Central Provinces, Berar, and the territories of various feudatory princes, of whom the most considerable are the Maharājah of Mysore, the Nizam, Scindia, Holkar, and the Guicowar.

I have spoken of the Vindhya Mountains—their greatest height is less than 5000 feet—as forming the southern limit of Hindustān. But we must not disassociate them from two other sets of hills. The Aravalli, of which the southern slopes are drained by the Nerbudda, are connected by lower ranges with the western extremity of the Vindhyas. The Sātpur, a parallel chain of no great height, are separated from them by the valley through which that river flows. It is in the Sātpur Hills that the Tāpti rises. This river and the Nerbudda flow in almost parallel lines till they join the sea in the Gulf of Cambay. The reader who really

desires to understand India must diligently study
her mountains and her streams. He will perceive
that one very important physical characteristic of
the region now engaging our attention is the hill
system which traverses the country south of the
Nerbudda. He will observe, too, that as the
tableland constituting the Deccan has the Vindhya
Mountains for its base, so it is supported on either
side by the long ranges known as the Eastern and
Western Ghāts, which give the key to the configuration of the peninsula. Both follow its form as
they run towards the south. And between them
and the sea is a low strip of land forming a sort
of belt, narrow on the Western side and broader
on the Eastern. From the Western Ghāts issue
the three great rivers of the Madras Presidency,
the Godavery, the Kistna, and the Cauvery, which
flow eastward across the central plain of the
Deccan into the Indian Ocean. The Western
Ghāts, which run parallel to the sea for some five
hundred miles, maintain a much higher level than
the Eastern, and sometimes rise to over eight
thousand feet. But the highest peak in Southern
India is found in the Anamully Hills—a spur of
the Eastern Ghāts : its altitude is 8850 feet. The
Eastern Ghāts are joined to the Western range
by the Neilgherries, or Blue Mountains, in whose
spacious, undulating plateau, 7000 feet up, and
"sweet half English air," are the sanatoria of
Ootacamund and Conoor. And here it may not
be amiss to insert a few words of Mr Andrew
Wilson's, pointing out a remarkable parallelism
between the Western Ghāts and the Himālayas,

which will serve to make the contour of both ranges more easily intelligible.

" Both are immense bounding walls, the one to the elevated plains of the Deccan, and the other to the still more elevated tableland of Central Asia. Carrying out this parallel, the Narbada (Nerbudda) will be found to occupy very much the same position as the Indus, the Sutlej as the Tāpti, and the Godaveri as the Brahmaputra. All have their rise high up on their respective tablelands ; some branches of the Godaveri rise close to the sources of the Narbada, just as the Indus and the Brahmaputra have their origin somewhere about Lake Mānasarowar, and yet the former rivers fall into the sea on opposite sides of the Indian Peninsula, just as the two latter do. So, in like manner, the Tāpti has its origin near that of the Narbada, as the Sutlej rises close to the Indus ; and if we can trust the Sind tradition, which represents the upper part of the Arabian Sea as having once been dry land, there may have been a time within the human era when the Tāpti flowed into the Narbada, as the Sutlej does into the Indus some way above the sea. There is no mountain group in the highlands of Central India where the three southern rivers rise quite so close together as do the three northern rivers from the lofty and inaccessible Tibetan Kailas, but still there is a great similarity in their relative positions."

So much in general as to the more striking physical characteristics of the Deccan. I will now add a very few words regarding the several provinces which are included in it. First, then, as to Central India, which the reader must not confound—as, if unversed in the subject, he is apt to do—with the Central Provinces. Central India is the name applied to a congeries of native states covering an area of 75,079 square miles, which are under the direct supervision of nine Political

Agents, all of them being subordinate to the Agent to the Governor-General for that territory. It includes a great part of what was known as Mahal Rachtra, "the Great Kingdom," the country of the Mahrattas, bordered on one side by the Vindhya Mountains, and on the other by the Western Ghāts ; a land for the most part fertile and well culti-vated. Eighty - two states are included in the Central Indian Agency, some of them being very small. The most considerable are the dominions of two princes of the Mahratta race, whose names are specially familiar to English readers : Scindia, the most powerful native sovereign of Hindustān, whose country—Gwalior—extends to 29,067 square miles ; and Holkar, who rules over 8402 square miles, and at whose capital of Indore the Agent to the Governor-General resides.

Another great Mahratta prince is the Guicowar, whose state, Baroda, is subject to the political control of the Government of Bombay. It is an open fertile tract, and covers an area of 8570 square miles. The Central Provinces lie to the south of Central India, and extend to 113,279 square miles. It is a country of highlands and valleys, of plateaus and plains, and presents grand alternations of picturesque scenery, fertile in places—in the Ner-budda valleys, for example, which have been de-scribed as "green from end to end with wheat" in the cold season—but in large part sterile and waste : only one-third of its whole area is under cultivation. Once its heights were clothed with magnificent forests. But these have largely dis-appeared before the axe of the charcoal-burner, and the fires of the *dhya* cultivator, whose method in husbandry is to clear a portion of the jungle, to set fire to the logs and brushwood when dried by the sun, and to scatter among the ashes after the first rainfall a handful of grain. Hyderabad, the Nizam's country, has an area of 80,000 square miles. It is a tract of considerable elevation, averaging 1250 feet above the level of the sea, and presenting much variety of surface and feature. It is generally fertile ; but its most productive part is the province of Berar, directly administered by the British Government, to whom it was assigned for the support of the Hyderabad contingent. Berar is a broad valley running east and west, and lying south of the Sātpur range ; its 17,700 square miles include many rich cotton-fields.

The area of the Bombay Presidency is 197,876 square miles, and the country is of a broken character. It may be roughly divided into two portions, the Nerbudda forming the boundary line. The northern portion is for the most part a low plain of alluvial origin ; the southern a level coast strip, rising into an upland country.

The Madras Presidency, of which the area is 149,092 square miles, presents three natural divisions : the long and broad east coast, the shorter and narrower west coast, and the central tableland. But this central tableland goes beyond the limits of Madras. It includes a considerable portion of the Bombay Presidency, Berar, the Nizam's country, and Mysore. Indeed, Mysore, with its area of 27,936 square miles, may be regarded geographically as a portion of Madras.

The whole of Southern India, there is reason
to believe, was once buried under forests. Their
remains are still extensive. The various mountain regions are all more or less wooded. The
forests of the Madras Presidency alone cover 5000
square miles and yield noble timber. " In the
valleys and upon the elevated plains of the central
plateau," we are told in the *Imperial Gazetteer of
India*, "tillage has driven back the jungle to the
hilly recesses, and fields of wheat and many kinds
of smaller grain or millets, tobacco, cotton, sugar-
cane, and pulses, spread over the open country.
The black soil of Southern India, formed from
the detritus of the trap mountains, is proverbial
for its fertility ; while the level strip between the
Western Ghāts and the sea rivals even Lower
Bengal in its fruit-bearing palms, rice harvests, and
rich succession of crops. The deltas of the rivers
which issue from the Eastern Ghāts are celebrated
as rice-bearing tracts. But the interior of the
central tableland of the Southern Peninsula is
subject to droughts. The cultivators here contend
against the calamities of nature by various systems
of irrigation—by means of which they store the rain
brought during a few months by the monsoon,
and husband it for use throughout the whole year."
But of this I shall have to speak in a subsequent
Chapter.

CHAPTER IV

BURMAH

THE fourth division of the Indian Empire, as we are considering it, is Burmah : a country of hills, forests, streams, and abundant rainfall, covering 170,000 square miles. Through the centre of it flows the Irawadi, the greatest of all its rivers. "The source of the Irawadi," Mr Blandford tells us, in his *India, Burmah, and Ceylon*, "is still unknown, and has been the subject of much discussion among geographers. The main stream probably comes from Tibet, breaking through the Eastern Himālaya, where it is known as the Lu-tse-Kyang, or Lu River, and it enters Upper Burmah under the name of the Kewhom, or Meh Kha, but this is known from native report only, in lat. 26°, where it unites with a smaller river, the Mali Kha, that comes from the north, and rises in the mountains that close the eastern end of the Assam Valley. A little below lat. 25°, where it receives the Mogoung River from the west, the Irawadi is a fine river, half a mile broad and from two to three fathoms deep, flowing at the rate of two miles an hour. Below this it enters the first defile, where at one place it is contracted by rocks to 70 yards in the dry season, and this defile continues to five miles above Bhamo. A second occurs below Bhamo, a third 40 miles above Mandalay, and a fourth between Thyetmyo and Prome. It receives several affluents from the east, the largest of which, the Shiveli, comes from Yunan, and is navigable in the rainy season; but its greatest tributary is the Chindwin, which joins it from the north-west, 58 miles below Mandalay. It enters its delta at Myanoung and gives off branches, one of which forms the Bassein River, a large navigable stream that enters the sea near Cape Negrais, and another communicates with the Rangoon River at the eastern extremity of the delta. The length of the Irawadi from the Kewhom in lat. 26° to the sea is 850 miles, all of which is navigable to boats. Steamers ascend it 700 miles to Bhamo, which is the starting place of the trade route to China."

Burmah groups itself naturally into four divisions. First, there is the central valley watered by the Irawadi and its most important tributary the Chindwin. Second, the province of Arakan, to the west of this valley, divided from it by the lofty Yoma range, the highest peak of which is the Blue Mountain (7100 feet), and running down to the Bay of Bengal. The greatest breadth of this strip of coast is 170 miles. The largest river is the Kuladan, which rises in the Yoma mountains and receives the drainage of their western half.

Third, the mountainous country east of the
Irawadi, inhabited by the Shans, and other tribes
in a low state of civilisation, which runs up to the
frontier provinces of the Chinese Empire. The
chief river watering this country is the Salween,
which forms the boundary between Burmah and
Siam. Fourth, the province of Tenasserim, a
long, isolated southern coast strip, through which
the Salween flows, passing Moulmein and empty-
ing itself into the Gulf of Martaban. The other
chief rivers of this province are the one which
bears its name, the Attaran, which joins the
Salween not far from the sea, and the Tavoy;
and all three run in longitudinal valleys, parallel
with the coast and the Yoma Mountains.

" The central valley and the two coast strips,"
writes Sir William Hunter, " are extremely fertile.
The outskirts of the hilly tracts are rich in teak
and other valuable trees, and forest produce. A
thousand creeks indent the sea-board; and the
whole of the level country, on the coast and in the
lower Irawadi valley, forms one vast rice-field.
The rivers float down cheaply the teak, bamboos,
and timbers from the north. Tobacco, of an
excellent quality, supplies the cigars which all
Burmese (men, women, and children) smoke, and
affords an industrial product of increasing value.
Arakan and Pegu, the two provinces of the coast,
and also the Irawadi valley, contain mineral-oil
springs. Tenasserim is rich in tin-mines, and
contains iron-ores equal to the finest Swedish;
besides gold and copper in smaller quantities, and
a very pure limestone. Rice and timber form the

staple exports of Burmah; and rice is also the universal food of the people."

A word should here be added regarding the Andaman and Nicobar Islands, which, as Mr Blandford observes, "may be regarded as the emerging summits of a submarine range of hills, linking the Arakan Yoma to the central hill range of Sumatra." There are four of the Andaman group and eighteen of the Nicobar, and their whole area is 3285 square miles. They are administered by a Superintendent, who, for certain purposes, ranks as a Chief Commissioner, and the main Andaman island is used as a penal settlement for Indian convicts.

PART II

RACES, LANGUAGES, AND LITERATURE

CHAPTER V

From the Physical Characteristics of India I pass on to speak of the Races which dwell in it. The transition is a natural one, for the geographical configuration of the country has largely determined the habitats of its population. Who its aborigines were we cannot say with absolute certainty. Probably they were Kolarians, whose chief seat was south of the Ganges in its lower course; men of the same stock as the Nigritians of the Indian Ocean, and represented now by some of what we call the wild tribes of India; by the Santāls about Bhāgalpur; the Karias and Mehtos of Singbhum and Chutia Nagpur; the Mundas, Larkas, and other Kols of Singbhum; the Mal-Parahias or Tuangs of Orissa; the Kurkus about the sources of Nerbudda, in the very heart of the Sātpur range; the Bheels of Malwa and Kandesh; the Kulis of Guzarat; the Mhairs of Rājputāna; and others elsewhere: numbering altogether about 4,000,000.

The first invaders of India seem to have been Mongolian and Dravidian tribes, who have left but faint oral traditions, and, of course, no written histories. Their descent upon the country took place in the dim antiquity of prehistoric times ; doubtless long before the date assigned by Hebrew chronologists to the Creation. The Mongolians came into the plains of Bengal, it is conjectured, through the north-eastern passes of the Himālayas, from Central Asia, where they dwelt side by side with the forefathers of the Chinese. The Dravidians * appear to have found their way into the Punjāb through the North-West Provinces of the same mountains, and to have established themselves at first along the southern coast of the Indus.

But both Mongolians and Dravidians were destined to give place to a mightier race. According to Hindu chronologists, who, indeed, are of no more authority than Hebrew, the Aryans entered India just three thousand years before Christ. It is from this date that they reckon their present era : the Kali Yuga or Black Age. The Aryan invaders settled in the Punjāb and remained there, apparently, for 1500 years. Then, about the time of the exodus of Israel from Egypt, they began to move towards the valley of the Ganges. In another thousand years they reached the delta of that great stream. As the Aryans advanced eastward from the

---

* I follow the usually received account of the Dravidians : but another view is taken, and is supported by weighty arguments, in the vast *Manual of the Administration of the Madras Presidency*, due to the indefatigable labour of Dr Charles Maclean.

Sind-Saga-Doāb to the Sunderbunds, they drove the Mongolian race into the Himālayas and beyond the Ganges, where they are still represented by the Thibeto-Burman tribes of Ladāk and Baltistān, Garwal, Nepaul, Bhutān, Sikkim, and Assam, and of the maritime countries of Arakan, Pegu, and Tenasserim : some 4,000,000 people in all. The southern advance of the conquerors towards Saurashtra on the west and Orissa on the east, pressed the Dravidians into the Vindhyan fastnesses. There, side by side with the Kolarian tribes, some of them still dwell and are known as Gonds in the Central Provinces, as Konds in the highlands of Ganjam and Orissa. But the great bulk of them descended into the Deccan, then thickly wooded, and were fruitful and multiplied, and replenished the earth and subdued it. Southern India is still mainly Dravidian : the portion of it between the Godaveri and Cape Comorin, we may say, is almost exclusively so. Hindustān is mainly Aryan. And the hill tribes of the North-West frontier, who probably number about a million, are no doubt for the most part descendants of Aryan stragglers, left there and reduced to primitive savagery by the conditions of so inaccessible and unproductive a situation.

I have said that Hindustān is mainly Aryan. But sections of its population are due to subsequent invasions. Between the years 100 B.C. and 500 A.D. various tribes of Central Asia, called for want of a more exact name Scythians, made many inroads into India ; and their descendants still form a

considerable element in the population of the
frontier provinces. About the year 1000 A.D.
began the series of Mohammedan invasions which
lasted till the middle of the sixteenth century of
our era. "They represent in Indian history the
overflow of the nomad tribes of Central Asia to
the south-east, as the Huns, Turks, and various
Tartan tribes disclose, in early European annals,
the westward movements from the same great
breeding ground of nations."

These, then, are the chief constituents of the
population of India. First, the wild tribes composed, according to the most probable conjectures,
of the various elements above enumerated, whose
numbers may roughly be estimated at 10,000,000,
or, perhaps, 11,000,000. Secondly, the Dravidians
of the Deccan—Tamils, Telugus, Canarese, and
others, amounting to about 54,000,000. Thirdly,
the Aryans, who are found chiefly in the country
which I have called Hindustān. But of these
only the Brahmins and the Rājputs—they number
some 20,000,000—are of pure Aryan blood. Pure,
or relatively pure; for in truth it is only in the
north of India, and especially in Kashmīr and
the Punjāb, that we find the unmodified Aryan:
as we descend the Gangetic valley, the lips, the
nose, the cheek-bones, the dark complexion, more
and more betray foreign ingredients, until in
Bengal and Orissa the traces of the nobler
race are almost undiscernible. The remaining
135,000,000 Hindus represent the fusion of Aryan
and non-Aryan elements. And, fourthly, the Mohammedans, dwelling chiefly in Bengal, the North-West

Provinces, the Punjāb, and Hyderabad, who number about 60,000,000. They are by no means a homogeneous race. Half of their number are the descendants of the converts made to Islām from Hinduism for many centuries, whether by might, persuasion, or compulsion. The other half are Tartars, Afghans, or Persians — Arabs, so-called; the descendants of successive hordes of Moslem invaders.

The 9,000,000 of Burmese, as we may roughly reckon them, are of Indo-Chinese race— with perhaps the exception of the Mon or Talaings of Pegu and Arakan, who are believed to be the posterity of Dravidian immigrants.

The Parsis, though numerically inconsiderable— they amount only to some 90,000 souls—occupy in wealth and influence a foremost position in the population. They are the descendants of refugees from Persia who fled from their country on the fall of the Sassanian dynasty in the seventh century of our era, and established themselves on the coast of Damān in Western India. Fifty thousand of them dwell in Bombay. But "there is not an advanced port of the Empire in Arabia, or the Somali coast of Africa, in Balūchistān, or even in the far-off Shan States of Burmah, which is not occupied by some of them."

The British element in the population of India is not numerically much larger than the Parsi. It may be roughly stated at 135,000. There is about the same number of Eurasians, the descendants of European fathers and native mothers; there are some 12,000 Jews, and perhaps as many Chinese.

CHAPTER VI

LANGUAGES

PROFESSOR SAYCE, in his most interesting *Intro-duction to the Science of Language*, tells us that the tongues at present spoken in the world fall into about a hundred families. One of the chief of these is the Aryan or Indo-European: the family of which the languages of Hindustān, Persia, Greece, Italy, Germany, and Slavonia are members: "daughters of the same mother, and heirs of the same wealth of words and flections." Of these, Sanskrit is, in some respects, the most interesting and important from a merely philo-logical point of view, for it is no doubt the nearest to the language of the ancient Aryans. I speak thus advisedly. It is most probable that at the time of the dispersion of the Aryans from their original home—wherever that may have been—their speech was already divided into dialects of which Sanskrit was merely one. "At the head of the Indian group of dialects," writes Professor Sayce, "stands Sanskrit, the classical language of Hindustān and its Sacred Books, which, though long since extinct, is still spoken by the Brahmans as Latin was in the Middle Ages. We must distinguish, however, between Vedic Sanskrit and classical Sanskrit, the older Sanskrit of the *Veda* differing in many respects from the later Sanskrit of the Hindu epics. . . . . Both Vedic and Post-Vedic Sanskrit were poor in vowels, possessing only *a*, *i*, and *u*, long and short, with the diphthongs *e*, *ai*, *o*, and *au*, and the linguals *r* and *l*; on the other hand, they were rich in consonants, among which the 'cerebral' or linguo-dental *t* and *d* are usually supposed to have been borrowed from the Dravidian tongues. The euphonic laws are strict and delicate, the final sounds of a word being affected by the initial sounds of the word following according to precise and well-observed rules. The syntax is comparatively simple, composition taking its place, especially in the later period of the language. The grammatical forms, however, are very full and clear, and it is to them that Sanskrit mainly owes the high position that it has occupied in the comparative study of Aryan speech. It has often preserved archaic forms that have been obscured elsewhere, though it must not be forgotten that this is by no means invariably the case; Greek and Latin, for instance, are sometimes more primitive than the old language of India. The declension is especially complete, preserving the dual as well as a locative and an instrumental. Other cases, however, which must have been once possessed by the parent-speech, have either disappeared or left faint traces behind them."

So much as to Sanskrit. The Prākrit dialects

followed upon it just as the Romanic dialects of
Europe followed upon Latin. One of them, the
Pāli of Maghada or Behar in North - Eastern
India—now, for many centuries, a dead language
—was transported by Buddhist missionaries to
Ceylon in the year 244 B.C., and became the
holy language of the Southern Buddhist Church,
the most authoritative Sacred Books of which
are written in it. "The modern Aryan languages
of India," continues Professor Sayce, "have developed out of the other Prākrits, and in their
present form are considered not to go back further
than the tenth century. Bengāli and Assamese
retain many features of Sanskrit; Sindhi and
Gujerāti in the north-west, Nepāli and Kashmiri
in the north, Hindi in the centre, and Marāthi
in the south, are all more or less changed from
the primitive type. Hindi is merely the modern
form of Hindui, a language which was much cultivated during the Middle Ages of recent Hindu
literature, while Hindustāni or Urdu, the language
of the 'camp,' is Hindi mixed with Arabic and
Persian—in fact, a *lingua franca* which grew up
at the time of the Mohammedan invasion in the
eleventh century."

We may say, then, speaking generally, that
the languages of Hindustān are Aryan. The
languages of the Deccan belong to another family,
the Dravidian. This is an agglutinative family,
whereas the Aryan is inflectional, a difference
lucidly explained by Professor Max Müller in his
Lectures on the Science of Language: "The chief
distinction between an inflectional and an aggluti-

nate language," he writes, "consists in the fact that agglutinative languages preserve the consciousness of their roots, and therefore do not allow them to be affected by phonetic corruption; and though they have lost the consciousness of the original meaning of the terminations, they feel distinctly the difference between the significative roots and the modifying elements. Not so in the inflectional languages. There the various elements which enter into the composition of words may become so welded together, and suffer so much from phonetic corruption, that none but the educated would be aware of an original distinction between root and termination, and none but the comparative grammarian able to discover the seams that separate the component parts." The Dravidian languages are usually reckoned as twelve in number. Six—Tamil, Telugu, Kanarese, Malayālam, Tulu, and Kudagu—are all highly developed tongues. Tamil is peculiarly rich in grammatical forms; and Telugu has been called, not without reason, "the Italian of India." Six less refined and developed varieties of Dravidian are Toda, Kota, Khond, Gond, Uraon, and Rajmuhāli, spoken by more or less barbarous tribes, and quite distinct from one another. The tribes descended from the aborigines speak some ten different dialects of Kolarian, which is a distinct linguistic family.

Finally, to complete this rough enumeration of the languages of India, there is the Tibeto-Burman family, which is neither inflexional nor agglutinative, but isolating. And here, for the benefit of the reader not versed in philological studies, a

word of explanation may be necessary. I will
take it from Professor Sayce: "In the isolating
languages, the separate terms or ideas which make
up the sentence are not subordinated to each
other and fused into a single whole, but every
word remains a separate and distinct sentence.
The Chinaman has to say, '*thyan — hi — leri
tsyari—sari—lei*' — literally, 'heaven — air — cold
begin—rise—come'—if he wants to state that
'the weather began to be cold'; and the Bur-
man's way of expressing 'we are going' is by
saying '*nā dō dhwā kra dhán*' — 'I multitude
go multitude which.' In cases such as these, the
ideas are each set down independently, instead of
being subordinated one to another, and the words
which embody them are accordingly contrasted
with each other like so many independent sentences." Of the Tibeto-Burman family Professor
Sayce reckons seven groups speaking some seventy
different tongues or dialects. The most important of these is Burmese.

CHAPTER VII

LITERATURE

WHAT has been said of the languages of India may serve, incidentally, to impress upon the reader the much needed lesson of the vastness of the country and the complexity of its civilisation. Let us now proceed to consider its literature. I do not think there is much of very high value in any of its non-Aryan tongues. Certainly there is not in the Tibeto-Burman. Nor, in my judgment, is there in the Dravidian languages, with three principal varieties of which—Tamil, Telugu, and Canarese—I have some acquaintance. Tamil, indeed, possesses many books ; but they are chiefly borrowed from the Sanskrit. The most pretentious original work in it is the *Tirāga Chintāmami*, which a high authority, the Rev. Dr Pope, somewhat hyperbolically characterises as being "at once the Iliad and Odyssey of the Tamil language." The *Kural* of Tiruvallular— a collection of verses compiled in the tenth century of our era by a Pariah, whose sister, Auvaiyār, has also left some admirable stanzas — certainly exhibits, in places, considerable poetical power.

41

Barth, in his very learned work on *The Religions of India*, characterises it as "instinct with the purest and most elevated religious emotion." In the eighteenth century of our era, the Italian Jesuit Beschi composed an immense epic poem in classical Tamil, the *Tembāvani*, on Biblical subjects. It is considered by some competent judges to have won him "a conspicuous rank among Dravidian poets." Many years have elapsed since I looked into the work, but I remember it appeared to me tasteless and frigid.

The modern Aryan tongues, so far as I am aware, contain no writings of any considerable merit. The only Indian literature of much real intrinsic value is the Sanskrit. And the most notable things in it are the Vedic Hymns, the two great national epics, the *Rāmāyana* and the *Mahābhārata*, and the *Upanishads*.

Of the *Vedas* the oldest is the *Rig-Veda*, preeminently called *The Veda*. "It is," writes Professor Sayce, "a collection of hymns and poems of various dates, some of which go back to the earliest days of the Aryan invasion of northwestern India ; the whole collection, however, may be roughly ascribed to at least the fourteenth or fifteenth century B.C. In course of time it came to assume a sacred character, and the theory of inspiration invented to support this goes much beyond the most extreme theory of verbal inspiration ever held in the Jewish or the Christian Church. The *Rig-Veda* was divided into ten *mandalas*, or books, each *mandala* being assigned to some old family ; and out of these were formed three new *Vedas*—the *Yajur*, the *Sāma*, and the *Ātharva*. The *Yajur* and the *Sāma* may be described as prayer-books compiled from the Rig for the use of the choristers and the ministers of the priests, and contain little besides what is found in the earliest and most sacred *Veda*. . . . . The *Ātharvana* may be described as a collection of poems mixed up with popular sayings, medical advice, magical formulæ, and the like."

In the *Rig-Veda* we have poems—sometimes very striking—on Nature : hymns to the Sun, the Rain, the Clouds, the Fire, the Sky, the Earth, the Wind, the Storm, the Dawn. But there is no subjective thought, no personal emotion. I shall have to speak in a later Chapter of the Vedic religious teaching. Here, by way of specimen of the poetry of our far-off Aryan ancestors, I will quote Max Müller's rendering of the 129th hymn of the tenth book of the *Rig-Veda*.

> " Nor Aught nor Naught existed ; yon bright sky
> Was not, nor heaven's broad roof outstretched above.
> What covered all ? what sheltered ? what concealed ?
> Was it the water's fathomless abyss ?
> There was not death—yet was there naught immortal,
> There was no confine betwixt day and night ;
> The only One breathed breathless by itself,
> Other than It there nothing since has been :
> Darkness there was, and all at first was veiled
> In gloom profound—an ocean without light—
> The germ that still lay covered in the husk
> Burst forth, one nature, from the fervent heat.
> Then first came love upon it, the new spring
> Of mind—yea, poets in their hearts discerned,
> Pondering, this bond between created things
> And uncreated. Comes this spark from earth

Piercing and all-pervading, or from heaven?
Then seeds were sown, and mighty powers arose—
Nature below, and power and will above—
Who knows the secret? who proclaimed it here
Whence, whence this manifold creation sprang?
The gods themselves came later into being—
Who knows from whence this great creation sprang—
He, from whom all this great creation came,
Whether His will created or was mute,
The Most High Seer that is in highest heaven,
He knows it—or perchance even He knows not."

As time went on, commentaries on the *Vedas*
were produced and received the name of *Brāhmanas.* They soon came to be regarded as little
inferior in sacredness to the *Vedas* themselves.
In truth they are, for the most part, incorrect and
inept explanations of Vedic texts, the meaning of
which had grown obscure. Herr Eggeling, the
accomplished author of the translation of the *Satta-
patha-Brāhmana* in the *Sacred Books of the East,*
remarks: " For wearisome prolixity of exposition,
characterised by dogmatic assertion and a flimsy
symbolism rather than by serious reasoning, these
works are perhaps not equalled anywhere." Most
intelligent readers of his bulky volumes will, I think,
agree in this judgment.

I should here remark that the *Purānas*—there
are eighteen of them and eighteen supplements—
are ancient legendary histories written when the
Vedic religion had become antiquated, some by
the votaries of Vishnu, and some by the votaries
of Siva—I shall have to speak of these deities in
a subsequent Chapter—for the purpose of exalting
the one or the other to the highest position. The

Tantras were composed to stimulate devotion to the female counterpart of Siva.

Next let us glance at the two great Sanskrit epics. The *Rāmāyana*, which consists of 24,000 stanzas, and is arranged in seven books, describes the history of Rāma, the seventh incarnation of Vishnu. The name of Rāma is a household word throughout all India. Hindu mothers delight to tell their children of his exploits. He is for the poet who sings of him " the finished type of submission to duty, nobility of moral character, and chivalric generosity "; and there are passages in the work which attain to a high order of inspiration. Further, as Barth observes, there are in it "accents of an ardent charity, of a compassion and tenderness, and a humility, at once sweet and plaintive, which ever and anon suggest the action of Christian influences, and which in any case contrast singularly with the pride and want of feeling—fruits of the spirit of caste—with which Hindu literature is replete."

The other great Sanskrit epic is the *Mahā-bhārata*. It is the longest epic in the world, extending as it does to 222,000 lines. It is, strictly speaking, rather a collection of epic poetry than an epic : and by far the most noteworthy portion of it is the *Bhagavat-Gīta*—" The Lay of the Divine One "—a work which may justly be considered the high-water mark of Sanskrit poetry. William von Humboldt celebrates it as " the most beautiful, perhaps the only true, philosophical song which exists in any known tongue." Warren

Hastings noted in it "a sublimity of conception, reasoning, and diction almost unequalled." Schlegel closes his Latin version of it with an invocation of the unknown author, "whose oracular soul is, as it were, wafted aloft into divine and eternal truth with a certain ineffable delight." It is in the form of a metrical dialogue in which Krishna, an incarnation of Vishnu, explains to Arjuna the supreme secret of religion and philosophy. Very noble are the portions of the poem in which Krishna reveals himself as the manifestation of that Great Universal Spirit with whom Arjuna is one. It is worth while to cite them in Sir Monier Williams's excellent translation.

> " Whate'er thou dost perform, whate'er thou eatest,
> Whate'er thou givest to the poor, whate'er
> Thou offerest in sacrifice, whate'er
> Thou doest as an act of holy penance,
> Do all as if to me, O Arjuna.
> I am the ancient Sage, without beginning,
> I am the Ruler and the All-sustainer,
> I am incomprehensible in form,
> More subtle and minute than subtlest atoms;
> I am the cause of the whole universe.
> Through me it is created and dissolved;
> On me all things within it hang suspended,
> Like pearls upon a string. I am the light.
> In sun and moon, far, far beyond the darkness;
> I am the brilliancy in flame, the radiance
> In all that's radiant, and the light of lights,
> The sound in ether, fragrance in the earth,
> The seed eternal of existing things,
> The life in all, the father, mother, husband,
> Forefather, and sustainer of the world,
> Its friend and lord. I am its way and refuge,
> Its habitation and receptacle,

I am its witness. I am Victory
And Energy ; I watch the universe
With eyes and face in all directions turned.
I dwell, as Wisdom, in the heart of all.
I am the Goodness of the good, I am
Beginning, Middle, End, eternal Time,
The Birth, the Death of all. I am the symbol A
Among the characters. I have created all
Out of one portion of myself. E'en those
Who are of low and unpretending birth,
May find the path to highest happiness
If they depend on me ; how much more those
Who are by rank and penance holy Brahmans
And saintly soldier-princes like thyself?
Then be not sorrowful ; from all thy sins
I will deliver thee. Think thou on me.
Have faith in me, adore and worship me,
And join thyself in meditation to me ;
Thus shalt thou come to me, O Arjuna ;
Thus shalt thou rise to my supreme abode,
Where neither sun nor moon hath need to shine,
For know that all the lustre they possess is mine."

Arjuna, filled with awe at this revelation, thus
addresses the Incarnate Deity :—

" Most mighty Lord supreme, this revelation
Of thy mysterious essence and thy oneness
With the eternal Spirit, clears away
The mists of my illusions. Show me then
Thy form celestial, most divine of men,
If haply I may dare to look upon it."

To this Krishna replies :—

" Thou can'st not bear to gaze upon my shape
With these thy human eyes, O son of Pandu,
But now I gift thee with celestial vision ;
Behold me in a hundred thousand forms,
In phases, colours, fashions infinite."

Then follows the description of Krishna's transfiguration :—

" Thus having said, the mighty Lord of all
   Displayed to Arjuna his form supreme,
   Endowed with countless mouths and countless eyes,
   With countless faces turned to every quarter,
   With countless marvellous appearances,
   With ornaments, and wreaths, and robes divine,
   With heavenly fragrance and celestial weapons;
   It was as if the firmament were filled
   All in an instant with a thousand suns,
   Blazing with dazzling lustre, so beheld he
   The glories of the universe collected
   In the one person of the God of gods."

The likeness between these portions of the *Bhagavat-Gīta*—there are many more such—and the Sacred Scriptures of Christianity must strike even the most superficial reader. Hence some scholars—conspicuous among them is Dr Lorinser —have been led to believe that the Sanskrit poet directly borrowed from the New Testament, copies of which, he thinks, found their way to India about the third century, the period, as he judges, of the *Gīta's* composition. On the other hand, there are those who assert that the Christian Evangelists were indebted to the Krishna legend : an assertion for which, however, there is no evidence. If, indeed, the *Gīta* is rightly assigned to the third century of our era, its author may have known something of Christianity, which certainly existed in India at that period. But, in truth, the date of the *Gīta* cannot be fixed. Mr K. T. Telang, a learned Hindu to whom we owe the translation of it given in the

Sacred Books of the East, refers it to the fourth century B.C., and gives many arguments, some of which are plausible enough, in support of his theory. What is certain is—to quote the words of a learned American author—that the work, "though not without its imperfections, like the rest, is one of the grand immortal forms in religious literature: an eternal word of the Spirit in man."

The *Mahābhārata* and the *Rāmāyana* are of great value as pictures of ancient Indian life and civilisation. In Sanskrit poetry they occupy a place by themselves. There are, however, two later epics, the *Raghu-vansa* and the *Kumāra-sambhava* which, though of far inferior inspiration, contain passages marked by much beauty of poetic diction and much elevation of thought. They are ascribed to Kālidāsa, who lived—as seems most probable—in the sixth century before Christ, and who is considered the father of the Sanskrit drama. The most famous of his plays is *Sakuntāla*, The Lost Ring, which Sir William Jones translated, and which Goethe warmly eulogised in some well-known verses.

It remains to speak of the *Upanishads*—the term Upanishad means mystic teaching—of which there are some one hundred and seventy. Only a few of them, however, such as the *Prāsna*, *Mundaka*, and *Māndukya Upanishads* belong to the period—the later period—of Vedic literature. They present the earliest and simplest form of the Vedānta philosophy which is accounted—as the name implies—"the end of the *Veda*"; its ultimate aim and consummation ; an idealistic monism deriving the universe from an eternal conscious spiritual principle which it calls *Atmān* —self. I shall have to speak in a later Chapter of the influence of the *Upanishads* in the development of Hinduism. Their importance to readers specially interested in Oriental metaphysics has been admirably pointed out by Mr Gough in his well-known work upon them. " They are an index to the intellectual peculiarities of the Indian character. The thoughts they express are the ideas that prevail throughout all subsequent Indian literature, much of which will be fully comprehensible to those who carry with them a knowledge of these ideas to its perusal. A study of the *Upanishads* is the starting-point in any intelligent study of Indian philosophy."

To enter upon an exposition of the various schools—they reckon six principal ones—of that philosophy, would take me beyond the scope of the present work. The practical outcome of them all is in the Vedānta, which for the last thousand years has dominated—and which still dominates, consciously or unconsciously—the Hindu mind. It may be thus briefly summed up. Being, absolute, pure, void, unconscious, is the Ultimate Reality. The veil of Māya hides It from us. The whole universe is " a fleeting show for man's illusion given." It seems, and is not. Humanity, Society, Civilisation, are mere delusions. Man is "a wandering shadow in a world of dreams." He is an unreal actor on the semblance of a stage, as his soul transmigrates through an innumerable series of bodies. And the way of deliverance from this web of illusion is entire detachment from the world and the things of the world, through a process of purificatory virtues which may be the work of many successive lives: the renouncement of family, of home; meditation, abstraction; the denial of desire. Thus does the sage lose all sense of individual personality, and return to the condition of simple soul. This is the *summum bonum*, the only real good—this loss of separate identity by absorption into the unconscious Absolute, the fontal Self. It is no great wonder that a people penetrated by these doctrines and beliefs should be unprogressive. It is no great wonder that such a people should have no history, no national polity, no science.*

* By way of appendix to this Chapter, I should like to call attention to the great value of the translations from the Sanskrit which find place in the forty-nine volumes of the *Sacred Books of the East*. Those volumes are a vast monument of the learning and zeal of my lamented friend, Professor Max Müller, and of the wisdom and liberality of the University of Oxford which enabled his great design to be carried out.

PART III

HISTORY

CHAPTER VIII

HINDU INDIA

LET me now proceed to indicate, in the briefest outline, and as if by a few strokes of a pencil, some of the more salient features of the history of India. I shall touch, first, on the course of events up to the middle of the seventh century of our era, when the long series of Mohammedan invasions began. That is the subject of this present Chapter. Of the two next Chapters, the one will deal with the period of Mohammedan domination, and the other with the British conquest.

Our materials for a knowledge of Hindu India are of the scantiest. It is not too much to say that there are no Hindu historians. To the Hindu mind, essentially idealistic, filled with a profound conviction of the illusiveness of life and the unreality of phenomena, the procession and succession of events, the rise and fall of dynasties, the fate of empires, seemed a tale of sound and fury signifying nothing. Our knowledge of India, till the chroniclers of Islam wrote of it, is derived from the evidence of language and material monuments, from legends beneath which facts may be traced in dim and uncertain outline, and from casual mention by writers of other countries.

The most ancient Indian legends are those collected in the Sanskrit epics, the *Mahābhārata* and the *Rāmāyana*, of which some account was given in the last Chapter. The wars which are their themes, are probably historical events. That celebrated in the *Mahābhārata* was a contest between the dynasties of Pandu and Kuru for the territory of Hastinapūr, apparently a place on the Ganges to the north-east of Delhi. General Cunningham, by the help of certain astronomical data, places its date in 1426 B.C. The *Rāmāyana*, which relates the invasion of Ceylon by the Hindu prince, Rāma, is a few centuries later. It is not necessary here to relate the main story of either of these epics, or to speak of the various episodes interwoven in them. Their historic value lies in what they disclose to us of the condition of the Indian Aryans at the time when they were written. It is clear that at the period to which the *Mahābhārata* refers, there were many reigning houses—states or principalities—in the country. Half a dozen, at least, are mentioned as belonging to the Gangetic district; among them the kingdom of Magada, afterwards to become so famous. And chiefs from widely distant parts, the banks of the Indus and the Deccan, are among the allies on either side. Both the *Mahābhārata* and the *Rāmāyana* represent a state of society possessing many of the features of the Homeric age: a society of primitive structure and simple arrangements; of athletic habits and warlike tastes; a society, too, of archaic sexual relations: Draupadī, the heroine of the *Mahābhārata*, is the wife in common of five brothers.

There is no trace in these ancient poems of the preponderating influence afterwards enjoyed by the Brahmins, or of the system of caste upon which that influence rests. During the periods to which both relate, the Brahmins appear to have been little more than animal sacrificers at religious rites. How and when they acquired their subsequent power, we cannot conjecture. They were certainly in possession of it when Buddhism comes upon the scene of Indian history in the sixth century before the Christian era. The *Laws of Manu*, though probably not reduced to their present shape until two centuries later, present an accurate picture of Indo-Aryan society as it then existed; the four-fold caste—I shall dwell upon it in a subsequent Chapter—the sacrosanct character of the Brahmins, the paternal despotism of the petty princes or Rājahs who bore rule, the village system which has come down to this day unchanged in its essential features. Such was the world into which Sākya Muni, afterwards known as Gotama Buddha, was born; himself the son of a Rājah who ruled over Kapila-vastu, a small principality situated on the southern slope of the Himālayas. Of him and his mission I shall have to speak when dealing with the religions of India. Here I will merely observe that Buddhism was essentially a reaction against Brahminism. It was not that Gotama laboured directly for the abolition of caste; or that he even, in terms, condemned it. He recognised it, just as he recognised the multitudinous Hindu deities.

But he emptied it, as he emptied them, of real significance. His teaching — to quote Köppen's admirable words — " put spiritual brotherhood in place of hereditary priesthood ; personal merit in place of distinctions of birth ; human intelligence in place of authoritative *Vedas ;* the self-perfected sage in place of the gods of the old mythology ; morality in place of ritualism ; a popular doctrine of righteousness in place of scholasticism ; a monastic rule in place of isolated anchorite life ; and a cosmopolitan spirit in place of old national exclusiveness."

It is to the Greeks that we owe the most trustworthy glimpses of India in the centuries immediately preceding the Christian era. Shortly after the death of Gotama Buddha in B.C. 543—if indeed that is the right date—Darius Hystaspes is said by some authorities to have invaded the Punjāb, and to have formed part of it into a satrapy. Two hundred years subsequently, Alexander the Great, on conquering the Persian Empire, resolved, as is alleged, to emulate that exploit ; and it is to his followers that we owe the first fairly accurate accounts of India and its inhabitants. Starting from Bactria — the modern Balkh — he crossed the Hindu Kush and descended to Kabul. Thence he made his way through the Khyber Pass, and fought that famous action against Porus on the Jhelum, or Hydaspes, which is familiar to every schoolboy. It would be foreign from my present purpose to speak of the various episodes of Alexander's Punjāb campaign. Shortly after his death, Eudemus, his lieutenant and representative at Taxila, on the Indus, was driven out of the country by the Hindu prince, Chandragupta, known to the Greeks as Sandrokottos, who then captured the city of Patna, and soon after acquired the kingdom of Magada. This monarch formed an alliance with Seleukos, the Greek sovereign of Persia and Bactria, whose daughter he married, and received at his court a Greek ambassador named Megasthenes. Nearly all that we know of the condition of Hindustān at this time is due to the account written by Megasthenes (300 B.C.). His experience seems to have been chiefly gained at Magada; but he has left us a detailed account of ancient Patna—Pali-both.a—with its wooden walls, its busy streets, its elephants, chariots, and horsemen. He was told that in all India there were 118 independent governments; and he relates that the army of Sandrokottos numbered 400,000 men. He mentions castes, gives an account of the administration of justice, and furnishes some curious particulars as to taxation.

The grandson of Chandragupta, Asoka, plays a great part in ancient Hindu history. He began his career as monarch by massacring all his brethren, and then greatly extended his dominions by force of arms. He is said to have reigned over Hindustān, the Punjāb, and Afghanistān. Four years after his accession, he openly took under his patronage the religion of Gotama, which may be said to have then entered upon a new career. He is often called the Constantine of Buddhism, and there is unquestionably a close and curious parallelism between the two monarchs. Each was, probably, much influenced by political considerations in declaring himself in favour of the new faith. Each was, as probably, influenced by similar motives in postponing his formal admission into the Church till the last years of his life. But of the two, Asoka appears to be by far the higher character. " The Wrathful," was the title given him in early life, and he unquestionably deserved it. But in his later days, when his heart had been touched and changed by the holy doctrine of the Buddha, men called him " The Just." And the monuments of his legislation, cut in the rock at his command, which are with us to this day, witness to a spotless purity of motive, a noble zeal for justice and mercy, a genuine liberality of mind, an enlightened toleration of spirit, which entitle him to rank high among the rulers of mankind His inscriptions tell us : " The King, beloved of the gods, honours every form of religious faith, but considers no gift or honour so much as the increase of the substance of religion ; whereof this is the root—to reverence one's own faith, and never to revile that of others. Whoever acts differently, injures his own religion, while he wrongs another's. The texts of all forms of religion shall be followed, under my protection. Duty is in respect and service. Alms and pious demonstrations are of no worth compared with the loving-kindness of religion. The festival that bears great fruits is the festival of duty. The King's purpose is to increase the mercy, charity, truth, kindness, and piety of all mankind. There is no gift like the gift of virtue. Good is liberality ; good it is to harm no living creature ; good to abstain from slander ; good is the care of one's parents, kindness to relatives, children, friends, slaves. That these good things may increase, the King and his descendants shall maintain the law. Ministers of morals shall everywhere aid the charitable and good. I will always hear my people's voice. I distribute my wealth for the good of all mankind, for which I am ever labouring."

With the conversion of Asoka (257 B.C.) began the alliance between Buddhism and the State in India, which lasted for nearly a thousand years. We should perhaps err in calling Buddhism the established religion of any part of the country. But for long it certainly seems to have been, in many regions, the most favoured. We read of a prince called Kanishka, who begun to reign in the year 10 of our era, and who was a very zealous Buddhist. "His dominions extended from Kabul to the Hindu Kush and Bolor Mountains, over Yarkand and Khokan ; through Kashmīr, Ladāk, and the Central Himālayas ; down over the plains of the Upper Ganges and Jumna as far as Agra ; over Rājputāna, Guzarat, and Sind, and through the whole of the Punjāb—a magnificent empire unequalled in extent from the time of Asoka to that of the Moghuls." Under the fostering care of this and like-minded princes, stately monasteries arose throughout the land, in which crowds of monks spent their lives in teaching the law of Buddha, and in developing those metaphysical speculations which have so irresistible an attraction for the Hindu mind. Missionaries went to and fro ; and from Kashmīr to Cape Comorin the

gospel of Gotama had free course and was glori-
fied. A son of Asoka is said to have evangelised
Ceylon. And gradually the doctrine of the Buddha
penetrated to regions much further from its original
home: to Thibet and China, to all Eastern Asia
from Korea to Siam. For glimpses of it in the
land of its origin, during the early centuries of our
era, we are indebted to the accounts of pious
Chinese pilgrims who came thither in search of
relics and sacred texts. Interesting in the highest
degree are these records of the geography, history,
manners, and religion of the people of India in
those far-off times. And we may entirely agree
with their translator, Mr Beal: "Never did
disciples more ardently desire to gaze on the
sacred vestiges of their religion: never did men
endure greater sufferings by desert, mountain, and
sea, than these simple Buddhist priests."

Fa Hian, the earliest of them, wrote at the beginning of the fifth century of our era. It took him
five years to arrive at mid-India. He resided there
for six years, and it was three more before he returned
to China from Ceylon—after a perilous voyage of
which he gives a most graphic account—with the
sacred books and images collected by him. Fa
Hian relates that throughout his travels he found
the religion of the Buddha everywhere flourishing,
with kings for its nursing fathers and queens for
its nursing mothers. And between it and Brahminism there seems to have been no open enmity.
Sung Yun visited India a century later, but did
not penetrate further than Peshāwar. He speaks
of the country east of the Indus as Buddhist. Of

far more importance was the pilgrimage of Hiouen-
Tshang. This most illustrious traveller was born
in the year 603 of our era, at Ch'in Liu, in the
province of Honan, and at the age of twenty
received full Buddhist orders as a Bhikshu or
priest. In A.D. 629 he left China on his perilous
pilgrimage, returning in A.D. 648 with precious
relics and statues of the Buddha. and with Buddhist
literature, which formed a load for twenty-two
horses. He found India divided into more than
a hundred states, of which he has left us as exact
an account as he could : geographical, social,
political, historical, and religious. St Hilaire calls
him one of those "elect souls in history, few of
whom have been able to carry disinterestedness so
far towards the limit where nothing is known but
the plain idea of goodness." It would appear that
the most powerful monarch in India at that time
was Sīlāditya, the king of the country which
Hiouen-Tshang calls Kie-jo-kio-she-kwo (Kanya-
kubja). The remains of its capital, Kanauj, may
still be seen on the banks of the Ganges. Hiouen-
Tshang received a cordial welcome from Sīlāditya,
a zealous Buddhist, well read in the Sacred Books,
whose virtues he celebrates in glowing terms. Of
the capital city and its inhabitants he gives the
following pleasant account : " It has a dry ditch
round it, with strong and lofty towers facing one
another. The flowers and woods, the lakes and
ponds, bright and pure, and shining like mirrors,
are seen on every side. Valuable merchandise is
collected here in great quantities. The people are
well off and contented : the houses are rich and

well formed. Flowers and fruits abound in every place, and the land is sown and reaped in due season. The climate is agreeable and soft: the manners of the people are honest and sincere. They are noble and gracious in appearance. For clothing they use ornamented and bright shining fabrics. They apply themselves much to learning, and are renowned for the clearness of their arguments. The believers in Buddha and the heretics are about equal in number. There are some hundred Buddhist temples with 10,000 priests. There are 200 Hindu temples with several thousand followers." Sīlāditya is stated to have reigned over Hindustān and the Punjāb, and to have exercised suzerainty over many princes beyond those regions. So much as to Hiouen-Tshang and his travels. The general impression which he leaves on the mind is, that though he found Buddhism still a considerable power, it had fallen below the position which it held in Fa Hian's day.

This is the last glimpse we get of Buddhism in India. Four centuries afterwards, it is gone, and its original birthplace knows it no more. Its disappearance is one of the most curious phenomena in history, and is quite unexplained. There is a tradition of sanguinary and exterminating persecutions by the Brahmins. But the tradition rests upon no evidence. Mr Rhys Davis thinks, " In the eighth and ninth centuries Buddhism became so corrupt that it no longer attracted the people, and when it lost the favour of the kings, it had no power to stand against the opposition of the priests."

CHAPTER IX

MOHAMMEDAN MASTERS

A THOUSAND years is the period commonly and roughly assigned by historians to Buddhist supremacy in India. The next thousand years are the millennium of Mohammedan invasion and conquest. The Hindus, speaking generally, have never been a warlike people. In most ages, foreign victors have made a prey of them. Thus, in the epoch at which we have just glanced, invaders, dubiously described as Scythians, swept in, horde after horde, through the north-west passes, and occupied portions of the Punjāb, and of the valley of the Ganges. It was in driving back these foreigners that Vikramāditya won his prominent place among Indian heroes. He is described as King of Ujjain, but what his achievements really were, or what was their date, we do not know. Of this great prince

> "Only a fading verbal memory,
> An empty name in writ, is left behind."

We also read of a people called Guptas—the Hindu name for them was Mlechhas or barbarians

—who made a home for themselves in the North-West Provinces. But when they came, or who they were, we are ignorant. The favourite conjecture seems to be that they were immigrants from the old Græco-Bactrian Empire who had become half Hinduised. Anyhow, they would seem to have made common cause with the Hindu princes, and to have fought side by side with them in the great battle of Korūr, in which the Indo-Scythians were completely overthrown. But the date of this conflict, esteemed "one of the decisive battles of the world," is matter of conjecture. It has been shifted forwards and backwards from 78 to 544 A.D.

The truth is, Elphinstone well remarks, that we must be content with guesses until the arrival of the Mussulmans at length puts us in possession of a regular succession of events with their dates. In the year 604 of our era—and 44 of the Hijra—the Moslems first appeared in India. It was a mere incursion. Not until a century afterwards did the Arabs seriously invade Sind with a regular army under the command of Mohammed Kāsim. The success which attended that expedition led the youthful general—he was only twenty—to plan a march upon Kanauj. But he was baffled by what Elphinstone calls "a sudden reverse," which shall be related in the well-chosen words borrowed by that writer from the Mohammedan historians. "Among the numerous female captives in Sind were two daughters of Rāja Dāhir, who, from their rank and their personal charms, were thought worthy of being presented to the Commander of the Faithful (Walīd, the sixth calif of the house of Ommeia). They were, accordingly, sent to the court, and introduced into the harem. When the eldest was brought into the presence of the calif, whose curiosity had been stimulated by reports of her attractions, she burst into a flood of tears, and exclaimed that she was now unworthy of his notice, having been dishonoured by Cāsim before she was sent out of her own country. The calif was moved by her beauty, and enraged at the insult offered to him by his servant; and, giving way to the first impulse of his resentment, he sent orders that Cāsim should be sewn up in a raw hide, and sent in that condition to Damascus. When his orders were executed, he produced the body to the princess, who was overjoyed at the sight, and exultingly declared to the astonished calif that Cāsim was innocent, but that she had now revenged the death of her father and the ruin of her family."

This characteristic catastrophe checked the advance of the Mohammedan arms in India for a time. But Kāsim's conquests remained in the hands of his successor for thirty-six years when, upon the downfall of the house of Ommeia, they were reoccupied by the Rājputs.

The next Moslem invaders of India were not Arabs, but Tartars, whom we may, with sufficient accuracy for our present purpose, call Turks. After the breaking-up of the empire of the Caliphs, which may be dated from the middle of the ninth century, there arose, among other independent

Moslem governments, that of Ghazni, which, under a ruler named Sebektegin, became a considerable power. Sebektegin was a slave, whom Alptegin, the ruler of Ghazni, himself originally of servile condition, had bought from a merchant of Turkestan, and who displayed such skill in the arts both of peace and war, that he rose to high offices of power and trust. It is related of him that "one day in hunting, while yet a private horseman, he succeeded in riding down a fawn; but when he was carrying off his prize in triumph, he observed the dam following his horse, and showing such evident marks of distress, that he was touched with compassion, and at last released his captive, pleasing himself with the gratitude of the mother, which often turned back to gaze at him as she went off to the forest with her fawn. That night the Prophet appeared to him in a dream, told him that God had given him a kingdom as a reward for his humanity, and enjoined him not to forget his feelings of mercy when he came to the exercise of power." He appears to have ruled his own people well. But he slaughtered and plundered the Hindus who dwelt on the northern bank of the Indus, and established a garrison at Peshāwar.

He was succeeded by his son, Mohammed of Ghazni, who assumed the title of Sultan. This prince made seventeen expeditions into India between 1001 and 1020 A.D. Of these, thirteen were directed to the subjugation of the Western Punjāb; one was an unsuccessful incursion into Kashmīr; the remaining three were "short but furious raids" against Kanauj, Gwalior, and Somnath respectively.

It is by the Somnath campaign that Mohammed of Ghazni is chiefly remembered. One of the few fragments of Indian history, so called, that have found currency in Europe, is the story of his breaking in pieces the idol of the great Somnath temple with his mace, after declining the ransom offered for it by its priests, to find the reward of his iconoclastic zeal in the treasure of jewels which poured to the ground from its interior. But, as modern writers have pointed out, the legend is a fond thing vainly invented, the idol of Somnath being merely a rude block of stone, one of the twelve lingams, or phallic emblems, erected in various parts of India. Another exploit of this Sultan Mohammed connected with his Somnath expedition, more or less popularly known in this country, is his carrying back the gates of the temple with him to Ghazni. It was these gates which Lord Ellenborough in 1842 proposed to send back to the place whence they came, after the storming of that town, as a memorial of " Somnath Revenged," announcing his intention to the native rulers and people of India in a proclamation, the bombastic language of which excited general wonder and dissatisfaction. As a matter of fact, the gates, which appear not to have been the ancient ones, but a modern forgery, got no further than Agra, and are still warehoused in the magazine there.

But although the legend about the jewel-bellied image of Somnath is a clumsy forgery, no doubt Mohammed of Ghazni amply merited his title of Image-breaker by the destruction of the idol of that temple and of many others. The one lasting result of his Indian campaigns was the conversion of the Punjāb into an outlying province of Ghazni. "He never set up as a resident sovereign in India. His expeditions beyond the Punjāb were the adventures of a religious knight errant, with the plunder of a temple or the demolition of an idol as their object, rather than serious efforts at conquest."

Mussulman historians extol Mohammed of Ghazni as one of the greatest sovereigns of any age. He appears, certainly, to have been among the greatest of his own. His military skill was unquestionably of a high order. And his administration of his kingdom displayed much talent for government. Notwithstanding the bloodshed and misery which he carried far and wide, he does not seem to have been wantonly cruel. Many anecdotes are current about him which illustrate his sense of kingly duty. One of the shortest, and not the least striking, is the following :— " Soon after his conquest of the Persian province of Irāk, a caravan was cut off in the desert to the east of that district, and the mother of one of the merchants, who was killed, went to Ghazni to complain. Mohammed urged the impossibility of keeping order in so remote a part of his territories, when the woman boldly replied, ' Why, then, do you take countries which you cannot govern, and for the protection of which you must answer at the Day of Judgment ? ' Struck with the reproach, he made the woman a liberal present and took effectual measures for the protection of the caravans." Another story about him illustrates his severity to military license. One day a peasant threw himself at the monarch's feet complaining that an officer of the army had forcibly entered into his house, more than once, to gratify a criminal passion for his wife. The king directed the peasant to say nothing, but to come to him directly the next time the officer made his appearance there. This the man did. Mohammed took his sword in silence, and wrapped himself round in a loose mantle, and the two went to the house. There they found the guilty couple asleep, and the king, first extinguishing the lamp, cut off the head of the adulterer with a single blow. He then ordered lights to be brought, and on looking at the dead man's face, burst into an exclamation of thanksgiving, and called for water, of which he drank a deep draught. Perceiving the astonishment of the peasant, he told him that he had suspected his own nephew to be the criminal; that he had extinguished the light lest his justice should give way to affection; that he now saw the offender was a stranger, and having vowed neither to eat nor drink until he had given redress, he was nearly exhausted with thirst.

The great stain upon this prince's character seems to have been insatiable avarice. The love of gain, not of glory, was the chief motive of his wars. On the other hand, it is claimed for him that "if he was rapacious in acquiring wealth, he was unrivalled in the judgment and grandeur with which he knew how to expend it." The mosque called *The Celestial Bride*, which he

built at Ghazni, was the wonder of the East. His
court was splendid. He founded a university at his
capital, and spent a large sum on its maintenance.
He was illustrious for his munificence to learned
men, and gained especial renown for his patronage
of Ferdousi. It was at his request that the poet
composed the great epic, *Shāhnāmeh* — a labour
of thirty years. But the reward which Mohammed
offered upon its completion was judged by Ferdousi
altogether inadequate. He rejected it, and with-
drew in indignation to his native city of Tūs, where
he composed a bitter satire against the too parsi-
monious prince. Mohammed, however, took no
offence, but sent the bard a lavish present. It
arrived too late. As the messenger, who bore it,
entered by one door of Ferdousi's house, the poet's
body was being carried out to burial by another.
His daughter, the chronicler adds, at first rejected
the gift, but subsequently accepted it, and devoted
it to procuring a supply of water to Ferdousi's
native city. The memory of Mohammed's avarice
lived after him, and inspired one of the most striking stories in Sādi's *Gulistān*. A certain person,
that poet relates, saw the monarch, then long dead,
in a dream. He was a mere skeleton, save the
eyes, which were entire. And those organs of
covetousness, as Orientals account them, gazed
eagerly from their sockets, insatiable and inde-
structible, like the passion which had animated
them.

So much may suffice regarding Mohammed of
Ghazni; on the whole, perhaps, the best type of
those Mohammedan conquerors from whom India

suffered so much in the Middle Ages. He died in 1030 A.D. His dynasty lasted till 1186, when the Ghorī family conquered Ghazni. The most famous prince of this house was Mohammed Ghorī, who reigned from 1156 to 1205 A.D., and laid the real foundation of the subsequent Mohammedan empire of India. His six Indian campaigns were not merely incursions for the sake of booty, of which, however, he amassed an immense amount. He annexed the districts which he occupied—they extended from the delta of the Indus to the delta of the Ganges— and provided means for their administration. At this period the ruling families of Northern India were all Rājputs who, when defeated by the Moslem invaders, quitted their homes rather than submit, and established themselves in the country border-ing on the eastern desert of the Indus, in which they have remained unto this day, and which is called after them Rājputāna.

When Mohammed Ghorī died—as a matter of fact, he was murdered by a party of Gakkars, a mountain tribe with whom he had had trouble—his Indian viceroy, Kūtab-ud-dīn, proclaimed himself King of India, and founded a line of rulers which lasted for nearly a century, and which is known as the Slave dynasty, from the fact that he started in life as a Turkī slave. He was a valiant and able ruler, and the celebrated minaret at Delhi, known as the Kūtab Minār, still exists as a memorial of him.

It was in 1288 that the last Sultan of the Afghan Slave dynasty—or rather dynasties, for there were several of them—was assassinated, and till

1320 the house of Khiljī reigned at Delhi.   The
most famous prince of this line was Alā-ud-dīn.
The great work of the twenty years of his reign
was to found the Mohammedan sway in Southern
India.   But before starting on his great expedition
to the Deccan, he had to meet five Moghul inroads
from the north.   It should be noted that by this
time there was a large Mohammedan population in
Northern India, consisting of Moghul invaders,
who, having failed in attempts at conquests, had
taken service with the kings of Delhi; of Afghans
who had followed the Ghorite sovereigns, and of
Turkīs who had been brought in by the Ghaznite
princes.   To these should be added the converts
to Islām made from time to time whether by
persuasion or compulsion, but chiefly by the latter
means.

The Khiljī dynasty disappeared in 1321, and
was succeeded in the Delhi kingdom by the house
of Tughlak, founded by a Turkī slave.   The second
of the race, Mohammed (1325-1351), was one of the
most extraordinary characters that ever reigned.   He
is described as the most eloquent and accomplished
prince of his age, an admirable Arabic and
Persian scholar, well versed in mathematics and the
physical sciences as they were then cultivated, in
Greek philosophy, and in medicine; a great
builder of hospitals and almshouses, and a patron
of learning, " Yet," proceeds the historian, "all
these splendid talents and accomplishments were
given him in vain; they were accompanied by a
perversion of judgment which, after every allow-
ance for the intoxication of absolute power, leaves

us in doubt whether he was not affected by some degree of insanity." He assembled a vast army for the conquest of Persia, "which, after it had consumed his treasures, dispersed for want of pay, and carried pillage and ruin to every quarter." He sent another army of 100,000 men through the Himālayan passes to conquer China; a disastrous expedition in which the troops perished almost to a man. To relieve his insolvency he introduced into his dominions a forced currency of copper tokens, the natural result being vastly to increase his financial embarrassment. When the husbandmen, beggared by his exactions, abandoned the culti-vation of their fields, and fled to the woods, he would order a man hunt. His army surrounded an extensive tract of country, and then gradually closing up towards the centre, slaughtered all the human beings within it, as though they were wild beasts. It is reported of him that, on one occasion, he commanded a general massacre of the inhabitants of the great city of Kanauj, who had in some way offended him. He compelled the whole population of his capital Delhi to remove to Deoghīri, in the Deccan, a journey of some seven hundred miles, through dense jungles, over high mountains and across great rivers, accomplished with infinite distress and prodigious loss of life, and entirely infructuous, for the plan failed. But the fort of Deoghīri, which still remains, is a token of the stupendous scale of his undertakings. "The rock round the hill is cut perfectly smooth and perpen-dicular for 180 feet — the only entrance being through a winding passage in the heart of the rock. The whole is surrounded by a broad, deep ditch, cut also in the solid rock." The net result of his reign was the dislocation of his empire, more extensive in the early part of it than the dominion of any Mohammedan prince who had preceded him. Bengal revolted under a Mussulman officer who became its Sultan. The Hindu Rājah of Karnāta asserted his independence, and founded a new dynasty at Vijayanagar which soon flourished in great power. The Hindu Rājah of Telingāna established himself at Warangōl. The Mohammedan army of the Deccan broke into mutiny and set up a Sultan of its own.

Of the subsequent princes of the Tughlak dynasty the most notable was Fīruz (1351-1388) distinguished for the number and excellence of his public works, which are stated to have comprised 50 dams across rivers to promote irrigation, 40 mosques, 30 colleges, 100 caravanserais, 30 reservoirs for irrigation, 100 hospitals, 100 public baths, and 150 bridges. The most considerable of his undertakings remaining to us is the great Jumna canal, a part of which has been restored by the British Government. Ten years after this monarch's death, Tamerlane descended on India through the Afghan passes, with his Tartar hosts, and, defeating the Tughlak king Mahmūd, under the walls of Delhi, took that city and gave it up to five days of massacre and plunder by his troops. He departed on the last day of the year, carrying off a vast amount of booty, and many men and women of all ranks who had been reduced to slavery. On the day of his departure

he is said to have "offered up to the Divine
Majesty a sincere and humble tribute of grateful
praise in the noble mosque of polished marble
erected on the banks of the Jumna by Fīruz." He
formed no permanent government in India. The
Tughlak dynasty continued to rule in Delhi till
1412, when it came to an end. The Sayyid
dynasty took its place and continued till 1450,
when it was succeeded by the Afghan house of Lodī
which endured to the year 1526. It was in that
year that Bāber, the sixth in descent from Tamerlane, invaded India, and winning the first battle
of Pānipat, founded the famous Moghul Empire.

Before I proceed to speak briefly of this last and
greatest of the Moslem dynasties of India, I should
note that during the period at which we have just
cursorily glanced, Mohammedan rule never extended over the whole of that country. In the
Deccan—which word, it will be remembered, I use
to denote all India south of the Vindhya Mountains
— there were a large number of petty Rājahs,
more or less independent. There were also, from
very ancient times, three considerable Hindu
monarchies, the Chera, the Chola, and the Pandya;
and the last mentioned of these, of which the
capital was at Madura, endured until the
eighteenth century. We possess no trustworthy
evidence regarding these old Hindu states, beyond
what is supplied by their inscriptions and architectural remains. But of the great monarchy of
Vijayanagar we have several accounts by Western
visitors. It existed from 1335 to 1565, and in the
time of its highest prosperity its dominion extended

from sea to sea, including well-nigh all the territory now known as the Madras Presidency. The
greatest of its monarchs appears to have been
Krishna Rāya, a contemporary of our Henry
VIII., by whom were constructed most of the large
annicuts still existing which cross the Tungabudra.
On the south bank of that river stood its capital,
from which it took its name : a magnificent city,
indeed, among the colossal ruins of which I have
often wandered, trying to reconstruct in imagination its palaces and aqueducts, its amphitheatres
and bazaars. An Italian traveller who visited it
at the beginning of the sixteenth century, describes
its buildings as far surpassing in splendour anything which he had beheld in Europe : and,
certainly, if they were on a like scale with its still
existing temples — as no doubt they were — we
may well credit the assertion. He tells us that
it was twenty-four miles in circumference, enclosing
several hills, and speaks with much admiration of
the cool channels flowing through its streets, and
the groves and gardens covering its suburbs. It
fell in 1565 before a combination of the five
Mohammedan princes of the Deccan, who overthrew its king in the sanguinary battle of Tālikot.
And great was the fall of it. With it seemed to
fall all independent Dravidian life.

The five Mohammedan princes who united to
overthrow the Hindu kingdom of Vijayanagar
were the "Sultans"—so they styled themselves—
of Bijāpur, Golconda, Berar, Ahmednagar, and
Ahmedābād. Their kingdoms had been formed out
of the territories of the Brahminī dynasty founded

by Hussain Ganga, one of the generals of Muhammed Tughlak, who successfully rebelled against his master, and who began to reign as an independent Moslem monarch in the Deccan in the year 1347. The date of the extinction of his dynasty is usually given as 1526. But long before that, as a matter of fact, the five Mohammedan principalities mentioned above had arisen in the Deccan, and had become practically autonomous.

Let us return to Bāber, who, as will be remembered, established himself at Delhi in the year 1526, and whose account of his eventful career in his *Memoirs* is one of the most fascinating autobiographies ever written. Strangely pathetic was his death. His son Humāyon being grievously sick, and given over by the physicians, the magnanimous monarch solemnly offered up his own life in substitution for the dying prince's, who forthwith began to recover. But Bāber's vital force gradually declined, until, in a few months, he passed away at the age of fifty (1530). The greatest of his line was undoubtedly the famous Akbar, his grandson, who comes upon the stage of history in 1556. It was in that year that this boy of thirteen, by the aid of his general, Beiram, won the decisive victory at Pānipat—the second important battle of that name—over the Afghans, who had dispossessed his father, Humāyon, of the throne of Delhi. The next year Humāyon died and he succeeded as Emperor. His reign lasted till 1605, and was therefore almost contemporaneous with that of our Queen Elizabeth. At first he was, naturally, much under the tutelage of Beiram, the ablest of his father's warriors and councillors. And his relations with this strong and masterful adviser curiously resembled those which existed between the present German Emperor and Prince von Bismarck, Beiram being the real author of the renewed greatness of the House of Tamerlane. He it was whose clear intellect, iron will, and unswerving steadiness of purpose, had reared again the Moghul throne at Delhi. But he had the defects of his qualities. Harsh, dictatorial, overbearing, he brooked no opposition, and those who ventured upon any, he put to death or sent into banishment. Akbar endured this thraldom for four years, and then found it intolerable. He was now seventeen. "He took occasion, when on a hunting party, to make an unexpected visit to Delhi on the plea of a sudden illness of his mother. He was no sooner beyond the sphere of the minister's influence, than he issued a proclamation announcing that he had taken the government into his own hands, and forbidding obedience to orders issued by any other than his authority." This fell upon Beiram like a thunderbolt. For a brief time he meditated upon various schemes for recovering his power. But as none of them seemed promising, he set out for Nagūr, announcing his intention of going on a pilgrimage to Mecca. While he lingered over his preparations for it, an imperial messenger arrived, bringing him a formal dismissal from his office, and a command to proceed on his pilgrimage without delay. He protested his submission to his master's will, and surrendered his standards, kettledrums, and other insignia of authority. But instead of embarking for Mecca, he raised an insurrection in the Punjāb. Akbar proceeded against him in person. He was defeated by a detachment of the imperial troops, and threw himself upon his master's mercy. The Emperor sent nobles of high rank to meet him and to bring him to the royal tent. On his arrival there, he prostrated himself at the sovereign's feet, and moved, whether by the reproach written on Akbar's face, or by recollections of their former relations, or by the realisation of his departed greatness, the strong man wept aloud. Akbar's own hands raised him up and seated him next to the imperial throne. He was invested with a dress of dignity, assured that his disloyalty should be forgotten, and offered his choice of high office at court, of one of the principal governments of the empire, or of an honourable dismissal upon his pilgrimage. His proud soul elected to proceed to Mecca, feeling, no doubt, that his occupation in public affairs was gone. But at Guzarat, when about to embark upon that pious expedition, he was cut off by the knife of an Afghan assassin, whose father he had killed, years before, in battle.

I have told this of Beiram at length, because it well illustrates the magnanimity which was one of the strongest features of Akbar's character, and which perhaps won for this great prince as many victories as his sword. A great prince, indeed; one of the greatest that ever swayed the rod of empire; great as a warrior; greater as an administrator; greatest as a man. It would take me far beyond my present limits to sketch, even in outline,

F

the conquests of his long reign. I can only remind my readers, touching upon a few salient points, how, before he was twenty-five, he had brought into subjection his turbulent military aristocracy, crushing his adversaries by his vigour, or attaching them to him by his clemency ; how next he subdued the Rājput princes—all save the Rāna of Chitūr (or Udaipūr)—and turned them into loyal feudatories ; how, subsequently, he recovered Bengal and Behar, and reduced Kabul, which had revolted under his brother, Mirza Hakim, binding that turbulent prince to him by a generous pardon and a restored trust ; how he added Kashmīr to his dominions—this was in 1586—and conquered Sind in the north-west, and Kandesh in the south. The net result was that he ruled over territories extending from the heart of Afghānistān, to Orissa and Sind, and across all India, north of the Vindhyas, and divided them into the thirteen provinces of Bengal, Behar, Berar, Khandesh, Ahmadnagar, Allahābād, Oudh, Agra, Malwa, Guzarat, Ajmere, Delhi, Lahore, Multan, and Kabul—a term which embraced Kashmīr, Swat, Bajaur, and Kandahār. As Elphinstone well writes, it was his "noble design to form the inhabitants of that vast territory"— some 150,000,000 of them — " without distinction of race or religion, into one community." Hence, one of his chief cares was to put an end to the religious disabilities pressing upon Hindus under previous Mussulman rulers. Quite early in his reign he abolished the jizia or capitation duty on infidels, an oppressive and irritating badge of Moslem supremacy. He abolished also the taxes

on Hindu pilgrimages, giving as his reason that
"although the impost fell upon a vain superstition,
yet as all modes of worship were designed for One
Great Being, it was wrong to throw an obstacle in
the path of the devout, or to cut them off from their
own way of intercourse with their Maker." On
the other hand, like the strong ruler he was, he
forbade certain Hindu practices which were
obviously opposed to public policy and to the
general welfare, such as trials by ordeal, child
marriages, and the enforced perpetuity of widowhood. He carried, however, his respect for individual freedom so far as to permit sutti, if it
was altogether voluntary. Upon one occasion,
having heard that the widow of the Rājah of
Jodhpūr's son was pressed by her father-in-law to
the funeral pile, he rode post-haste to the spot,
and prevented the intended sacrifice. He himself
married into two Rājput princely houses, and one
of his Hindu wives—the daughter of the Rājah
of Jeypūr — is said to have been his favourite
queen. Hindus were largely employed by him in
the public service, and were advanced to the highest
and most responsible offices. His famous finance
minister, Rājah Tōdar Mall—also distinguished as a
military commander—the principal author of the
land revenue settlement which, in some of its chief
features, endures to this day, was a Hindu. So
was Rājah Mān Singh, one of his most trusted
and distinguished generals, who ruled the province
of Bengal from 1589 to 1604. In fact, we may
say that in Akbar's reign was realised the august
conception of civil and religious liberty worthily

enshrined by Milton in words written after that monarch had passed away. " The whole freedom of man consists either in spiritual or civil liberty. As for spiritual, who can be at rest, who can enjoy anything in this world with content-ment, who hath not liberty to serve God? The other part of our freedom consists in the civil rights and advancements of every person, accord-ing to his merit." It is worth while to remember that while Akbar was carrying out this enlightened policy in his Indian Empire, Queen Elizabeth was racking and hanging her Catholic subjects in Eng-land, and King Philip the Second was burning holo-causts of Protestant victims in the fires of the Inquisition throughout Spain and the Low Coun-tries. Even the measure of toleration granted in France by the Edict of Nantes (1598), fell far below the ideal of religious equality realised by the greatest of the Moghuls.

As might have been expected, Akbar's tolera-tion in matters of religion was most unacceptable to the more rigid of his Mohammedan subjects. In Islām, I need hardly observe, there is no priest-hood. The place of a sacerdotal order is filled by the Doctors of the Law—the very source and fount of which is the Qu'rān. Akbar was obliged, in the interests of the public peace, to adopt stringent measures for keeping the more fanatical of these sages in order. It is not unusual for persecutors who are withheld from persecuting, to complain that they themselves are persecuted. Such com-plaints were made against Akbar by the Moham-medan Scribes and Pharisees. They must be largely discounted. Certain it is, indeed, that he effectively broke down their power, and banished the more refractory of them to distant regions of Central Asia. They, in return, accused him of apostatising from Mohammedanism, and of founding a new religion of his own under the name of The Divine Faith. But it is undeniable that throughout his life he conformed to the creed of Islām, and that he died in the free and open profession of it. Unquestionably, however, he held it in a very different spirit from that which animated, and still animates, the vast majority of its adherents. As unquestionably he displayed an intelligent interest in other creeds. The disputations held in his palace every Friday, when Christians, Brahmins, Buddhists, and Parsis expounded their views with as much freedom as Moslems, witness to the openness and candour of his mind. He had much sympathy with the religion of Zoroaster. For Christianity he professed the utmost respect, and he manifested it by inviting Catholic priests to Agra and allowing them to build a church there. It is said, too, that one of the best loved of his wives was a Christian. The so-called sect founded by him does not appear to have really been more than a coterie of friends who held the Deism, of a Pantheistic type, which he regarded as the root of the matter, and which is the doctrine of the great Mohammedan mystics. We may fitly take leave of the subject of Akbar's religion in the well-weighed words of Elphinstone. "He excelled all his predecessors in his conception of the Divine Nature," and "the general freedom which he allowed to private judgment was a much more generous effort in a powerful monarch than in a recluse reformer."

In Akbar we have, I think, the well-nigh perfect type of an Indian ruler; and in his policy the true norm of Indian administration. I must not omit to notice how admirably Nature had equipped him for the great task committed to his hands. Strongly built, and handsome in person, he excelled in all manly exercises and feats of physical strength and skill. It is related of him that he would spring upon the backs of elephants who had killed their keepers and compel them to do his bidding. " He sometimes underwent fatigue for the mere pleasure of the exercise, as when he rode from Ajmere to Agra (220 miles) in two successive days, and in many similar journeys on horseback, besides walks on foot of twenty or thirty miles a day. His history is filled with instances of romantic courage, and he seems to have been stimulated by a sort of instinctive love of danger, as often as by any rational motive." He was extremely sober and abstemious in his personal habits, and was satisfied with very little sleep. Under the massive strength of his character there ran a deep vein of tenderness. One of the most touching episodes in his life is his grief when Rājah Bīr Balu, to whom he was deeply attached, was slain during a campaign against the Afghans. He mourned for him like David for Jonathan, and was for long inconsolable. He greatly delighted in the society of learned men. Among his most intimate and cherished friends were the two brothers, Feizi and Abdul Fazl. Both were persons of much culture, and to Feizi belongs the distinction of being the first Mussulman profoundly versed in Hindu literature. To Abdul Fazl we owe the *Akbarnāmeh*, a detailed account of Akbar's home and history. Both were employed by him in weighty diplomatic affairs. Abdul Fazl also obtained high military rank, and, for some time, held the office of Prime Minister. His great influence with Akbar earned for him the hatred of Selim, the Emperor's eldest son, and successor under the title of Jehānghīr; and he was cut off in an ambuscade instigated—though Akbar never knew it—by that prince. Akbar was deeply affected by the intelligence of his death, and for two days could neither eat nor sleep. Some years before he had sustained the loss of the other of the two illustrious brothers, and the narrative of his behaviour upon that occasion well illustrates the strong sensibility of his nature. It was midnight when tidings reached him that Feizi was in the last extremity, and caused him to hasten to the chamber of the dying man, who was already nearly insensible. Akbar raised his head and, addressing him by the endearing epithet " Shekhji," said, " Why don't you speak? I have brought Ali the physician to you." But Feizi's speech was now decayed, and no answer came. Akbar threw his turban on the ground in a passion of grief, and burst into lamentation. But the thought of the dying man's brother brought back his self-control, and he went off to sympathise, and condole with, Abdul Fazl.

I spoke just now of Akbar's revenue system

which conferred upon India the boon of simple
and just taxation in the place of the arbitrary
and capricious demands made by former rulers
upon the cultivators of the soil. The principal
features of it were that the land was accurately
measured and marked out, that the money equivalent of the share of the state was determined
on fixed and rational principles, and that the fees
formerly levied by the officers of the Government
—a vast source of extortion and vexation—were
abolished. In the *Ain-y-Akbāri*, or Regulations
of Akbar, which forms the third volume of the
Akbarnāmeh, there is a precise account of it. To
that work also—made accessible to the English
reader through several translations — we owe a
minute and most interesting account of the establishment and regulation of all the branches of
Akbar's service, "from the Mint and the Treasury
down to the fruit, perfumery, and flower offices,
the kitchen and the kennel," the whole — I am
quoting from Elphinstone—presenting "an aston-
ishing picture of magnificence and good order."
Akbar's life, in the midst of the splendour of his
court, was as simple as dignified. European
travellers who visited him describe him as affable
and majestic, merciful and severe; loved and
feared of his own, terrible to his enemies. He
lies buried at Agra, where so many magnificent
structures were reared by him, in a mausoleum
which is no unworthy sepulchre of so great a
prince. "It is a sort of pyramid," writes Bishop
Heber, "surrounded externally with cloisters,
galleries, and domes, diminishing gradually on

ascending it, till it ends a square platform of
white marble, surrounded by the most elaborate
lattice work of the same material, carved with a
delicacy and beauty which do full justice to the
material, and to the graceful forms of the Arabic
characters which form its chief ornament."

There arose no king like unto Akbar among
the Moghuls who came after him. His son Selim,
who had embittered his last days by spasmodic
attempts at rebellion, succeeded him, and took the
pompous title—I am not aware for what reason—
of Jehānghīr, "Conqueror of the World," by which
name he is generally known. This "Conqueror
of the World" appears to have been, upon the
whole, not a bad ruler, according to the Eastern
standard of rule. He was equitable and tolerant
to his Hindu subjects, as became the son of a
Rājput princess. But the old Tartar ferocity, of
which we find no trace in Akbar, was strongly
marked in him. Rebellious children are the great
curse of Oriental dynasties, partly owing to the
absence of the settled rule of succession now
usually prevailing in the kingdoms of the West
through the custom of primogeniture. Kushrū,
Jehānghīr's eldest son, who had endeavoured to
supplant him even in Akbar's lifetime, broke into
open revolt against him soon after his accession.
The revolt was quelled within a month, and
Kushrū was brought in chains to his father at
Lahore. In order to intimidate the young prince,
Jehānghīr ordered seven hundred of his principal
accomplices to be impaled in a row, and caused
him to be conducted along the line on an elephant,

while a mace-bearer, mocking the agonies of the sufferers, called upon him to receive the salutations of his friends.

In the sixth year of his reign Jehānghīr married Nūr Jehān, whose romantic history, and striking personality, merit a few passing words. This very beautiful and accomplished woman was the daughter of a Persian nobleman who, reduced to poverty in his own country, emigrated to India to seek his fortune. Nūr Jehān was born on the journey, just as the caravan reached Kandahār. And as the father had no means of supporting the baby, or even of paying for her journey, she was exposed by the road over which the travellers were to proceed next morning. A principal merchant of the caravan, struck with the child's beauty, had compassion on her, and announced his intention of providing for her. He further provided for the immediate needs of her relatives, and, subsequently, introduced her father and eldest brother to Akbar. After fulfilling some subordinate offices in that monarch's service, they were advanced to higher ones, upon their merits becoming manifest to his judging eye. When Nūr Jehān grew into girlhood she often accompanied her mother to the harem of Akbar, where she was seen by Jehānghīr, who became violently enamoured of her. This coming to the ears of Akbar, he thought it advisable to remove the damsel from the prince's sight, and caused her to be married to a young Persian of good family named Shīr Afghan Khān, who had recently entered his service, and to whom he gave a jaghir

in Bengal. In a few years Jehānghīr succeeded
to the throne, and, shortly after that event, he
determined to gratify his passion for the fair
Persian, whom he had by no means forgotten, and
directed his foster brother, the Viceroy of Bengal,
to negotiate the matter with her husband. But
in the course of an interview at which this was
attempted, Shīr Afghan Khān, so far from proving
complaisant, entirely lost his temper, and stabbed
the Viceroy to death, himself being immediately
despatched, in return, by the viceregal attendants.
Nūr Jehān, shocked at this tragedy, for several
years rejected all Jehānghīr's overtures ; but in
the event yielded to his importunities, and their
marriage was celebrated with great pomp. Her
influence over him was unbounded, and she was
treated with a consideration never before shown
to the consort of a Mohammedan sovereign. Her
name appeared on the coinage beside the
Emperor's, and he took no important step in the
government of his dominions without consulting
her. She was a woman of great natural capacity,
and was usually a wise and prudent counsellor.
Her power was, upon the whole, exerted for good.
She repressed Jehānghīr's caprice and tyranny,
and induced him to be more sparing in the use
of wine, to which as a young man he had been
immoderately addicted. Her personal devotion to
him was unquestionable, and upon one occasion
she hazarded her life to deliver him from captivity
to a rebellious general by whom he had been
captured. At the end of his reign she was much
mixed up in intrigues having for their object to oust

from the succession Shāh Jehān, a son of Jehānghır who had married her niece, in favour of another and younger son, Sheriār, who had married her daughter by her first husband. But these intrigues failed, after causing a great deal of bloodshed, and on Jehānghīr's sudden death of an asthma in 1627, Shāh Jehān succeeded, and after slaying Sheriār, his only surviving brother, was firmly established upon the throne. Nūr Jehān's influence expired with her husband, to whose cherished memory she devoted the remaining nineteen years of her life. She was treated with the greatest respect by the new monarch, and was allowed a pension of £250,000 a year. Shāh Jehān had proved himself a general of much ability during his father's lifetime. Among other achievements he had succeeded in bringing to an honourable termination the conflict with the Rāna of Udaipūr, the greatest of the Rājput chiefs, and following the wise policy of Akbar, had assured to the vanquished prince a high position among the military paladins of the Empire.

Shāh Jehān's wars, chiefly with the potentates of the Deccan, need not detain us here. His civil administration of his dominions seems entitled to high praise. The historian, Khāfi Khān, declares that for the good order and arrangement of his territory and finances, and the good administration of every department of the state, no prince ever reigned in India that could be compared with Shāh Jehān. And Elphinstone allows that after all deductions are made for fraudulent exaction by the collectors of revenue, and corruption in the ministers of justice, and for acts of extortion by custom house officers, and for arbitrary deeds by governors of provinces, "there will still remain enough to convince us that the state of India under Shāh Jehān was one of great ease and prosperity."

But Shāh Jehān's fame rests chiefly upon the splendour of his court and of the structures which he erected. He was the most magnificent of the Moghuls, and kept his state upon that wonderful peacock throne—a blaze of diamonds and precious stones—which is estimated to have cost six and a half millions sterling, and is reckoned among the wonders of the world. He rebuilt Delhi on a regular plan, and adorned it with edifices of unrivalled magnificence, among which may be specially mentioned the palace—now the fort—the Great Mosque, a work of extraordinary elegance and grandeur, and the Tāj Mahāl, "a dream in marble, designed by Titans and executed by jewellers": it is the mausoleum of Mumtāz Mahāl—the niece of Nūr Mahāl—whom he passionately loved, and whom he lost after fourteen years of marriage, within twelve months of his accession to the throne. Here I should note that his sons did unto him as he had done unto his father—and more also. His reign closed with a fratricidal war between four of them, resulting in his captivity to Aurungzebe—the third—in which he languished for the last eight years of his life.

Aurungzebe's most pressing care after his usurpation was to get rid of his three brothers. In the first year of his sovereignty he put to

death Dāra. In the second he completely broke
the power of Shuja, who fled into Arakan and
there perished miserably. In the third Murād
was slain in prison. Thus began Aurungzebe's
reign of forty-nine years (1658-1707) under the
title of Alamghīr, "the Conqueror of the Universe." As a matter of fact, the portion of the
universe which he conquered consisted of the Mohammedan kingdoms of Southern India. Three
of these, Bedar, Ahmadnagar, and Ellichpur, had
submitted to him before he attained the empire.
It was not till 1680 that he annexed Bijapur.
In the next year Golconda was subdued by his
troops. His court was magnificent. His administration, at all events during the earlier part of
his reign, was careful and exact. He was unquestionably an able, valiant, and accomplished
prince. Mussulman historians regard him as the
greatest of the Moghul rulers, greater even than
Akbar. In this they are wrong. He was certainly
a more zealous Mohammedan. But the intoler-
ance bred of his zeal is the secret of his failure
as a ruler. He was a crowned and sceptred
bigot. While extending his dominions, and carrying his empire to wider limits than any of his
predecessors, he undermined the foundations of his
rule. He reimposed the insulting poll tax (jizia)
on non-Mussulmans throughout his territories. He
sought to exclude all except Mussulmans from
the public service. He desecrated shrines and
destroyed sacred images of the Hindus. He
prohibited many of their religious festivals. The
dream of his life was the conversion of India to

the faith of Islām. The effect of his proselytizing measures was to create disaffection and alarm throughout the country. His character and career present a curious similarity to the character and career of Louis XIV. of France, whose reign was almost contemporaneous with his. To the men of their own time, both seemed magnificent and illustrious. In Dryden's play of which Aurungzebe is the hero, he is presented as an ideal of magnanimity, and some of the noblest verses the poet ever wrote are put into his mouth. To Boileau, Louis XIV. was the embodiment of all kingly qualities: "Tout brille en lui, tout est roi," he declares. Far other is the judgment of history on "the Conqueror of the Universe" and the "Grand Monarque." In each it finds the same unscrupulousness, arrogance, and cruelty; in each it detects theological fanaticism usurping the place of pure religion and undefiled. It shows us how each, in the plenitude of his despotic egotism, by attempting to force his creed upon dissentient subjects, brought about the disruption of his realm and the ruin of his house. The palm of wickedness must be, indeed, conceded to the Most Christian King. The ravage of Rājputāna was as atrocious an act as the ravage of the Palatinate. But there is nothing in the exploits of the sixth Moghul to equal in turpitude the Revocation of the Edict of Nantes and the Dragonnades.

Aurungzebe's reign of half a century came to an end in 1707. He was then eighty-nine years old, "none of his senses," writes the historian Khāfi

Khān, "being impaired, except his hearing, and that in so small a degree that others could not perceive it." His last days were embittered by the not unnatural fear of such treatment from his sons as his father had experienced from him. It is related that not long before his end, upon Prince Āzim seeking permission to visit him at Ahmed-nagar, where he was then encamped, on the ground of illness and desire for change of air, he observed "that is precisely the pretext I used to Shāh Jehān."

There is no need for entering here upon the history of his successors to the imperial throne, the last of whom, Mohammed Bahādur Shāh, died forty years ago in captivity at Rangoon. They reaped the heritage of trouble which he had sown. It was in Aurungzebe's time that the Mahrattas came forward under Sivajī as a new Hindu power in Western and Central India: indeed, the last twenty years of his life were employed in waging an unsuccessful war against them. Immediately after his death, they began to close in upon the empire. They were aided in their work of destruction by the Rājputs, who in 1715 became practically independent; and by the Sikhs, a body of peaceful religionists, founded towards the end of the fifteenth century by Nānak Shāh, who were converted in 1710-1716 by a bitter persecution into an armed nationality. In 1729, the Persian, Nādir Shāh, swooped down upon India, sacked and plundered Delhi, and retired with a booty valued at 32,000,000 sterling —Shāh Jehān's peacock throne being among the

spoils. Then followed a tempest of invasion by the
Afghans, resisted successfully by the Mahrattas
until their decisive overthrow at the third battle
of Pānipat (1761), in which 200,000 of them are
said to have perished. The victorious Ahmed
Shāh returned home without attempting to profit
by his success. But, as Elphinstone observes,
this third battle of Pānipat really marks the close
of the Moghul Empire. "Its territory is broken
into separate states; the capital is deserted; the
claimant to the name of Emperor is an exile and a
dependant, while a new race of conquerors has
already commenced its career, which may unite the
empire under better auspices than before."

CHAPTER X

THE ENGLISH CONQUEST

IT is difficult for us to realise in how short a time the British Empire in India has grown up. A century ago it comprised only Bengal, Behar in Eastern Hindustān, a small territory round Bombay, and a somewhat larger round Madras. Two Indian princes — the Nawab Vizier of Oude and the Nawab of the Carnatic—were the protected allies of the English. Three others—the Nizam, Scindia, and Tippu—were their dreaded foes. Now, the whole country owns the sovereignty of the King-Emperor : and five-eighths of it are under his direct rule. It has been remarked by De Toque-ville that the conquest and government of India are really the achievements which give England her place in the opinion of the world. No doubt this is so. It is equally beyond doubt that our greatness in India was forced upon us. Our Indian Empire was acquired, not by the deliberate design, but against the will of the people of England. I shall proceed in this Chapter to sketch in outline what Sir Henry Maine has well called "that wonderful succession of events which has brought the youngest civilisation in the world to instruct and correct the oldest, which has re-united those wings of the Indo-European race—separated in the infancy of time to work out their strangely different missions."

Thomas Stephens, the Jesuit, is the first Englishman known to have visited India in modern times. The date of his visit is 1578. His letters to his father, giving an account of it, stimulated the spirit of curiosity and adventure among us, and four years afterwards, three English merchants, whose names are worth remembering—Newberry, Fitch, and Leeds—made their way to the country overland. The Portuguese, who were already there, threw them into prison, first at Ormuzd, and then at Goa. Newberry, in the event, settled down as a shopkeeper at the last-mentioned place : Leeds entered into the service of Akbar : and Fitch, after long wanderings, found his way back to England. In 1600, "the Governor and Company of Merchants of London trading to the East Indies" were incorporated by Royal Charter with a capital of £70,000. They prospered exceedingly, their profits seldom falling below 100 per cent., and in 1612-13 their capital was raised to £400,000. Other rival Companies were started from time to time, the most formidable being "The General Society trading to the East Indies," incorporated in 1698 with a capital of £2,000,000. In 1708 this "English" Company was amalgamated with the original "London" Company, under the style of "The United Company of Merchants of England trading to the East Indies." That is "The East India Company," which has lasted till our time.

It is not necessary here to chronicle the conflict of English traders in India with Portuguese and Dutch during the seventeenth century. We may, however, note that the three great English cities of India then had their origin. Madras was founded in 1638, and was the first English territorial possession in that country. It was created an independent Presidency in 1653. The island of Bombay, which formed part of the dowry of Catherine of Braganza, came into our possession in 1665, 'and was made the seat of the Western Presidency twenty years afterwards. The beginnings of Calcutta must be referred to the year 1686. It was originally subordinate to Madras, and was not made an independent Presidency till 1716.

The eventual struggle for the possession of India was not between the English and the Portuguese, or between the English and the Dutch, but between the English and the French, and took place in the eighteenth century. In 1674 the French founded their settlement of Pondicherry, some hundred miles lower than Madras on the Coromandel coast. And there, for seventy years, they peaceably pursued their commercial operations, although differences with the Madras Government arose, from time to time, and led to angry correspondence. But in 1743 war broke out between England and France. And in 1746 a French fleet, under La Bourdonnais, captured Madras. The English Government removed to Fort David, a similar settlement only twelve miles from Pondicherry. In 1748 a fleet arrived from England under Admiral Boscawen, and siege was laid to

Pondicherry.   It was then that Clive, a civilian who had obtained an ensign's commission, first won military distinction.   The siege of Pondicherry was unsuccessful, and was raised in three months. Shortly afterwards, hostilities between France and England were brought to a close by the Peace of Aix-la-Chapelle, and Madras was restored to the British.

But Dupleix, the Governor of Pondicherry, nourished the dream of a French Empire in India; and during the next fourteen years he laboured with all his might to realise it.   He was no soldier. Battles, he said, confused his genius.   But he was a consummate politician: and the story of his intrigues with the native potentates, through whom he sought to compass his designs, would fill a vast volume.   In the wars which they produced, the English and the French were ranged on different sides: At first, the plans of Dupleix, ably seconded by his half-native wife, were crowned with success. In the early part of 1751 the ascendency of France was established throughout Southern India. Suddenly the situation was changed by the dauntless courage and admirable strategy of Clive.   His capture and defence of Arcot, in 1751, were the beginning of an unbroken series of English triumphs, finally crowned by the victory of Eyre Coote at Wandiwash in 1760 over Count Lally, General Bussy, and the whole French army, and by the capture of Pondicherry in 1761. Dupleix, who had been recalled to France in 1754, died ten years afterwards, ruined and broken hearted. Lally was judicially murdered in 1766.   And in

1769 the French East India Company ceased to exist.

Meanwhile Clive, promoted in 1755 to be Governor of Fort St David, had been called to Calcutta by the tragedy of the Black Hole—"that great crime, memorable for its singular atrocity, memorable for the tremendous retribution by which it was followed." On 23rd June 1757, the Battle of Plassy was fought and won. It is the date of the beginning of our Indian Empire. In 1758 Clive was appointed by the Court of Directors the first Governor of Bengal. His work during the next two years was the permanent establishment of British influence in the North Circars and at the Court of Hyderabad. In 1760 he returned to England, and was raised to the Irish peerage. He remained at home for five years, living in great splendour upon his income of £40,000 a year—a very large one in that age—cultivating Parliamentary interest, and defending himself against a party among the Directors of the East India Company who were jealous of his greatness. During those five years, affairs in Bengal were grossly mismanaged by the officials who held power there. Lord Macaulay goes so far as to say that their misgovernment was carried to a point such as seems hardly compatible with the very existence of society. "A succession of revolutions: a disorganised administration: the natives pillaged, yet the Company not enriched: every fleet bringing back fortunate adventurers who were able to purchase manors and to build stately dwellings, yet bringing back also alarming accounts of the financial prospects of the Government: war on the frontier, disaffection in the army: the national character disgraced by excesses resembling those of Verres and Pizarro: such was the spectacle which dismayed those who were conversant with Indian affairs. The general cry was that Clive, and Clive alone, could save the empire which he had founded." Clive responded to the cry, after assuring his position with the Directors of the East India Company, and in May 1765 once more reached Calcutta and assumed office as Governor. He remained in India only a year and a half. But during that short time he accomplished two great works. He reorganised the Company's service, prohibiting that private trade which had been the source of frightful oppression and corruption, and establishing a liberal scale of official salaries. And he procured from the Moghul Emperor the grant of the Dewāni or fiscal administration of Bengal, Behar, and Orissa, which constituted the English the legal rulers of the country. He left India in 1767, for the last time, broken in health, and a poorer man than when he had returned to it. Of the "causes which embittered the remainder of his life and hurried him to an untimely grave," it is not necessary to speak here. But whatever blots are found on his career, Lord Macaulay's verdict upon him is certainly well warranted: "His name stands high in the roll of conquerors; but it is found in a better list; in the list of those who have done and suffered much for mankind."

To Lord Clive must be given the first place among the founders of the Indian Empire. The second belongs to one even greater—Warren Hastings. It is from his appointment as Governor-General, in 1774—he was the first to fill that office —that we must date the foundation of the existing system of Indian Government. His name, like Clive's, has become a household word among us through the brilliant essays of Lord Macaulay. But certain it is that, in several important particulars, Macaulay was betrayed into injustice towards him by too implicit reliance upon traditions which have only more recently been discredited. It has been conclusively shown by the late Sir James Stephen that the charge of contriving the judicial murder, or something very like it, of Nuncomar, is untenable. And Sir John Strachey has given good reasons for thinking that the Rohilla war was by no means so flagitious an undertaking as it had for a century been believed to be. It is undeniable that whatever faults may stain Warren Hastings' long administration of the Indian Government—it lasted from 1774 to 1785—his services to the State were of the highest order. And the verdict of posterity ratifies the verdict by which the House of Lords, after a seven years' trial, acquitted him of the charges urged by the majestic eloquence of Burke. Here again we may quote Lord Macaulay with full assent: "Those who look on his character without favour or malevolence, will pronounce that, in the two great elements of all social virtue, in respect for the rights of others, and in sympathy for the sufferings of others, he was deficient. His principles were somewhat lax. His heart was somewhat hard. But though we cannot with truth describe him either as a righteous or as a merciful ruler, we cannot regard without admiration the amplitude and fertility of his intellect, his rare talents for command, for administration, and for controversy, his dauntless courage, his honourable poverty, his fervent zeal for the interests of the State, his noble equanimity, tried by both extremes of fortune, and never disturbed by either."

Warren Hastings was succeeded as Governor-General by Lord Cornwallis, whose first term of office lasted from 1786 to 1793, and who established on durable foundations the system of British administration which his predecessor had initiated. He is best known by his least successful achievement—of which I shall have to speak in a subsequent Chapter—the Permanent Settlement of Bengal. In 1790-92, he commanded in person the British army in the second Mysore war—the first had been waged under Warren Hastings in 1780-84—in which the Nizam of the Deccan and the Mahratta Confederacy co-operated as allies of the British. It resulted in the submission of the Mysore ruler, the redoubtable Tippu Sultan, who was deprived of half his dominions and made to pay a fine of two millions sterling. With the exception of the disastrous Permanent Settlement of Bengal, carried out under the stringent orders of the Court of Directors, Lord Cornwallis's administrative measures were wisely conceived and admirably executed. It has been observed by a well-informed writer, "The Corn-

wallis Code, whether for revenue, police, criminal
and civil justice, or other functions, defined and
set bounds to authority, created procedure, by a
regular system of appeal guarded against the mis-
carriage of justice, and founded the civil service of
India as it exists to this day."

Lord Mornington—created Marquis Wellesley
in 1799—ruled India from 1798 to 1805 : and unquestionably was one of her greatest rulers.   As
Clive must be regarded as the founder of the territorial system of the British Empire, and Warren
Hastings as the founder of its administrative system,
so Lord Wellesley was the founder of its political
system.   The friend and confidant of Pitt, his
policy was shaped by the imperial spirit of that
great statesman.   On arriving in India he found
French influence dominant at the courts of the
principal Mohammedan prince, the Nizam, and
the great Mahratta potentate Scindia, while the
ruler of Mysore, Tippu Sultan, had openly sought
the aid of Napoleon Bonaparte, then in Egypt,
against the English, and had declared himself "a
citizen of the French Republic."   Lord Wellesley
resolved to crush this curious citizen of the French
Republic, and having induced the Nizam to receive
and pay for a British force, and to discard his
French officers, he sent into Mysore two British
armies, to whose assistance his brother Arthur
Wellesley, the future Duke of Wellington, brought
a considerable body of the Nizam's troops.   Tippu
perished at the siege of Seringapatam (1799): a
youth who represented the ancient Hindu dynasty
was proclaimed Mahārājah of Mysore, and Arthur

Wellesley was entrusted with the settlement and administration of that country. Lord Wellesley's next great achievement was to break up the Mahratta Confederacy in Southern India which aimed at, and very nearly achieved, supreme power there. It was Arthur Wellesley who gave the death blow to it at the battle of Assaye (1803). There is no exaggeration in saying that he was the saviour of our rule in India. The course he pursued in that famous fight was daring in the extreme. But it was the truest wisdom: a retreat would almost certainly have been fatal to him. The battle of Assaye is second in importance only to the battle of Plassy. It was followed, as a natural consequence, by the paralysis of French influence and French intrigue. It was supplemented by Lord Lake's great victories of Delhi and Laswāri. And England became indisputably the dominant power in the East. Here we may note that the Duke of Wellington gave to our rule in India not merely military strength, but moral force. He did much to raise the tone of official life there, and to purify the public service. To corruption, in all its forms and disguises, he was the unflinching foe. And the prudence of his policy towards the native chiefs is as remarkable as his military skill. Like Akbar he knew how successfully to conciliate the foes he had subdued. His, too, was a sword "that only conquers men to conquer peace."

Lord Wellesley left India in August 1805. He had found the Moghul Empire in complete dissolution. He had raised the British Empire on its ruins. He had brought the North-West

Provinces under British rule. He had acquired the greater part of the territory in South-Eastern India, now constituting the Madras Presidency. And in South-Western India he had reduced the Mahratta ruler, the Peshwa, to vassalage, thus preparing the way for the destruction of that Prince's power in the fourth Mahratta war (1818), when the dominions of the vanquished potentate were annexed by Lord Hastings. They now form a portion of the Bombay Presidency.

It was in 1813 that the Marquis of Hastings— he was then Lord Moira — came to India as Governor-General. After the departure of Lord Wellesley, Lord Cornwallis was again nominated to the office, but died within a few months of his arrival. Next Sir George Barlow officiated in it for two years, when he was sent to the subordinate Government of Madras, upon the appointment of Lord Minto, whose rule of six years (1807-13), was marked by no incident which need be mentioned in this brief sketch. The most important event of the Marquis of Hastings' long Governor-General-ship (1814-1823), was the fourth and last Mahratta war which has been already mentioned. But his reign was also memorable for the Nepaul war (1814-15), in which General Ochterlony achieved the brilliant march to Khatmandu, and dictated there the peace which assured to us the hill stations of Naini Tāl, Massūri, and Simla, and for the suppression (1815) of the Pindari bands of mar-auders who desolated Central India. Then came Lord Amherst (1823-28), and the first war with Burmah, which resulted in the cession to us of a

portion of that country. The next Governor-
General was Lord William Bentinck, who twenty
years before had been Governor of Madras : "the
benevolent Bentinck" who—to quote Macaulay's
inscription on his statue at Calcutta—"never forgot
that the end of government is the welfare of the
governed ; who abolished cruel rites : who effaced
humiliating distinctions : who allowed liberty to the
expression of public opinion : whose constant study
it was to elevate the intellectual and moral character
of the nation committed to his charge." His reign
lasted from 1828 to 1835. And it was in 1833 that
Macaulay was appointed legal member of his
Council, being the first to hold that office.

Lord Auckland's Governor - Generalship — it
lasted from 1836 to 1842—was made memorable by
our intervention for the first time in the affairs
of Afghānistān. For two years the country was
occupied by British troops. Then came the murder
of Sir William Macnaughten, the Political Officer,
and the destruction of our army in its attempt
to make its way back to India through the passes.
In 1842 Lord Ellenborough succeeded Lord Auckland as Governor-General, and two British armies,
under Generals Pollock and Nott respectively,
made their way to Kabul, which they sacked,
blowing up the great bazaar with gunpowder. In
1843 Lord Ellenborough annexed Sind. In 1844
he was recalled, and was succeeded by Sir Henry
Hardinge, subsequently advanced to the peerage
as Lord Hardinge.

Lord Hardinge held office as Governor-General
for four years. The chief event of his reign was

the first Sikh war. As was stated in a previous
Chapter, the Sikhs were a sect founded by Nānak
Guru out of Hindus, Mohammedans, and others
in the fifteenth century. At first gentle religionists, the savage persecution of the Moghul
Emperors in the early eighteenth century converted them into valiant warriors. About the
beginning of the nineteenth century one of them,
Runjeet Singh, established himself as their personal
ruler, making Lahore his capital, and extending
his conquests south to Multān, west to Peshāwar,
and north to Kashmīr. Up to his death in 1839,
he was faithful to an alliance into which he had
entered with the British. But when he had passed
away, troubles arose, issuing in the invasion in
1845 of our territories by a Sikh army of 60,000
men with 150 guns. They were opposed by Sir
Hugh Gough, afterwards raised to the peerage
as Lord Gough, who in three weeks fought four
pitched battles with them, at the last of which,
Sobrāon, they were decisively overthrown. Peace
was then concluded, Dhuleep Singh, the infant son
of Runjeet, being recognised as Maharājah, a
portion of Sikh territory being annexed by the
British, and the Rājput, Golab Singh, a Sikh
general, being constituted Maharājah of Kashmīr
for a payment of a million in hard cash towards
the expenses of the war, one of the most disgrace-
ful transactions that stain our rule in India.

In 1848 Lord Dalhousie went out as Governor-
General, at the comparatively early age of thirty-six.
He held the office for eight memorable years,
leaving the impress of his vast energy, iron will,

and intense devotion to duty, upon every branch of the administration. The second Sikh war broke out before he had been in the country six months. It ended within a year in the decisive victory of Guzarat. Lord Dalhousie determined upon the annexation of the whole of the Punjāb as the only way of ending its chronic misgovernment. And the event has justified his policy. The country soon became tranquil, and has steadily advanced in prosperity. And the Sikhs are among the most loyal and contented subjects of the British Crown. Dhuleep Singh received for his relinquishment of the sovereignty a grant of £58,000 a year, and lived as an English gentleman upon an estate in Norfolk. In 1852 the second war with Burmah broke out. It resulted in the annexation of a further portion of that country. In 1856 the kingdom of Oudh, long a prey to anarchy and oppression, was annexed, the ex-king being allowed a pension of £120,000 a year, upon which he settled down in a suburb of Calcutta. Further accretions of territory took place during Lord Dalhousie's reign by the lapse to the British Government of the states of Sattāra, Jhansi, and Nagpur, upon the death of their respective Rājahs without heirs male. But Lord Dalhousie's long term of office was distinguished not merely by the extension of British territory, but also by his indefatigable exertions to promote the moral and material well-being of the people over whom he ruled. He was the real founder of the Indian Universities. He set on foot vast and most beneficent schemes of public works. Under him the railway system of

India was begun.   He introduced into the country
the half - anna post.   The admirably successful
system of administration in the Punjāb and in
Burmah was initiated by him.   He went home to
die—his constitution, never strong, quite broken
down by his labours and anxieties.

Lord Dalhousie's friend, Lord Canning, the
illustrious son of the illustrious George Canning,
was the next Governor-General.   In little more
than a year from his assumption of office, the Indian
Mutiny broke out.   It would almost seem as if some
presage of a great calamity must have arisen in
his mind when, on the eve of his departure from
England, he said, at a farewell banquet given by
the Court of Directors: "I wish for a peaceful
term of office: but I cannot forget that in our
Indian Empire that greatest of all blessings
depends upon a greater variety of chances, and a
more precarious tenure, than in any other quarter
of the globe.   We must not forget that in the
sky of India, serene as it is, a small cloud may
arise, at first no bigger than a man's hand; but
growing bigger and bigger, may at last threaten
to overwhelm us with ruin."   It would be difficult
to depict more accurately than in these prophetic
words the course of the Indian Mutiny.   The
affair of the greased cartridges, which seemed to
the official mind a mere bagatelle, was, as a matter
of fact, the occasion of a commotion which shook
the British Rāj to its foundations.   In May 1857
the sepoys at Meerut rose on their officers, and
began the work of massacre.   It was not until
the middle of the year 1858 that Sir Hugh Rose,

afterwards Lord Strathnairn, finally suppressed the insurrection in Central India. There is no need to touch here even upon the outlines of the tragedy which filled that space of time. The massacre at Cawnpore, the siege and storming of Delhi, the defence and relief of Lucknow, the heroic deeds associated with the names of Havelock, Lawrence, Outram, and Colin Campbell, are fresh in all memories. But it is well to turn the mind's eye to Lord Canning, unmoved throughout that season of stress and storm; realising the ideal of the "just man, firm of purpose," depicted by the Roman poet; declining to swerve one hair's breadth from the course of justice in obedience to the "rabid and indiscriminate vindictiveness" which, as he wrote to the Queen in September 1857, was "abroad, even among those who ought to set a better example." "As long as I have breath in my body," he protested to Lord Granville, a short time afterwards, "I will pursue no other policy than that I have been following: justice, and that as stern and inflexible as law and might can make it, I will deal out: but I will never allow an angry or undiscriminating act or word to proceed from the Government of India as long as I am responsible for it."

The suppression of the Mutiny was followed by the extinction of the East India Company as a ruling body. In 1858 an Act for the better government of India transferred the administration of that country to the Crown, acting through a Principal Secretary of State. Shortly after the passing of this measure, a great Durbar was held at Allahābad, at which Lord Canning—who had now become Viceroy — published the Royal Proclamation, announcing that the Queen had assumed the Government of India, and declaring the policy of justice and religious toleration which would be pursued by herself and her successors.

In March 1862 Lord Canning went home in a moribund state, and was succeeded by Lord Elgin, who died in November of the following year. Then came the five years' Viceroyalty of Sir John Lawrence —afterwards raised to the peerage—whose wise and firm administration had saved the Punjāb during the Mutiny. The next Viceroy was Lord Mayo, whose short term of office—he was cut off by the hand of an assassin in 1872—was marked by a great development of public works. His successor, Lord Northbrook, held the Viceroyalty for four years, and was followed in 1876 by Lord Lytton, who in 1877 held a great Durbar at Delhi, when the Queen was proclaimed Empress of India, and who in 1880 made way for the Marquis of Ripon. The first year of the new Viceroy's rule was marked by the conclusion of the war with Afghānistān, occasioned by the murder of Sir Louis Cavagnari. The remaining three were years of peace, devoted chiefly to legislative measures recommended by the name of Liberal. Of these measures the most notable was the so-called Ilbert Bill, which proposed to extend the jurisdiction of the rural criminal courts over European British subjects, irrespective of the race or nationality of the presiding magistrate. This project was vehemently opposed, not only in India but also in England,

and was ultimately amended by its restriction to
the Courts of District Magistrates and Sessions
Judges.

Whatever view we may take of some portions
of Lord Ripon's policy, there can be no question
as to his high character, rectitude of purpose, and
unswerving loyalty to his sense of duty. Few
English rulers have so largely won the confidence
and affection of the native population. When he
retired in 1884, he was succeeded by the Marquis
of Dufferin, who in the next year was driven by
the hostile attitude of the Burmese king to annex
the country over which that monarch ruled:
thereby completing the conquest of the territories
which form the Indian Empire.

PART IV

RELIGIONS

CHAPTER XI

HINDUISM

I now come to speak of the religions of India. The broad lines of demarcation are between Hinduism, Mohammedanism, Buddhism, and Christianity. Three-fifths of the people of India profess Hinduism. But, as we shall presently see, it would be difficult to give any accurate definition of Hinduism: to say what it is, where it begins, and where it ends. There is not the same difficulty about Mohammedanism, which is the religion of some 60,000,000 of the inhabitants of the Indian Empire; or about the Buddhism of the Southern Church, which is the religion of the 9,000,000 who dwell in Burmah. These are definite and homogeneous creeds. There are 2,500,000 of Christians, of various kinds. The Sikhs, Jains, and Parsis, however considerable from other points of view, are numerically a mere handful. In this part of my work I shall speak first of Hinduism, devoting to it the present Chapter. The next will deal with the other non-Christian religions of India. Then will follow one on Christianity.

The *Rig-Veda* is confessedly the work of trans-

cendent authority on the beliefs and practices
which make up Hinduism. All other Indian
Sacred Books are subordinate to it. The name
sruti, or revelation, is uniquely applied to it. Less
holy writings are called *smriti*, or tradition. The
Vedic religion is the first phase of that poly-
theistic idea of the universe which, after the
transformations, and developments, and corrup-
tions of three thousand years, still subsists in
India, and dominates the minds of the great
majority of her people. Let us consider it a
little.

The gods of the *Vedas* are personifications—
there is no better word available—of physical forces
and phenomena. The religious beliefs enshrined
therein are founded on that nature worship which
was originally common to all the branches of the
Indo-European family. The Light, the Sun, the
Dawn, the Wind, the Fire, are celebrated in the
Vedic hymns with vivid and picturesque imagery,
as manifestations of Divinity. In the god Varuna
—the name is the same as the Greek word for
Heaven, Οὐρανός — the attributes of power and
majesty found in the other objects of worship are
combined. But Varuna appears to be merely the
chief of many deities—*primus inter pares*—who
keep watch over the universe. To say that there
is absolutely no moral element in this old Vedic
religion would be incorrect. Sin is recognised as
evil, righteousness as good. But if we proceed to
inquire what constitutes sin, and what righteousness, we find little trace of those ethical conceptions
which lie at the root of modern European life.

"The Vedic minstrels," writes Barth, "feel the weight of other duties besides those of multiplying offerings to the gods, and the punctilious observance of religious ritual; but we must admit that the observance of these is with them a matter of capital importance, and that their religion is preeminently ritualistic: the pious man is, by distinction, he who makes the soma* flow in abundance, and whose hands are always full of butter; while the reprobate man is one penurious towards the gods, the worship of whom is the first duty." Of the features of modern Hinduism most repugnant to the European mind there is no mention in the *Vedas;* the atrocities of Siva and Kāli; the licentiousness of Krishna; the grotesque adventures of Vishnu; child marriage, sutti, and perpetual widowhood.

So much as to the religion of the Indo-Aryans up to, say, B.C. 1200; the religion treasured up in those Vedic hymns which, as Weber remarks, "they had brought with them from their ancient homes on the banks of the Indus, and which they had there used for invoking prosperity on themselves and their flocks, in their adoration of the dawn, in celebration of the struggle between the god who wields the lightning and the powers of darkness, and in rendering thanks to the heavenly beings for preservation in battle." How this Vedic religion passed into Brahminism we have no means of determining. But it did so pass, as its naturalism was metaphysically construed and sacerdotally

* The fermented drinkable juice of a plant so named, offered in libation to the gods.

developed in the *Brāhmanas.* The Vedic deities
became gradually more and more shadowy in the
popular mind. The rites performed by the priestly
caste—the Brahmins—assumed an ever greater and
greater importance. In the word *caste,* indeed, we
have the key to the explanation of this second phase
of the Indo-Aryan religion. The fourfold division
of the people into Brahmins, Kshatriyas, Vaishyas,
and Sūdras is, no doubt, foreshadowed even in the
Rig-Veda; the priesthood appears there as constituting a distinct profession and as hereditary.
But in this second period, the caste distinctions are,
so to speak, stereotyped ; they assume the rigidity
which finds expression in the *Laws of Manu.* The
Brahmin alone knows the rites of religion with
their hidden and mystic meaning ; and his supremacy is established. In this period, which may be
roughly considered to extend from 1000 to 500 B.C.,
sacrifices hold a great place ; and, as Barth
remarks, "among the victims, which consist of all
imaginable kinds of domestic and wild animals,
there is one which recurs with ominous frequency,
viz., man."

But while the Brahmins were thus building up
a stupendous system of rites, they were busy with
the philosophic speculations which are enshrined in
the *Upanishads.* These sacred books are metaphysical treatises, largely pantheistic in tone,
largely mystical, largely allegorical. The origin
and destiny of things, the nature of deity, the constitution of the soul, the genesis of mental error, of
moral evil, are their main themes. But, to quote
Barth again, "these singular books are still more

practical than speculative. They address themselves more to man as man, than to man as thinker.
Their aim is not so much to expound systems, as
to unfold the way of salvation. They are preeminently exhortations to the spiritual life, per-
plexed and confused, indeed, but delivered at times
with a pathos which is both lofty and affecting. It
seems as if the whole religious life of the period,
which we miss so much in the ritualistic literature,
had become concentrated in these writings. [They
regard] the separated condition of the soul, which
is the cause of mental error, as also the cause of
moral error. Ignorant of its true nature, the soul
attaches itself to objects unworthy of it. Every act
which it performs to gratify this attachment, en-
tangles it deeper in the perishable world; and, as
it is in itself imperishable, it is condemned to a
perpetual series of changes. Once dragged into
the *samsāra*, into the vortex of life, it passes
from one existence into another without respite and
without rest. This is the twofold doctrine of the
karman, *i.e.*, the act by which the soul determines
its own destiny, and of the *punarbhava*, *i.e.*, the
successive rebirths which it undergoes. This
doctrine, which is henceforth the fundamental
hypothesis common to all the sects and religions
of India, is found formulated in the *Upanishads* for
the first time."

Unquestionably, this doctrine had sunk deeply
into the popular mind, when Sākya Muni began
to preach and to teach, and to lay the foundations
of the religion which, numerically considered, is
still the most prevailing of the world's creeds. I

shall have to speak of it, particularly, in the next Chapter. Here I would remark that though the spiritual greatness of its founder has impressed a distinct character on Buddhism, it is as truly both a development of and a reaction against Brahminism, as Christianity is a development of and a reaction against Judaism. Its underlying doctrine is essentially that doctrine of the *Upanishads* at which we have just glanced. On the other hand, it may be called, with entire accuracy, "a protest against the tyranny of Brahminism and caste." We must remember, however, that the protest was rather implicit than explicit. The Buddha was no conscious revolutionist. He does not appear to have controverted the cosmogony or the theology of the Brahmins. His teaching seems to have been purely ethical; its substance that existence, in any form, must necessarily be evil; and that the only way to get rid of evil is to get rid of the desire of existence. The Buddha was born, and lived, and died a Hindu. "His whole teaching," Mr Rhys Davids emphatically observes, "was Brahminism; he probably deemed himself to be the most correct exponent of the spirit as distinct from the letter of the ancient faith; and it can only be claimed for him that he was the greatest, the wisest, and the best of the Hindus." But in declaring that his law was "a law of grace for *all*," in receiving *all* who came to him without distinction of birth or status, in opening to *all* his kingdom of righteousness wherein reigned "universal brotherhood and spiritual equality," he undoubtedly struck a fatal blow to the system of caste which is the corner-stone of Brahminism. In the long run, Buddhism and Brahminism were found incompatible.

The death of the Buddha occurred, probably, in B.C. 543. And within two or three centuries his doctrine became the fashionable religion in India. How it lost its hold upon the people we do not know. But we do know that by the tenth century of our era it had practically disappeared. During those thousand years a great transformation had taken place in the Brahminical religion. It had overcome Buddhism by new combinations of belief, philosophy, and epic legend, of which the *Baghavat-Gīta* is the chief literary symbol. The religion of the *Vedas* had practically disappeared; it had given place to the religion of the *Purānas*. The worship of Siva had arisen, and in the eighth century of our era it was widely and successfully propagated by Sankarachārya—a great name in Hindu theology. His work it was to mould the Vedantic philosophy into final form, and to base thereon a popular religion. He died at the age of thirty-two, after having preached his doctrines throughout India; and is to this day venerated as an incarnation of Siva. Personally, he was a Deist, holding the visible world to be the creation of an omnipotent deity—the sole and supreme God. But among the masses his religion became a religion of fear and of the coarsest idolatry. It is recorded that one of his latest utterances was, " Oh Lord, pardon my three sins; I have in contemplation clothed in form Thee, who art formless; I have, in praise, described Thee, who

art ineffable ; and in visiting shrines I have ignored
Thy omnipresence."

It is claimed by the votaries of Sankara that
all the chief sects of modern Hinduism were
founded by his disciples. There are, besides the
Sivites—of whom there are thirteen varieties—the
Vishnavites, worshippers of Vishnu ; the Sauras,
worshippers of Surya, the Sun ; and the Gana-
patras, worshippers of Ganesa, the lord of the
demons ; to whom we may perhaps add the
Saktists, worshippers of the Sakti or female energy
of Siva, as they seem to constitute a distinct body.

What is the genesis of Siva himself cannot with
certainty be determined. Some learned men regard
him as a modification of Rudra, the storm god of
Vedas. Others consider that "the recognition of
his godhead is a survival of some ancient form of
demon worship." Certain it is that the religion of
the lower Indo-Aryan races *is* a religion of demon
worship, and that to them Siva, the Destroyer,
specially appealed. But Siva is not only the
Destroyer. He is also the Reproducer—"I bring
to life, I bring to death." To the more highly
educated Hindus, he is the symbol of death merely
as a change of life. It is as regarding him in this
deeper significance that the ordinary Brahmin is a
votary of his, with the *lingam* as his expressive
emblem. I may here remark that phallic worship,
like tree worship, was probably borrowed by Hinduism—one of the most receptive of religions—from
the aboriginal tribes. The procreative and productive energies of nature were among the first
facts to impress with wonder and awe the mind of

primitive man, awaking to speculation on the origin of things. The mystery of sex is unquestionably one of the greatest mysteries. And the early religious conceptions which were associated with the *lingam* and the *yoni*, must be distinguished from the morbid prurience and lascivious mysticism into which they naturally degenerated.

This by the way. Next in popularity to the worship of Siva, which is still the most prevailing element in the religion of the Hindus, comes the worship of Vishnu, the deity chiefly honoured by the trading classes. Vishnu is specially known as the Preserver, and is, at all events, so far as his name goes, a Vedic deity. In the *Rig-Veda* he is spoken of as a form of the sun or penetrating solar ray. In practice he is regarded by the numerous sects of his votaries as the Supreme Deity, just as the Sivite sects attribute that pre-eminence to Siva. He is worshipped for the most part in his Avatārs or Incarnations, of which they reckon ten, the most notable being those in which he was made man, first as Rāma and then as Krishna—the favourite deity of the Hindu women, who adore him as Bāla Gopāla, the Infant Cowherd. It may here be noted that the Vishnavite sects are marked by perpendicular white lines shaped like a trident, from the roots of the hair to the eyebrow; while the Sivite sects employ three horizontal lines drawn across the forehead. It must not be supposed that Sivism and Vishnavism are opposed, or incompatible creeds. They merely represent different aspects of Hindu theology, and their professors dwell together in unity. It may

be added that Siva and Vishnu are, in practice,
chiefly adored in the persons of their consorts,
the wife of Vishnu being Lakshmī, while Siva's
consort is the goddess called Kālī, Durgā, Jagad-
hātū, or Mahī. It was out of devotion to the
female energies of Nature, as represented by these
consorts of Siva and Vishnu, that the *Tantras*
were composed; the latest of the religious writings
of the Hindus, and the most grossly licentious.

Although it may be said, generally, that all
Hindus are worshippers either of Siva, Vishnu,
or of their female energies, there is another principal god and person of what is popularly called
the Hindu Trinity, namely, Brahmā, the Creator.
In the general mind, however, he holds an insignificant place. He is regarded, apparently, as
functus officio, and there seems to be only one
shrine of importance throughout the whole of
India specially sacred to him. It is at Pushkāra,
near Ajmere. "The worship which was once his
due," writes Sir Monier Williams, "was transferred to the Brahmins, regarded as his peculiar
offspring, and, as it were, his mouthpieces; while
his consort, Sarasvatī, once a river goddess, was
regarded as the goddess of speech and learning,
and inventress of the Sanskrit language and letters."
But, besides these three principal deities, there are
innumerable minor ones, or semi - divine beings
—30,000,000 of them are reckoned, and for the
most part they are infamous conceptions — who
are the objects of worship. Hinduism is the most
tolerant of religions. The educated Brahmin
regards popular legends as merely broken lights

of the Supreme Reality. The uneducated Hindu is ready to worship anything. Mr Wilkins, in his *Modern Hinduism*, relates: "An old Brahmin pundit and priest, with whom I frequently conversed on these subjects, told me that in his own daily worship he first made an offering to his own chosen deity, Vishnu, and that when this was done, he threw a handful of rice for the other deities to scramble for it; it was his hope, he explained, that by thus recognising the existence and authority of them, though he had no clear notion in his mind about any of them, he would keep them in good humour towards himself."

The truth is that modern Hinduism is as complicated, as irregular, as multiform as the roof of a pagoda. We have seen that it is a development of Brahminism, just as Brahminism was a development of Vedism. But it no more resembles its original than the rank vegetation of an Indian forest represents the original germs or seeds. Sects, rites, doctrines, are innumerable. Articles of faith, fundamental dogmas, great lines of thought there are none. Theism, Pantheism, Polytheism, Fetichism, Nature Worship, Demon Worship, Ancestor Worship, Animal Worship — all are there, dissolved, so to speak, in an element of Pantheistic philosophy. The Brahmin seeking absorption in deity, the fakir earning the paradise of Siva by years of self-torture, the recluse honouring Vishnu by works of mercy, the Saktist revelling in sexual impurity, the Gond, the Pariah, on his knees before a shapeless stone — all are equally orthodox. Each of

the huge army of deities is so various in his form
and qualities, that he may be realised in another.
Siva, the Lord of Death, is, as we have seen, the
Lord of Life also; he is the Destroyer, but he
is the Producer too.   More, he is a great ascetic
and the model of ascetics.   But he is a great
voluptuary, and is honoured by debauch.   His
five faces, six arms, three eyes, and thousand
appellations express the variety of his attributes.
Vishnu, again, the Preserver, the Force which
upholds the universe—*rerum tenax vigor*, as the
Latin poet sings—is known in his incarnations,
and especially in the form of Rāma and of Krishna.
But the worship and legends of these two deities
have become almost indefinitely varied and multiplied.   The beliefs which have grown round the
trunk of Vishnavism — if I may so speak — are
countless.   It has associated elements of Buddhism,
of Mohammedanism, nay, of Christianity.   For,
surely, there is something more than an analogy
between Christianity and Krishna worship; while
the Lutheran and the Krishnaite doctrines of the
all-sufficiency of faith are most curiously alike in
their essential antinomianism.   It is significant
that learned Brahmins have been quite willing
to regard Christ himself as an incarnation of
Vishnu for the benefit of the Western world.

And here I should note that when we speak
of Hinduism as a religion, the word has a much
more restricted sense than that which it bears
when we apply it to Buddhism, Mohammedanism,
or Christianity.   In all those creeds there is an
ethical element.   In modern Hinduism there is

none. In this faith there is an absolute divorce between religion and morality. In it murder may assume the character of a religious duty—as, for example, among the Thugs. So may theft. There were sects—like the Thugs they have been suppressed by the strong arm of the British Government—who honoured Siva by larceny. The promiscuous intercourse of the sexes is a chief incident of the religious festivities of the Saktists. Dancing girls are among the endowed ministers of temple worship; and commerce with them is regarded as meritorious, as an act of devotion to the idol whose brides they are. Modesty, as we understand it, the Hindus know not. Their religion does not limit a married man to exterior decency, to say nothing of conjugal fidelity. Things which, in the language of the Apostle, it is shame even to speak of, are done by them not in secret but openly. All daily reverence the *lingam* and the *yoni*. The native conception of the relation of the sexes is merely animal. Love in the sense which it bears in the Western world—as hallowed by Christianity and disciplined by chivalry — is unknown in Hindu life. Children are married, and are immediately separated until they arrive at maturity. Then they are brought together, but the wife is merely her husband's first servant. The widow is an outcast and object of loathing, the very sight of her is an ill omen. But I shall have to speak of this later on.

In fact the religion of the ordinary Hindu is superstition, as Cicero defines it : *vanus deorum timor*. Vain fear of unseen powers, and the desire

of propitiating them, rule his life. This is the
foundation upon which the power of the Brahmins
rests. The world, a well-known text declares, is
under the power of the gods; the gods are under
the power of the mantras*; the mantras are under
the power of the Brahmins; therefore the gods are
under the power of the Brahmins. One of the
most curious of Hindu superstitions is connected
with shaving—an essential preliminary of every
religious rite. It is summed up in the text:

> "Sins as huge as Mount Meru or Mandara,
>   Sins of various kinds,
>   These all adhere to the hair of the head;
>   For these sins do I undergo this shaving."

And, as it is forbidden by religion that a man
should shave himself, the barber is a person of
much importance. He is a regular officer of the
Hindu village; and an endowment in land is set
apart for him. It is his right to shave the people
of the village, and, unless my memory is at fault,
the Courts have upheld that right by injunction.
Religion also prescribes that a man must be shaved
fasting.

Another matter of great importance in Hinduism
is the sacred thread. Manu orders, " In the eighth
year from the conception of a Brahmin, in the
eleventh from that of a Kshatriya, and in the
twelfth from that of a Vaishya, let the father
invest the child with the tokens of his class:"
that is the sacred thread, the frontal mark, and
the sacred top-knot. The marks on the forehead

* Mantras are religious formulas used by the Brahmins.

have already been described, and the top-knot
needs no description. The sacred thread, a cord
or skein over the left shoulder, hanging down
under the right arm like a sash, is the outward
visible sign of the three twice-born classes. Sūdras
have no right to assume it, though some do. It
is not, in fact, put on by the father, but by the
guru, or spiritual director of the family, who, at
the same time, teaches the child a mantra, a short
Sanskrit text, or the name of some deity, which
must be kept a profound secret, and repeated one
hundred and eight times a day. A rosary is
often used to help the recitation.

Very conspicuous persons in modern Hinduism
are the religious mendicants. There are some five
millions of them, of various kinds, described by a
learned Hindu gentleman, Mr Jogendra Nath Bhattachārya, in his valuable book on *Hindu Castes and
Sects*, as "sleek in body and pestilential in morals."
This authority proceeds : "When a mendicant has
acquired a character for sanctity by any one of the
usual processes, he has only to give out that he
has found an idol by miracle, with injunctions to
erect a temple to it. The necessary funds for the
purpose being never supplied miraculously to the
devotee, he invites subscriptions from the pious ;
and when the temple is built, a part of it naturally
becomes his dwelling house. With the further
contributions made by the visitors to the shrine, he
is enabled to live in comfort. When a shrine is in
the struggling stage, the high priest generally leads
a pure life, and spends a large part of his income
in feeding the poor pilgrims. But the high priests

of the temples that have a well-established character for sanctity, are usually just the kind of men
that they ought not to be.   There are thus five
stages in the careers of the successful monks and
nuns.   First the beggar, then the charlatan, then
the temple-promoter, then the princely high priest,
and last of all the debauchee.   The theme is one
to which justice could be done only by the genius
of a Shakespeare."

Of course these pungent remarks of this
extremely well-informed Hindu gentleman must
be accepted with reservation.   All religious mendicants in India are not of that type.   There is
much fanatical asceticism which is perfectly sincere.
Some devotees have given proof of their sincerity
by causing themselves to be buried alive.   Others
have practised, and still practise, the most horrible
self-torture.   " In our days cruel mortifications are
becoming rare.   Yet there are still Akacamukhiris
and Urdhvatalines, who pose themselves in im-
movable attitudes, their faces and their arms raised
to heaven, till the sinews shrink and the posture
assumed often stiffens into rigidity; as well as
Nagas, Paramahanavas, Avadhutas, and others,
who, in spite of English interdicts, expose themselves to the inclemency of the weather in a state
of absolute nudity."

Enough has been said, perhaps, to indicate
how in modern Hinduism only the faintest traces
are discernible of the Vedic beliefs whence it has
sprung.   Assuredly we must account it a religion
in the last stage of decadence and decay.   " It is
true," to quote the words of Professor Max Müller

in his *Westminster Abbey Lecture*, "there are millions of children, women, and men in India who fall down before the stone image of Vishnu, with his four arms, riding on a creature, half bird, half man, or sleeping on the serpent, who worship Siva, a monster with three eyes, riding naked on a bull, with a necklace of skulls for his ornament. There are human beings who still believe in a god of war, Kārtikeya, with six faces, riding on a peacock, and holding bow and arrow in his hands ; and who invoke a god of success, Ganesa, with four hands and an elephant's head, sitting on a rat. Nay, it is true that in the broad daylight of the nineteenth century, the figure of the goddess Kāli is carried through the streets of her own city, Calcutta, her wild, dishevelled hair reaching to her feet, with a necklace of human heads, her tongue protruded from her mouth, her girdle stained with blood. All this is true ; but ask any Hindu who can read, and write, and think, whether these are the gods he believes in, and he will smile at your credulity. How long this living death of national religion in India may last, no one can tell."

The dictum,

> "Segnius irritant animum demissa per aures
>   Quam quæ sunt oculis subjecta fidelibus,"

is as true as it is hackneyed. Anyone who wants to realise what modern Hinduism is would do well, should opportunity offer, to visit Benares, its centre, its very heart — Benares, the sacred city on the sacred Ganges : more hallowed by

the countless votaries who flock thither, than Jerusalem by the ancient Hebrew, than Mecca by the
Moslem, or Rome by the Catholic, of our own
day. So holy is it that death on its soil is the
gate of life, the abundant entrance to the Paradise
of Siva : and this to every one : to the Mussulman,
the Christian, the eater of beef, the slayer of the
cow, no less than to the thrice born, learned in
the *Vedas*, or the fakir, slowly self-immolated by
years of penance. This marvellous city was
already famous when Rome was a mere collection
of shepherds' tents, when Mecca was an unwalled
village, nay, long before Joshua smote Adoni-
Zedec, King of " Jebusi, which is Jerusalem," with
his four confederate chieftains, and slew them and
hanged them on five trees. Wonderful, indeed,
is the spectacle which Benares presents with its
25,000 Brahmins ; its 2000 temples and innumerable shrines ; its 500,000 idols, of all varieties of
hideousness and obscenity ; its streets full of pilgrims jostled by sacred cows who feed peaceably
on their offerings, and by gambolling and gibber-
ing apes ; its clear air darkened by the columns
of smoke from the funeral piles which are turning
the devout dead into ashes to be mingled with its
sacred stream, in whose lustral waters thousands
of the devout living are seeking to wash all their
sins away.

There is, however, another consideration which
must not be lost sight of, when we survey the
gloomy and repulsive, the absurd and obscene
features of modern Hinduism. And I do not
know who has better expressed it than Barth,

in words which may serve to conclude this Chapter :—

"It would be to display great ignorance indeed of the immense resources of the religious sentiment, to presume that the effect of such things as these must be necessarily and universally demoralising. The common people have a certain safeguard in the very grossness of their superstition, and among the higher ranks there are many souls that are at once mystically inclined and pure-hearted, who know how to extract the honey of pure love from this strange mixture of obscenities. That is a touching legend, for instance, of that young queen of Udayapura, a contemporary of Akbar (in the end of the sixteenth century), Mirā Bāī, who renounced her throne and her husband rather than abjure Krishna, and who, when close pressed by her persecutors, went and threw herself at the feet of the image of her god, exclaiming, 'I have abandoned my love, my wealth, my kingdom, my husband. Mirā, thy servant, comes to thee, her refuge ; oh, take her wholly to thyself! If thou knowest me to be free from every stain, accept me. Except thee, no other will have compassion on me ; pity me, therefore. Lord of Mirā, her well-beloved, accept her, and grant that she be no more parted from thee for ever !' Upon this the image opened, and Mīrā Bāī disappeared in its sides."

CHAPTER XII

In this Chapter, I shall glance, briefly, at the principal non-Christian creeds, other than Hinduism, which are professed in the Indian Empire. These are Buddhism, Jainism, Mohammedanism, the religion of the Sikhs, and the religion of the Parsis. I shall not think it necessary to dwell upon the various forms of Fetichism found among the less civilised tribes, such as the Bheels, who adore stones covered with red lead and oil; or to speak of the recently formed Deistical sects, which do not number more than eight or ten thousand adherents between them, and which certainly have not the promise of the future.

Of all the religions of the East, Buddhism is perhaps the most interesting to us in the Western world. Through "the mists of fabling time," the great figure of its founder shines, clear and distinct upon us, in this far-off twentieth century, and wins the homage of the best men of the most various schools of thought. Philosophers like Schopenhauer, and physicists like Huxley, have been content to sit at his feet and to learn of him ;

158

Catholic and Anglican prelates, Wesleyan and Baptist missionaries, consent to the judgment of the French rationalist, that "with the sole exception of the Christ, there is no more touching figure than his among the founders of religions," so entirely is he "without spot and blemish," "the finished model of the heroism, the self-renunciation, the love, the sweetness which he commands." It is difficult, indeed, to understand how any one can rise from the perusal of the works, made accessible to us by recent scholarship, in which is contained the genuine record of his life and teaching, without the profoundest veneration for his moral and spiritual greatness. It is no wonder that for twenty-five centuries, his personality and his religion have afforded more widely than any other, stay in life and hope in death, to "troublous and distressed mortality": it is no wonder that 450,000,000 of the human race still turn to him with the disinterestedness of pure affection, as the highest and noblest ideal of which they have knowledge. Of these, 9,000,000 dwell in the Burmese province of the Indian Empire. What the faith of the Buddha really is to them, has been of late told us, in the fascinating pages of Mr Fielding's work, *The Soul of a People*. I must content myself with thus indicating a document where the actual working of Buddhism, as a living religion, may be fully seen. Such space as I have to give to it here, must be devoted to a succinct account of its tenets, which I shall borrow from my work, *Ancient Religion and Modern Thought*, for two reasons; the first being, that I do not know how to put the matter more clearly and concisely; and the second, that Mr Rhys Davids, probably the greatest living authority on Buddhism, was good enough to characterise it as correct and complete.

" The foundation of the gospel of the Buddha is the illusoriness of the world, the subjection of all that is to the great law of mutability, the misery inseparable from the condition of man so long as he remains in 'the whirlpool of existence.' In the account which is given of the workings of his mind in the first watch of the great night which he spent under the bo-tree, he is represented as going through the chain of 'the Twelve Causes and Effects,' and tracing back all the evil that is in the world to ignorance, the prime illusion, the fundamental error of those who cling to individual existence. And in his sermon to the seventy Brahmins he declares, 'to know as truth that which is true, this is perfect rectitude, and shall bring true profit.' And then he goes on to point out as the primary truth—' Everywhere in the world there is death, there is no rest in either of the three worlds. The gods, indeed, enjoy a period of bliss, but their happiness must also end, and they must also die. To consider this as the condition of all states of being, that there is nothing born but must die, and therefore to desire to escape birth and death, this is to exercise oneself in religious truth.' For death is in itself no deliverance from the burden of being. To die is merely to pass from one state of existence to another. So long as *tanhā*—thirst, passion, desire—remains, the source

of being remains.   To root out '*tanhā*' is the only
way of escaping 'the yawning gulf of continual
birth and death.'   It is this which is expressed in
the Four Truths, thought out by the Buddha, in
that great night after he had followed the Twelve
Causes and Effects—the Four Noble Truths, as
they are called, regarding Suffering, the Cause of
Suffering, the Cessation of Suffering, and the
Path which leads to the Cessation of Suffering,
which may be reckoned great fundamental doctrines
of the Buddhist Church.

"But there are two other tenets of no less
importance.   In common with almost all Oriental
thinkers, the Buddha believed in Transmigration
—a hypothesis in support of which a certain
amount of evidence may be adduced, and which,
as Mr Rhys Davids observes, 'is incapable of
disproof, while it affords an explanation, quite
complete, to those who can believe in it, of the
apparent anomalies and wrongs in the distribution
of happiness or woe.'   The doctrine of *Karma*,
which plays so great a part in Buddhism, and which
is the main source of its moral excellence, is the
complement of the doctrine of Transmigration,
and the link which connects it with the 'Four
Noble Truths.'   It is the teaching of the Buddha
that there is no such thing as what is commonly
called a soul.   The real man is the net result of
his merits and demerits, and that net result is
called *Karma*.   A god, a man, a beast, a bird,
or a fish—for there is no essential difference
between all living beings—is what he does, what
he has done, not only during his present existence,

but very far more, among his countless previous existences in various forms. His actual condition is the result of the deeds done in his former births, and upon his present deeds, plus the past, will depend his destiny in future existences, divine, human, or animal. And the character of his acts depends upon his intention. 'All that we are,' the Teacher insists, 'depends upon what we have thought.'

"Thus life in all its grades, from the highest to the lowest, is, in the strictest sense, a time of probation. 'Two things in this world are immutably fixed,' the Buddha is reported to have said upon another occasion, 'that good actions bring happiness, and that bad actions bring misery.' In the pregnant Buddhist phrase, 'we pass away, according to our deeds,' to be reborn in heaven, or in hell, or upon the earth, as man or animal, according to our *Karma*. To say that a man's works follow him when he dies, that what he has sown *here* he shall reap *there*, falls far short of this tremendous doctrine. His works *are* himself, he *is* what he has sown. All else drops from him at death. His body decays and falls into nothingness, and not only his material properties (*Rūpa*) but his sensations (*Vedanā*), his abstract ideas (*Sannā*), his mental and moral predispositions (*Sankhārā*), and his thought or reason (*Vinnāna*)—all these constituent elements of his being pass away. But his *Karma* remains, unless he has attained to the supreme state of *Arahat*—the crown of Buddhist saintship—when *Karma* is extinguished and *Nirvāna* is attained."

Such is *Karma*—a great mystery, which the limited intellect of ordinary man can but contemplate, as it were, "through a glass darkly": only the perfectly enlightened mind of a Buddha can fully fathom it. As I observed, it is closely connected with the Four Noble Truths. The cause of demerit is *tanhā*, which appears to present some analogy to concupiscence, as Catholic theologians define it : "a certain motion and power of the mind whereby men are driven to desire pleasant things that they do not possess." That is the cause of sin, of sorrow, and of suffering. To root out this thirst is the only way to obtain salvation, release from the evil which is of the essence of existence, and, as the fourth of the Noble Truths teaches, "the means of obtaining the individual annihilation of desire" is supplied by the eight-fold Path of Holiness. Abolition of self, living for others, is the substance of the Buddhist plan of salvation. Scrupulously avoiding all wicked actions, reverently performing all virtuous ones, purifying our intentions from all selfish ends—this is the doctrine of all the Buddhas. Thus does man conquer himself; and, "having conquered himself, there will be no further ground for birth." And so the Chinese poet, commenting upon the *Pratimoksha*:

> " The heart, scrupulously avoiding all idle dissipation,
> Diligently applying itself to the holy Law of Buddha,
> Letting go all lust and consequent disappointment,
> Fixed and unchangeable, enters on *Nirvāna*."

This is the blissful state which results from the extinction of desire: this is the highest conquest of self; it is the fulness "of deep and liquid rest forgetful of all ill." Those who have attained to this "peace which passeth understanding" even the gods envy, we are told. "Their old *Karma* is being exhausted; no new *Karma* is being produced; their hearts are free from the longing after future life; the cause of their existence being destroyed, and no new yearnings springing up within them, they, the wise, are extinguished like this lamp."

Buddhism proper, as we saw in the last Chapter, has disappeared from the land of its birth. It survives there only in the form of Jainism—if indeed we are correct in regarding Jainism as a survival of it. That is a point on which scholars differ, and which is not likely to be conclusively settled. What is certain is that Jainism came into notice when Buddhism had disappeared from India, and that the affinities between the two systems are very striking. The chief difference between them is, that the Jains observe caste. The Jina, or Conquering Saint, is in the Jain system what the Buddha is in the Buddhist. He is the Perfect One who has subdued all worldly desires; who has completely effected that liberation (*moksha*)—the highest end and aim of intelligent beings — by means of right intuition, right knowledge, and right conduct. And the chief canons of this right conduct are: Do harm to no living thing; Do not lie; Do not steal; Be temperate, sober, and chaste; Desire nothing inordinately. All which certainly sounds like an echo of the teaching of the Buddha. Jainism now numbers about a million and a half adherents in India, among whom are some of the wealthiest and most cultivated natives of that country. Several fine Jain temples have recently been built in Calcutta.

From Buddha, the gentle Aryan sage, to Mohammed, the fierce Semitic warrior, is a vast descent. Still, only inveterate prejudice can blind us to the real spiritual greatness of the Founder of Islām. Our ancestors identified him with the devil:

> "The prince of darkness is a gentleman,
> Modo he's called, and Mahu."

We have come to think otherwise of Mahu or Mohammed. For a full estimate of his career and teaching, I may be permitted to refer the reader to a Chapter in my work, *The Claims of Christianity*. In this place I will merely quote a sentence from Mr Freeman, which, I believe, expresses correctly the judgment formed of him by most candid and competent scholars. " I cannot conceal my conviction that, in a certain sense, his belief in his own mission was well founded. Surely a good and sincere man, full of confidence in his Creator, who works an immense reform, both in faith and practice, is, truly, a direct instrument in the hands of God, and may be said to have a commission from Him."

The doctrine of Mohammed has been summed up epigrammatically and correctly by Deutsch: " Judaism as adapted to Arabia." Its essence is a severe and lofty Theism. The Divine Unity, making, upholding, governing, perfecting all things, is the rock on which Mohammed builds: his shield

K

and hiding place. The consciousness of dependence upon the Absolute and Eternal is the keynote of Islām. It is all briefly comprehended in the two words, " Allah akbar." Religion meant for Mohammed self-chosen submission to the will of a Moral Governor of the Universe. The sovereignty of God and the free volition of man are the postulates of his system. It was the unquestioning belief in this living and life-giving Theism taught by him —a belief summed up in the formula, " There is no God but God, and Mohammed is the Prophet of God "—that sharpened the swords of the earlier Moslems and gave them victory in the battle. It is the same faith which in our own day makes the Moslem preachers the most successful of proselytizers ; potent to expel from many dark places of the earth barbarous and impure idolatries, and to train millions of converts to better things by its doctrines of righteousness, temperance, and judgment to come. " It must be confessed," writes a distinguished Anglican clergyman, the Rev. Isaac Taylor, " that over a large portion of the world, Islām, as a missionary religion, is more successful than Christianity. It is eminently adapted to be a civilising and elevating religion for barbarous tribes. When it is embraced by a negro tribe, paganism, devil worship, fetichism, cannibalism, human sacrifices, infanticide, witchcraft, at once disappear. Hospitality becomes a religious duty ; drunkenness becomes rare ; gambling is forbidden ; immodest dances and the promiscuous intercourse of the sexes cease : female chastity is regarded as a virtue ; polygamy and slavery are regulated, and their evils are restrained. All the more civilised tribes of negroes, the Mandingoes, Foulahs, Jolofs, and Houssas are Moslems, while in Lagos the hold of Christianity is feeble, and in Sierra Leone Christianity is actually receding before Islām. How little have we to show for the vast sums of money and all the precious lives lavished upon Africa! Christian converts are reckoned by thousands; Moslem converts by millions."

In India there are nearly sixty millions of Moslems. His Most Gracious Majesty, the Emperor of that country, has more Mohammedan subjects than any other ruler; and in some respects they may be truly described as the backbone of the population. Islām, of course, has not escaped the influence of its environment in India. It has adopted various superstitious practices. It has, to some extent, declined from the sternly ascetic standard laid down in the *Qu'rān*. But Indian Mussulmans manifest a manliness, a self-respect, a devotion to duty, very attractive to Englishmen. And, as a rule, they make far more trustworthy officials than the supple and quick-witted Bengalis, who easily outstrip them in the examinations which are the portal to the public service. Their practical exclusion from their fair share of appointments under Government is unquestionably a public evil, and is justly resented by them as a wrong. "They feel themselves superior," Mr Spenser Wilkinson well remarks in *The Great Alternative*, "both as believers in one invisible God, and as men of warlike race and character, to the classes who enter at the examination door."

And they *are* superior. Their creed and worship give them a very real superiority over the idolatrous races by which they are surrounded. It is an interesting question how far this superiority is likely to influence the future of religion in India. Western civilisation is undermining Hinduism— this is beyond doubt. And what is to take its place? Christianity? Of that, as we shall see in the next Chapter, there seems small prospect. There are careful and competent observers who consider the faith of Mohammed far more likely to spread in India, as the foul deities of the Hindu Pantheon fall into discredit. Thus Sir Alfred Lyall writes in his *Asiatic Studies*:

"The Mohammedan faith has still at least a dignity, and a courageous, unreasoning certitude which in Western Christianity have been perceptibly melted down and attenuated, by the disease of casuistry, and by long exposure to the searching light of European rationalism : whereas the clear, unwavering formula of Islām carries one plain line straight up toward heaven, like a tall obelisk pointing direct to the sky, without shadow of turning. It thus possesses a strong attraction for Hindus, who are seeking an escape from the labyrinth of sensual Polytheism, but who yet require something more concrete and definite than is offered by their indigenous speculations about Deism or Pantheism : while the vigour and earnestness of the message announced so unflinchingly by Mahomed, conquer the hearts of simple folk, and warm the imagination of devout truth-seekers."

Mr Talboys Wheeler, in his *History of India*, goes further : "The people of India," he writes, "are drifting slowly but surely towards the religion of Islām, rather than towards Christianity. Few impartial observers will deny this fact."

There have indeed been times in the past history of India when a fusion of Hinduism and Mohammedanism seemed probable. Ramamander, Kabīr, Chaitayana, the great medieval missionaries, appealed to the adherents of both creeds alike. The Sikh religion is, in fact, the result of such a fusion. It now numbers 10,000,000 of adherents, of whom eleven - twelfths dwell in the Punjāb. Nānak, its founder, a Hindu, who died at Kirtipore, on the banks of the Ravi, in the year 1539, described himself as a successor of Mohammed, though one of his first sermons is said to have been on the thesis: "There are neither Hindus nor Mohammedans." Undoubtedly, he derived from the Prophet of Islām the strict monotheism which is the foundation of his teaching. The *Adi-Granth*, the Sikh Bible, describes God as "One, sole, self-existing, the meaning and the cause of all, who has seen numberless creeds and names come and go." It insists upon the brotherhood of men, does not recognise caste, and inculcates pure and simple ethics. This *Adi-Granth*—fundamental book, the term means—was not published till the time of Nānak's fifth successor, Guru Arjun (1584-1606), and the tongue in which it is written is now obsolete. It consists of the poetical pieces left by Nānak and the Gurus who succeeded him, including compositions by Arjun himself, and of selections from the writings of certain Hindu teachers.

"Since the publication of the *Granth*," writes Barth, "there cannot, in a dogmatic reference, be any longer much question of the profound influence of Islām on the thinking of the founders of this religion. But from first to last, both as regards the form and the foundation of its ideas, this book breathes the mystic pantheism of the Vedānta, reinforced by the doctrines of *chakti*, of grace, and of absolute devotion to the *guru*. It is especially distinguished from the sectarian literature in general, by the importance which it attaches to moral precepts, by the simplicity and spiritualistic character of a worship stripped of every vestige of idolatry, and especially by its moderation in regard to mythology, although we find in it a considerable number of the personifications of Hinduism, and even detect at times in it a sort of return to the Hindu divinities. But it would be difficult to eliminate from all this what is due to Mussulman influence. . . . The worship of the Sikhs is simple and pure. With the exception of Amritsar, which is the religious centre of the nation, and a few sanctuaries in places consecrated by the life or the death of gurus and martyrs, they have no holy places. Their temples are houses of prayer. Here they recite pieces and sing hymns extracted from the *Granth;* and the congregation separates after each believer has received a piece of the *karāh prasād*, ' the effectual offering,' a kind of pastry ware consecrated in the name of the guru. As tolerant as they were formerly fanatical, they do not object to admit to their religious services strangers, whom they allow even to participate in their communion. It is true that under this tolerance there lies concealed no little lukewarmness, and that, in the opinion of the best judge in this matter, Dr Trumpp, the translator of the *Adi Granth*, 'Sikhism' is a religion which is on the wane."

It remains to speak of the religion of the Parsis, which is of extreme interest as a survival of one of the world's greatest creeds, though professed by only some 100,000 people. They are the descendants of those Zoroastrian exiles, who, in the seventh Christian century, after the destruction of the Sassanid dominion, sought a refuge in India from the proselytizing violence of the conquering Mussulmans. And, during all that tract of years, they have kept the monotheistic faith of their fathers, and the monogamous structure of the family, although borrowing, as was natural, some Hindu and some Mohammedan customs. The Zoroastrian religion exhibits, in the judgment of Geiger, "a purity and sublimity of religious thought such as no nation of antiquity in the East, with the single exception of the Israelites, has been able to attain to ; embracing conceptions approximating closely to a pure monotheism, representing the Deity as free from human adjuncts, and working out the spiritual part of theology with exactness and precision." Its Sacred Books were sealed to the Western world, until towards late in the last century, Anquetil Duperron, a young Frenchman, without money, without friends, and but modestly equipped with scholarship, conceived the design of penetrating their secrets, and of unveiling their mysteries. There are few more romantic stories than his in the history of scholarship. And though his translation of the *Zend*

Avesta, published in 1771, is often wide of the sense of the original — which is not wonderful, seeing that he possessed neither grammar nor dictionary of its language — he laid securely the foundation upon which many illustrious scholars have since built. "The importance," writes Professor Darmestetter, "of the *Avesta* and of the creed of that scanty people the Parsis, in the eyes of the historian and the theologist, is that they present to us the last reflex of the ideas which prevailed in India during the five centuries preceding, and the seven following the birth of Christ : a period which gave to the world the Gospels, the *Talmud*, and the *Qu'rān* : . . . enabling us to go back to the very heart of that most momentous period in the history of religious thought which saw the blending of the Aryan with the Semitic, and thus opened the second stage of Aryan thought."

Zoroaster himself is of course a somewhat shadowy person to us, though there can be no question as to his historic reality. As little can there be that in the venerable document known as *The Five Gathas*, we possess a record of his actual teaching. Dr Haug inclines to consider him a contemporary of Moses. Pliny places him several thousand years earlier. Bunsen writes, "Zoroaster the Prophet cannot have lived later than B.C. 3000 (250 years before Abraham therefore), but 6000 or 5000 years before Plato may very likely be more correct, according to the statement of Aristotle and Eudoxus." What is certain is, that he was the preacher of Monotheism to

his people — the antique Aryans who were the
ancestors alike of Iranians and Indians. And it
is probable that his reform produced the schism
between the worshippers of the Vedic Gods and
the worshippers of Ormuzd. Most curious is it
to reflect how, after long centuries, the remnant of
the posterity of those who had followed his reform,
were driven to accept the hospitality of the descendants of those who had rejected it. Of course the
importance of the religion of the Parsis is historical.
They have never sought to make proselytes in
the country of their exile : nor is their creed likely
to exercise any influence upon the future of religion
in India. In number—as we have seen—they are
a quite insignificant element of the population of
the country. But socially they are far from insignificant : their intelligence, industry, and integrity
have given them a position of much importance
in the second greatest of Indian cities—Bombay.

CHAPTER XIII

CHRISTIANITY

THERE is a considerable body of excellent people in the world—chiefly in England and in the United States of America—whose thoughts turn to India as "the most interesting country in the mission field." They ardently desire its conversion to Christianity, and especially to some form—they do not, as a rule, greatly care what—of that variety of Protestantism which is known as Evangelical. Let us endeavour to see in this Chapter how far their desire seems likely to be gratified.

Christianity is no stranger in India. The tradition * that one "Thomas" introduced it there is very ancient. But whether this Thomas was—to quote Gibbon—"an Apostle, a Manichæan, or an Armenian merchant," has been much disputed among the learned. Certain it is, however, that Indian Christianity, so far as we can follow it back in history, presents traces of a special cultus of

* That very considerable authority, Dr Burnell, writes in *The Indian Antiquary* (vol. iv., p. 182): "The Manichæan mission to India in the third century A.D., is the only *historical fact* that we know of in relation to Christian missions in India, before we get as low as the sixth century."

154

St Thomas the Apostle. Certain it is also that Christian communities existed in India—on the Malabar coast—in the fifth century : and that they then became Nestorian. The Portuguese in the sixteenth century brought these heretical Christians into communion with Rome—the Acts and Decrees of the Synod of Diamper in 1599 setting the seal to the work. And the Inquisition, established at Goa in 1560, carefully watched over it, displaying, indeed, an amount of fiery zeal which astonished the Western world. But when, in 1663, the capture of Cochin by the Dutch overthrew the Portuguese power on the seaboard of Western India, the Jacobite Patriarch of Antioch sent a Bishop to Malabar, who received the adhesion of a considerable number of the Christians dwelling in that region; the speculative differences between the Jacobites, who deny the two natures in Christ, and the Nestorians, who assert not only two natures but two persons, appearing to them of less account than independence of Rome. That independence they have since maintained, and at the present day they number about 300,000. Side by side with these Jacobite Christians, are the Catholics of the Syrian rite in communion with the Holy See, who number some 200,000.

Another body of Indian Christians, who also are spiritual subjects of the Pope, is composed of the descendants of the converts made in the sixteenth century by Catholic missionaries. The rounding of the Cape of Good Hope by the bold navigators of Portugal had rendered India accessible, though the voyage occupied twelve months. And the Franciscans were the first to take advantage of this great change in order to spread the Christian faith. A small company of their friars arrived in the Deccan in 1500, and within a few months one of them, Father Peter of Covilhao, sealed his testimony with his blood. His brethren continued his work for forty years with a fair measure of success. Then—in 1542—St Francis Xavier landed at Goa and began his abundant labours. " Besides doing much to re-form the life of the Portuguese settlers them-selves," observes a recent writer, "he completed the conversion of the Paravas on the fishery coast, founded the Christianity of Ceylon, and converted thousands in the native states of Travancore and Cochin. To this day the lands where he laboured are the most Christian districts in India. His favourite disciples, the poor Parava fishermen, have never lost the faith they received from him, and numbers of them, during the last terrible famine in Southern India, refused to pur-chase food and life by even a day of simulated apostacy." He may be regarded as the pioneer of the Jesuit missionaries, whose heroic self-denial, quenchless zeal, and indefatigable activity in spread-ing Christianity, have never been surpassed. Two of the greatest names among them are those of Robert de Nobile, the founder of the Madura mission, and Beschi, who, as we have seen in a previous Chapter, attained high distinction as a Tamil poet, and who was honoured by the people with the title of Vīramamuni, "the heroic devotee." It has ever been the laudable endeavour of the

Jesuits, as far as their religion allows, to become all things to all men; and so in India, they were led to recognise and respect many native customs and prejudices, more or less questionable; especially those connected with caste. This, Sir William Hunter opines, "is the secret of the wide and permanent success of the Catholic missions." Anyhow, it was the source of the chief troubles of the Jesuit missionaries — troubles involving disputes which greatly divided them among themselves, and which had to be referred, in the event, for the decision of the Pope. The persecution of the Society of Jesus by the Portuguese Government in 1759, and its suppression fourteen years afterwards by Clement XIV., struck a heavy blow at Catholicism in India. Then came the persecution of Christians by Tippu Sahib in the countries subject to him. In one year (1784) he is said to have compelled some 30,000 Catholics of Canara to embrace Mohammedanism, forcibly circumcising them, and deporting them to the country above the Ghāts. But in 1814 the Society of Jesus was re-established, and began anew its missions in India; and various other Catholic agencies have been labouring during the present century for the evangelisation of that country. The number of Catholics throughout the Indian Empire is now close upon 2,000,000, to whom must be added 300,000 for the French and Portuguese settlements. It is worthy of note that more than one half of the Catholic clergy, including several Bishops, are natives.

"The Roman Catholics in India," writes Sir

William Hunter, "steadily increase; and, as in former times, the increase is chiefly in the South. . . . The Roman Catholics work in India with slender pecuniary resources. The priests of the Propaganda deny themselves the comforts considered necessaries for Europeans in India. They live the frugal and abstemious life of the natives; and their influence reaches deep into the life of the communities among whom they dwell." It should here be noted that great trouble and inconvenience have been caused to Catholics in India by what is known as the Padroado; the right of patronage over bishoprics and beneficies in the East, granted by the Popes to the Portuguese crown, and issuing in a general jurisdiction of the Archbishop of Goa. The condition on which this right was granted was that the Portuguese sovereigns should provide the necessary funds for the maintenance of the Catholic clergy in India. And it might have been supposed that when the decadence of the Portuguese power rendered the fulfilment of this condition no longer possible, the right of patronage would be held to have lapsed. But that was not the view taken by the Portuguese. And when Gregory XVI., in 1838, limited the Goanese jurisdiction to the possessions of Portugal, the Indo-Portuguese clergy broke into open schism. At last, in 1886, Leo XIII. concluded a new Concordat with Portugal which restricted the Padroado to the ecclesiastical province of Goa, raising the Archbishop of that see to the dignity of Patriarch, but reserved to the King of Portugal a voice in the selection of the Bishops of Bombay, Trichinopoly, and Mangalore—dioceses within the Indian Empire—an arrangement causing much discontent to the British Catholics resident there. While erecting Goa into a Patriarchate, Leo XIII. created seven Archbishoprics—Agra, Bombay, Verapoli, Calcutta, Madras, Pondicherry, and Colombo—besides raising all the existing Indian Vicariates Apostolic, and the Prefecture Apostolic of Bengal, to the rank of Episcopal sees. This may seem a very liberal hierarchical provision indeed, for some two millions of Catholics. But doubtless the Pope had in consideration the future as much as the present.

The first Protestant missionaries came to India at the beginning of the eighteenth century, and appear to have been Danish Lutherans. At all events they were under the patronage of the King of Denmark, though they were but coldly received by the local Danish authorities in India. Funds from Denmark failed them in a few years; and they were then taken into the pay of the Society for Promoting Christian Knowledge, English Protestant missionaries not being at that time forthcoming. It was the same Society that in 1750 sent out the famous Schwartz, also a Lutheran, who became the founder of the Protestant Tinnevelli missions. Towards the end of the century, the Baptist missionaries, Carey, Marshman, and Ward made their appearance. They busied themselves much, as their Lutheran predecessors had done, with translations of the Bible into the Indian vernaculars. In 1814 the first Protestant Bishopric in India was established at Calcutta. In 1814 the

Church Missionary Society sent out a few clergy, and in 1820 the Society for the Propagation of the Gospel, which had been at work in the country for some years, appointed Dr Mill Principal of Bishop's College, Calcutta. At the present time there are some thirty-five Protestant sects labouring for the conversion of India to their various forms of Christianity. It is not easy to give with accuracy the number of their adherents, as some of them include among their converts inchoate proselytes: persons under instruction and not as yet baptized. For these, assuredly, credit cannot fairly be taken, as, however promising their dispositions, they are not formally Christian. Making due deduction for them, the number of native Protestant Christians in India is probably not much over half a million.

It does not seem a very great result for long years of aspiration and effort—more especially when the quality of the converts is considered. But is there any reason to believe that, as Sir Monier Williams affirms in his interesting work on Hinduism, "Christianity is spreading its boundaries more widely, and striking its foundations more deeply?"—that—as he somewhat oddly expresses it — "the good time will arrive when every tongue of every native of India, from Cape Comorin to the Himālaya mountains, shall confess that Jesus Christ is Lord, to the glory of God the Father?" It seems to me, I own, that there are no tokens of a consummation so devoutly to be wished; but rather that the wish is father to the thought. The success of the Protestant missionaries is infinitesimal. And I look in vain for any

promise of a more abundant harvest.   Indeed, Sir
Monier Williams elsewhere observes, " The desire
of India for Christ is not articulate."   But in the
absence of articulation, what evidence is there that
such a desire exists ?   The Protestant missionaries
without exception—at least I never, while in India,
heard of an exception — lead quite respectable
lives, and sometimes even display earnest religious-
ness and much zeal.   But certain it is, that they do
not appeal to the popular imagination as did the
great Hindu ascetics, who forsook all to follow an
ideal.   Nor are their arguments, whether on behalf
of their own religion, or against the religion of
others, largely found persuasive or convincing.
The uneducated Hindus are not touched by their
preaching.   The educated despise it.   The Christian heaven depicted by them presents no attraction to their hearers.   The conception of happiness
cherished by the multitude is purely sensuous.
Higher minds look forward to what is called
makti : absorption in deity.   Some half a million of
youth—including 75,000 girls —attend their schools.
But the proportion of their pupils who join their
sects is exceedingly small.   The vast majority of
young Hindus educated by the missionaries, are
just as anti-Christian as are those educated in the
Government Colleges.   Mr Kerr, the author of a
well-known and justly esteemed work on *Domestic
Life in India*, tells us, that upon one occasion an
extremely interesting and highly cultured Brahmin
young man was asked by a missionary, whether
now that he had read Paley's *Evidences* he did not
feel drawn to Christianity ?   The youth's reverence

for truth would not allow him to say with his lips what he did not believe in his heart. He hung down his head, made no reply, and, after some silence, "looked up with rather a sly smile."

There seems to me, I confess, small prospect that Protestantism, in any or all of its varieties, will make substantial progress in India. And I am not much more hopeful for Catholicism. My own observations and inquiries, while in that country, brought me to the conclusion expressed by the Abbé Dubois, after three decades of most unsparing and self-denying, and not altogether unfruitful missionary labour: "Let the Christian religion be presented to these people under every possible light, . . . the time of conversion has passed away, and under existing circumstances there remains no human possibility of bringing it back."

I must refer my readers to the Abbé's own *Letters on the State of Christianity in India*, for the grounds upon which he arrived at a conclusion so distasteful to himself. The chief of them is the utter alienation of the Hindu mind from the fundamental positions of Christianity. In one extremely curious and significant passage he remarks: "Should the intercourse between individuals of both nations, by becoming more intimate and more friendly, produce a change in the religions and usages of the country, it will not be to turn Christians that they will forsake their own religion, but rather (what in my opinion is a thousand times worse than idolatry) to become mere atheists; and if they renounce their present

customs, it will not be to embrace those of Europeans, but rather to become what are now called
Pariahs." It should be observed that, although
the Abbé completely despaired of the higher
castes ever becoming Christians, he thought that
a certain number of converts might be made
among the lower castes and the out-castes. Of
his own labours he remarks, "For my part, I
cannot boast of my successes in this sacred career
during the period that I have laboured to promote
the interests of the Christian religion. The
restraints and privations under which I have lived,
by conforming myself to the usages of the country,
embracing, in many respects, the prejudices of
the natives, living like them, and becoming all
but a Hindu myself—in short, by being made all
things to all men, that I might by all means save
some—all these have proved of no avail to me to
make proselytes. During the long period I have
lived in India in the capacity of a missionary, I
have made, with the assistance of a native
missionary, in all between two and three hundred
converts of both sexes. Of this number two-thirds
were Pariahs or beggars ; and the rest were composed of Sūdras, vagrants, and out-castes of
several tribes, who, being without resources,
turned Christians, in order to form connections,
chiefly for the purpose of marriage, or with some
other interested views."

It may be of advantage to compare with these
extracts from the Abbé Dubois, the following
passage in Mr Baines' General Report on the
Census of 1891 :—

" The greatest development [of Christianity] is found where the Brahmanic caste system is in force in its fullest vigour, in the south and west of the Peninsula and amongst the Hill Tribes of Bengal.   In such localities it is naturally attractive to a class of the population whose position is hereditarily and permanently degraded by their own religion ; as Islām has proved in Eastern Bengal, and amongst the lowest class of the inhabitants of the Punjāb.   We have seen that in the early days of Portuguese missionary enterprise it was found necessary to continue the breach that Brahmanic custom had placed between certain grades of society and those above them ; but, in later times, and in foreign missions of the Reformed Church, the tendency has been to absorb all caste distinctions into the general communion of the Christianity of that form.   The new faith has thus affected the lower classes more directly than the upper, who have more to lose socially, and less to gain." . . .

In this connection, the following observations in Mr V. H. Narasimmiyengar's Mysore Census Report (1891) may be worth considering :—

" Roman Catholicism is able to prevail among the Hindus more rapidly and easily, by reason of its policy of tolerating among its converts the customs of castes and social observances, which constitute so material a part of the Indian social fabric. In the course of the investigations engendered by the census, several Roman Christian communities have been met with, which continue undisturbed in the rites and usages which have guided them in their pre-conversion existence.   They still pay worship to the Kalasam at marriages and festivals, call in the Brahmin astrologer and purohita, use the Hindu religious marks, and conform to various other amenities, which have the advantage of minimising friction in their daily intercourse with their Hindu fellows and brethren."

And here I will put before my readers a letter addressed to me some years ago by a highly culti-vated and highly placed Hindu gentleman, now no more, whose character was on a level with his intellect and his position. His views may be of special interest to those who are professionally engaged in the diffusion of Christianity in India :—

"You have asked me to set down in writing some of the thoughts which I have expressed, from time to time, in conversation, regarding the chances of Christianity in India. I do so with much diffidence, the source of which is not any doubt in my own mind on the subject, but my fear to give offence by speaking too plainly. I am quite sure that many educated European gentlemen would agree with me. Indeed, I think most whom I have met would. For I have observed that very few of them are Christians of the missionary type. But they usually wrap up their meaning and trim their phrases, so as not to hurt the religious prepossessions and prejudices among which they have grown up. I am confident you know me well enough to be sure that I should be very sorry to say anything that would distress or annoy *you*. But I am also confident that you wish me to be entirely candid. And as what I am writing is intended for your eye alone— though you are quite at liberty to make any use of it you see fit, but without mentioning my name—I shall set down my thoughts just as they come to me, trusting to your often experienced kindness to pardon my crudity of expression.

"The chances of Christianity in India! Well, I suppose it will be universally admitted to have little chance among Moslems, Jains, Sikhs, Parsis, and Buddhists. I should say its chances are best among the wild tribes who inhabit the Vindhyan ranges. In these there is the raw material of a good many converts, though they could hardly become Christians of the British type. I fancy, however, that what you specially wish from me is my opinion as to the chances of Christianity among the educated portion of the Hindus properly so called —my own co-religionists. Let me put it in this way. The missionaries come to me and say: 'You ought to be a Christian.' I reply, 'Why? What should I gain by it? What I should lose is clear enough.' They rejoin, 'Whatever you might lose, your gain would vastly preponderate. You

would gain the true religion : the one and only true religion.'
To that 1 demur. Christianity 'the one and only true
religion !' Well, in the first place, I might object that the
thirty or forty sects of you had better first agree among your-
selves as to what Christianity is, before you ask us to embrace
it. But let that pass. What is certain is that Christianity,
in all its forms, is losing its hold in Europe, a fact which is
perfectly well known to the educated Hindu, and is not, *prima
facie*, a recommendation of that religion to him. The tone of
the great masters of modern European literature, from Goethe
till now, is alien from Christianity, if not opposed to it. There
is hardly an exception. At the last census in France, out of a
population of some 35,000,000, 7,500,000 returned themselves as
'of no religious belief.' Is the Christian faith more prevailing
in Italy or in Germany ? In England it probably is, among
certain classes—especially the Lower Middle. But I remember
Emerson, in his *English Traits*, tells us, ' The Church·at this
moment is very much to be pitied. She has nothing left but
possession. If a Bishop meets an educated gentleman and
reads fatal interrogation in his eyes, he has no resource but to
take wine with him.' But you are offended at our superstitions. Is the religion of Spanish peasants, Neapolitan lazzaroni,
or British Salvationists a bit more rational ? Has not Cardinal
Newman told us that a popular religion is ever a corrupt
religion ? And then the grossness of our popular cult offends
you. You are shocked, for example, at the worship paid to
the *lingam* and the *yoni*. But is not this the real worship—
though cryptic—of multitudes in England ? The popular
literature of that country, so largely erotic, seems to suggest
that it is. In France the worship is less veiled. Contemporary
French fiction and poetry are, for the most part, pæans in
honour of the things represented by those symbols. I speak
specially of England and France, because those are the
European countries with whose languages and literature I am
personally familiar. But if I may trust what reaches me by
hearsay, it is not very different in other parts of the Western
world. Though indeed I do find that you Europeans, on the
whole, are, in this matter, upon a lower plane than we are.
Our phallic worship is of the reproductive powers of Nature.
Yours is of mere sensual gratification. Your Aphrodite is,

as Swinburne sings, the goddess 'of barren delights and unclean.'

" You must remember, my dear missionaries, that we look at Christianity as you do at Hinduism, from the outside. Things which use has made familiar to you, excite our wonder ; just as things which use has made familiar to us, excite yours. Bear with me, then, if I say that I think you and your Bible Societies have rendered a very doubtful service to the cause you have at heart, by the translations of your Sacred Books into our vernaculars, which you have disseminated broadcast in this country. To the man of the people, these writings, if he chances to be able to read them, are simply unintelligible. To the educated, they are amazing ! The beauty and pathos and sublimity of some parts of them are unquestionable. There are in the Psalms things as fine as anything in our own religious literature. But side by side with these strains of inspiration, are found savagery and imprecations certainly not breathing the wisdom that comes down from above. Your Bible is the most unequal book I ever saw ; as might, indeed, be expected from its extremely composite character. Heights, and depths, and shallows—all are there. There is the most unqualified fetichism — Moses reminds me of an Obi man among the negroes. But you turn the page, and you come upon such flashes of divine intelligence as might shine out of the depths of eternity. I am thinking, just now, chiefly of the Old Testament. But if I am to speak of the New, I confess freely the charm of the Gospels, and the high ethical tone, and elevated religious sentiment, of much in the Epistles. The figure of the Author of Christianity is certainly one of the noblest—perhaps the noblest—in the annals of humanity. I will go so far as Mill, and allow that we 'must place the Prophet of Nazareth in the very front rank of the men of sublime genius of whom our species can boast ; probably the greatest moral reformer and martyr to that mission who ever existed upon earth ; nay, possibly, what he supposed himself to be—not God, for he never made the smallest pretension to that character, and would, probably, have thought such a pretension as blasphemous as it seemed to the men who condemned him but—a man charged with a special, express, and unique commission from God to lead mankind to truth and virtue.' I do not wonder that the virtue which went out from him drew the Western world after him. But what is any candid mind, viewing the matter, like myself, from the outside, to make of the theology into which St Paul converted his religion? No, my dear missionaries, the educated Hindu knows too much of what history and criticism have done for your Sacred Books, while you were busy translating them, to take them at your valuation. If *you* knew as much, I feel persuaded you would agree with me that the claims made for the Bible by orthodox Protestantism, and I suppose I must say orthodox Catholicism too—for Catholics appear to be in the same boat — are quite as untenable as the claims made by orthodox Hindu theologians for the *Vedas*, or by orthodox mullahs for the *Qu'rān*. To which I would add, that the claim made for Christianity as the *one* religion seems not a whit more tenable. That has been well put by a very learned clergyman—the Rev. Mark Pattison—in words imprinted on my memory: ' Reflection on the history and condition of humanity, taken as a whole, gradually convinced me that this theory of the relation of all living beings to the Supreme Being was too narrow and inadequate. It makes an equal Providence, the Father of all, care only for a mere handful of the species, leaving the rest (such is the theory) to the chances of eternal misery. If God interferes at all to procure the happiness of mankind, it must be on a far more comprehensive scale than by providing for them a church of which far the majority of them will never hear.' Religions are the accidents of time and place : some better ; some worse ; all imperfect ; ' broken lights.' An absolute religion is a contradiction in terms. Religion is essentially relative. I think a wise Hindu, or a wise Mohammedan, or a wise Buddhist, would do well to make the best of the religion in which he is born. That is what I try to do."

The sincere and candid soul who wrote thus, perhaps knows more about these matters now.

> " The shadow cloak'd from head to foot,
>   Who keeps the keys of all the creeds,"

has summoned him beyond the veil. But his

words will not have been written in vain, if they help Christian missionaries to realise the difficulties which their message or rather messages, for their teaching is multiform, present to the cultivated Hindu, and arouse them to the need of an ampler apologetic, a diviner dialectic. And here I gladly insert a note with which my old and valued friend, Sir Alexander Arbuthnot, has favoured me, pointing out some admirable aspects of their work, too frequently overlooked by unsympathetic eyes.

"Remarks are often made upon the comparatively small success which has attended the efforts of Christian missionaries, and especially of Protestant missionaries, to convert to the Christian faith the Hindu and Mohammedan inhabitants of India. It is said, and is truly said, that hitherto their converts are chiefly natives of the lower castes, such as the Pariahs, the Shanars, and the like, and that the conversion of the higher classes, and especially of the better educated, is an event so remote as to justify us in regarding as futile the efforts which they have made during the century which has just closed, and are still making with undiminished zeal. Expression is given to this view in the striking letter from a Hindu gentleman which Mr Lilly is publishing in his forthcoming book on India ; and the sentiments expressed in that letter are, I am aware, held by many Englishmen, and not exclusively by those who, for one reason or another, are hostile to missionary effort.

"It is impossible to say how far the views to which I have referred will be justified as time goes on. The conversion to Christianity of the nations of Europe was the work of several centuries, and it may be that the conversion of the various peoples who inhabit the vast Indian continent will be a matter of even greater difficulty ; but however this may be, I cannot help thinking it a mistake to regard missionary enterprise in India as a waste of labour. On the contrary, I am convinced that looking at the question merely from a political point of view, the existence of our Christian Missions is an important factor in maintaining the prestige of the British Government in that land. I write from some practical observation of the work of the various missionary bodies, which, although dating back a good many years, is, I believe, fully applicable to the present state of things. I served in India for a period which covered from first to last some thirty-eight years, and during a part of that time my public duties as Director of Public Instruction in the Madras Presidency brought me into frequent contact with mission work. While thus employed I was greatly impressed by the admirable manner in which the work was done. I could not help feeling that the example of self-denying zeal which was afforded by many of the English missionaries, toiling, not for profit, not to gratify any ambitious aims, but with the single object of disseminating the faith which they believed to be the true faith, and of thereby promoting the spiritual and moral progress of the people among whom they worked, was a spectacle which could not fail to redound to the credit of the English nation and to raise the prestige of the British name. For instance, the presence in an Indian district of such a man as the late Bishop Caldwell, who for many years carried on the Edeyenkoody Mission in Tinnevelly, combining as he did devotion to his work with learning, judgment, and knowledge of the natives which were not surpassed by any Englishman throughout the land, was an example which could not fail to impress the native mind and to exercise a beneficial influence over numbers besides the actual converts to Christianity. I am persuaded that this aspect of missionary work is too little regarded by those who denounce it, and that if it be only on account of its value from a secular point of view, that work is deserving of liberal, nay, of enthusiastic support. With the other far more important aspects of the question I cannot attempt to deal in this brief note."

PART V

INDIA OF TO-DAY

CHAPTER XIV

UNTIL the paramount power of England was established, the whole of India never acknowledged a single ruler. For well-nigh a thousand years prior to its final conquest by the British, it was a perpetual battle-field, as we have seen in former Chapters. The reader will remember that, eventually, the struggle lay between us and the Mahrattas, represented chiefly by Scindia, the Guicowar and Holkar. The eventual triumph of British arms restored to India such unbroken peace as she had not known since the days immediately before the invasion of Alexander. And it has unquestionably been the constant endeavour of British administrators to enable the country fully to realise the blessing of peace. The words which that extremely well informed and acute observer, the Abbé Dubois, wrote a century ago have since received abundant confirmation :—" The justice and prudence which the present rulers display in endeavouring to make the people of India less unhappy than they have been hitherto ; the anxiety they manifest in increasing their material comfort ; above all, the inviolable

173

respect which they constantly show for the customs
and religious beliefs of the country ; and lastly, the
protection they afford to the weak as well as to
the strong, to the Brahmin as to the Pariah, to
the Christian, to the Mahomedan, and to the
Pagan : all these have contributed more to the
consolidation of their power than even their victories
and conquests."

Three-eighths of the country have been left
under the immediate sway of native rulers of
different grades, and possessing various degrees
of independence ; but all utterly unconnected with
one another, their only bond being the suzerainty
of the Emperor, the one independent sovereign.
There are about eight hundred feudatory states
in India, some of them very tiny.   Foremost among
them must be reckoned the seventeen principalities
ruled by Rājputs, who represent the purest Hindu
blood : the Rāna of Udaipūr, indeed, claims
descent from Rāma, the hero of the Rāmāyana,
who is generally worshipped as an incarnation of
Vishnu. The government of these Rājput states
is of a patriarchal character, the land being par-
celled out between the sovereign and his subjects,
who, as members of the same clan, are accounted
his kinsmen. The Mahārājah of Kashmīr is also
a Rājput, descended from Gholab Singh, to whom,
by a most disreputable transaction, that lovely
country was sold on the annexation of the Punjāb
in 1849. The most considerable Mohammedan
prince in India is the Nizam of Hyderabad, whose
dominions comprise an area of 82,698 square miles.
His importance is indicated by the fact that he is

entitled to a salute of twenty-one guns, an honour conferred upon only two other native feudatories, the Maharājah of Mysore and the Guicowar of Baroda. At the more important of the courts of native princes, the British Government is represented by a Resident, whose duty it is to watch over the administration, and, by timely and authoritative counsels, to prevent mis-government and oppression. The whole of Rājputāna is supervised by a Political Officer residing at Abū, who is styled Agent to the Governor-General. Similarly, the native states of Central India constitute an Agency, the Agent being placed at Indore. One of the most important reforms carried out in the feudatory principalities of late years is the conversion of their military forces into Imperial Service Troops. The effect of this measure, Colonel Durand well observes in *The Making of a Frontier*, has been that "small, compact bodies of well-trained, disciplined, and regularly paid troops were substituted for an armed rabble in all native states. The duty of the great chiefs to share in the defence of the Empire was emphasised; the readiness of the Supreme Government to give their troops a place of honour, and its open and avowed trust in the loyalty of the great martial races, were proclaimed to the world. It was a great scheme, giving to the fighting races, and to their hereditary leaders, a chance of wearing the sword, of resuming the honourable profession of arms, the only one for many races and castes in which a man of good blood can engage. The plan has worked splendidly. The Imperial Service

Troops now represent a force of some 20,000 men, the pick of the population of the Native States."

So much may suffice as to the territories under native rule. The rest of the Indian Empire—five-eighths of the whole—is directly under British administration. This vast region is divided into thirteen * provinces : Madras, Bombay, Bengal, the North - Western Provinces and Oudh, the Punjāb, Burmah, the Central Provinces, Assam, Ajmere, the Berars, Coorg, Balūchistān, and the Andamans. They vary much in extent, the area of Coorg being only 1583 miles, while 171,430 square miles are comprised in Burmah. They vary also in the method of their rule. Madras and Bombay are each administered by a Governor appointed by the Crown, who is assisted by a Council composed of two eminent members of the Covenanted Civil Service. Bengal, the North-West Provinces, the Punjāb, and Burmah are under Lieutenant-Governors, Oudh † and the Central Provinces and Assam are under Chief Commissioners, nominated by the Viceroy. Balūchistān is administered by the Agent to the Governor-General as Commissioner. The Andamans are under a Superintendent and Chief Commissioner. The Resident at Mysore is Commissioner of Coorg. Berar is administered by a Commissioner who is subordinate to the Resident at Hyderabad. And Ajmere is under a Commissioner who is subject to the Governor-General's

* Fourteen.   See Appendix A.
† The Lieutenant-Governor of the North-West Provinces is also Chief Commissioner of Oudh.

Agent for Rājputāna. The authority exercised by the Viceroy over the Lieutenant-Governors, and other rulers of provinces appointed by him, is direct and effective. The Governors of Madras and Bombay he "superintends and controls," in the words of the Act of Parliament (3 & 4 Will. IV., c. 85), "in all points relating to the civil and military administration" of their provinces, and can compel them to obey "his orders and instructions in all cases whatsoever." He also controls finance, and consequently public works throughout India: he supervises the army, he directs internal and external diplomacy. He is assisted by a Council of six, composed of the Commander-in-Chief in India, a legal member, a financial member, a military member, and two distinguished and ex-perienced civil servants. He holds office for a term of five years, and is himself subject to the control of the Secretary of State for India, who, again, is assisted by a Council.

Laws are made for all India by the Legislative Council of the Viceroy, and for various parts of it by the Legislative Councils of Local Governments. In these assemblies there are members who are supposed to bear a representative character, as they are appointed on the recommendation of certain local bodies.

The various provinces of India are divided into districts: the district is the territorial unit; the unit of administration. Of these districts there are 250. At the head of each is a Collector-Magistrate, or Deputy-Commissioner, who, as a rule, is taken from the Indian Civil Service,

M

appointments to which are obtained by open competition at examinations held in London. This official, who receives a salary ranging from £1200 to £2000 a year, fills a position of great importance, involving many and diverse responsibilities and anxieties. The tract of country which he rules is sometimes very extensive: one of the districts in the Madras Presidency with which I am personally acquainted is larger than Denmark. "Upon his energy and personal character," writes Sir William Hunter, "depends ultimately the efficiency of our Indian Government. His own special duties are so numerous and so various as to bewilder the outsider; and the work of his subordinates, European and native, largely depends upon the stimulus of his personal example. His position has been compared to that of the French *préfet*, but such a comparison is unjust in many ways to the Indian District officer. He is not a mere subordinate of a central bureau, who takes his colour from his chief, and represents the political parties or the permanent officialism of the capital. The Indian Collector is a strongly individualised worker in every department of rural well-being, with a large measure of local independence and of individual initiative. As the name of the Collector-Magistrate implies, his main functions are twofold. He is a fiscal officer, charged with the collection of the revenue from the land and other sources; he is also a revenue and criminal judge, both of first instance and in appeal. But his title by no means exhausts his multifarious duties. He does in his smaller local sphere all that the Home

Secretary superintends in England, and a great deal more ; for he is the representative of a paternal and not of a constitutional government. Police, gaols, education, municipalities, roads, sanitation, dispensaries, the local taxation, and the imperial revenues of his district are to him matters of daily concern. He is expected to make himself acquainted with every phase of the social life of the natives, and with each natural aspect of the country. He should be a lawyer, an accountant, a surveyor, and a ready writer of State papers. He ought also to possess no mean knowledge of agriculture, political economy, and engineering." In most parts of India there is an officer called a Commissioner who has under his supervision several districts. But in Madras this functionary does not exist. Instead of Commissioners, there is in that Presidency a Board of Revenue, to which all the District Collectors are directly subordinate.

The Collector-Magistrate, or Deputy Commissioner, is assisted in his duties by a vast number of subordinates. First come those Assistant Collectors, or Commissioners and Magistrates, who, like him, belong to the Covenanted Civil Service of India. Next in the official hierarchy are Deputy Collectors and Magistrates, who are sometimes Europeans or Eurasians, but more commonly natives. And then Tahsildars, or as they are called in Bombay, Mamlatdars, who are also Subordinate Magistrates, whether of the First or Second Class, and who are almost always natives.

Besides these administrative magistrates, there

are also in each district purely judicial functionaries, of whom the Chief is the Judge—District
and Sessions or District Judge is his full title—
and he is ordinarily taken from the Covenanted
Civil Service. In civil causes he has unlimited
jurisdiction, as he has also in criminal—except
over European British subjects — but capital
sentences passed by him must not be carried out
without the confirmation of the High Court to
which he is subordinate, and to which an appeal
from his decisions lies. There are four High
Courts in India, namely, of Bengal, Madras,
Bombay, and the North-West Provinces, besides the Chief Courts of the Punjāb and Lower
Burmah, which exercise the powers of a High
Court. In the smaller provinces those powers
are exercised by a Judicial Commissioner. Of
the Judges of the High Courts, at least one-third,
including the Chief Justice, must be barristers
of not less than five years' standing. Another
third are taken from the Covenanted Civil Service,
and some from the local bars, which are largely
composed of Hindu and Mohammedan advocates.
Besides their appellate jurisdiction, the High Courts
of Calcutta, Madras, and Bombay have an original
jurisdiction also in the cities in which they are
located; and European British subjects can be
tried only by a High Court for grave offences.
Not very far short of 3,000,000 suits are brought
annually before the civil courts in India;
and close upon 2,000,000 people are arraigned
before the criminal tribunals. The system of
criminal law prevailing in the Indian Empire is

largely based upon the English, and is embodied in the Indian Penal Code, the work chiefly of Lord Macaulay. The law of contracts and torts also is substantially English, as is the law of evidence. The law of marriage and inheritance is determined by the customs, usages, and Sacred Books of the various classes of the community. The public peace is kept by a large number of police—some 150,000 altogether—who, like the constables in England, are usually armed only with a truncheon.

No one can deny that this system of civil and criminal administration is vastly superior to anything which India ever possessed under former rulers. Its defects arise chiefly from causes extraneous to it. The unblemished integrity and unswerving devotion to duty of the officials, whether English or Indian, who occupy the higher posts, no one will call in question. The character of the subordinate officials is not always so entirely above suspicion, and the course of justice is too often perverted by a lamentable characteristic of the Oriental mind. "Great is the rectitude of the English, greater is the power of a lie," is a proverbial saying throughout India. Of course, false evidence is to be found in all countries. But in few regions, perhaps, is oral testimony of so little value as in India. Nay, Mr Rudyard Kipling goes so far as to assert that there "you can buy a murder charge, including the corpse all complete, for fifty rupees." This may be one of his humorous exaggerations. But he is strictly accurate in asserting that, "when a native begins perjury, he perjures himself thoroughly; he does not boggle

over details." Perhaps the least satisfactory of
the Government departments is the Police. A
recent writer observes, " It is difficult to imagine
how a department *can* be more corrupt." This, too,
may be an over-statement. But, taken on the
whole, the rank and file of the Indian police are
probably not of higher integrity and character than
those of New York.

Next, a few words must be said regarding the
finances of the Indian Empire. The currency is a
silver one, and hitherto the accounts of the Government of India have been so rendered as to show the
revenue and expenditure under each head in tens
of rupees, for which the symbol Rx is used. It
has come down to us from the days when ten
rupees were equivalent to one pound sterling.
One hundred thousand rupees are called a lac,
and a hundred lacs make a crore. So that
a crore of rupees represented a million of money.
Unfortunately, the exchange value of the rupee has,
of late years, been greatly depreciated—it has now
sunk to sixteen pence—whence financial difficulties
and problems too far-reaching and intricate to be
discussed here. One result of them was the appointment of a Royal Commission, which has recommended a gold currency for India. Sovereigns
have now become a legal tender in that country,
and are at present interchangeable with rupees at
the rate of one sovereign for fifteen rupees, and the
accounts of the Government of India are now drawn
up so as to show the total revenue and expenditure
under each head in pounds. The gross revenue
in 1899-1900 was £68,637,164, and the gross

expenditure £65,862,541. But with regard to these figures it may be well to quote the explanation given in the Moral and Material Progress Statement 1899-1900.

In the gross revenue are included very large receipts, amounting altogether to about one-third of the whole, which (being derived from the working of the railways and canals, the operations of the Postal and Telegraph Departments, the interest received on loans to municipalities, landholders, etc., and on the investments of the Currency Department, the contributions by officers towards their pensions, the sale of stores, and the receipts of the various administrative departments) are rather of the nature of a set-off against the corresponding charges than revenue proper ; and, on the other hand, there are included in the gross expenditure, first, the refunds and drawbacks, assignments and compensations, which are a direct set-off against the revenue ; secondly, the charge incurred for the production of opium, which is subject to variations caused by the state of the season and of trade ; thirdly, the charge for the maintenance of public works, which necessarily increases as more works are brought into operation. The financial position of the Government can be much better appreciated by looking at the Return of Net Income and Expenditure which is annually laid before Parliament : i.e., the revenue after the deduction of the refunds and drawbacks, assignments and compensations, and opium charges ; and the expenditure after the deduction of the various departmental receipts.

A Statement of the Net Revenue and Expenditure of the Indian Empire for 1899-1900 is given in Appendix B. It should be noted that at least one-third of the annual net revenue is withdrawn from the country. This constant depletion is a most serious matter, far too large to be discussed here, but ever to be kept in mind when considering the impoverishment of India.

The main source of Indian revenue, as will
have been seen, is the land tax, and the collection
of this tax is one of the chief duties of Indian
administration.   The accepted theory may be
roughly stated as being that the Government
is the lord paramount, or over-lord, of the land,
and is entitled to a certain share of the produce.
The claims of the Moghul Emperors, and of
the more powerful Hindu dynasties upon the
industry of their subjects, were extremely
onerous.   As Sir Henry Maine has tersely expressed it, " From the people of a country of which
the wealth was exclusively agricultural, they took
so large a share of the produce as to leave nothing,
practically, to the cultivating groups except the
bare means of tillage and subsistence."   Under
the British Rāj the assessment is fixed so as to
represent what is held to be the *fair* share of the
State.   " It was fixed permanently "—I am quoting
the Moral and Material Progress Statement for
1899-1900—"a hundred years ago on certain tracts
paying about £2,850,000 a year ; and it is fixed
periodically for terms of twelve to thirty years over
the rest of India.   On large estates, ranging from
a few hundred to many thousand acres each, the
periodical assessment is a share, generally about
one-half, of the rental enjoyed by the proprietors ;
on small estates cultivated by peasant proprietors
the periodical assessment is imposed on the cultivated
area at a rate per acre fixed with reference to the
productiveness of the land, and representing about
one-half of the estimated letting value.   The
permanently settled tracts comprise the greater

part of Bengal, about one-third of Madras, and certain southern districts of the North - West Provinces. Of the temporarily settled tracts, the North-Western Provinces, the Punjāb, Oudh, the Central Provinces, and Orissa mainly contain estates held by proprietory brotherhoods or large proprietors ; while in Bombay, Burma, Assam, and Berar, and in the greater part of Madras, the land is held and tilled by petty proprietors."

In different parts of India, different systems of land tenure prevail. Here I can give only the briefest account of the five principal ones, referring the reader who desires ampler information to Mr B. H. Baden-Powell's elaborate work quoted in Chapter II. The zemindāri system obtains chiefly in Bengal under the Permanent Settlement effected by Lord Cornwallis in 1793. The term zemindār was originally applied to hereditary Hindu chieftains who exercised a more or less ample jurisdiction, civil and criminal, in their territories, and paid the revenue assessed upon their lands to the officers of the Mohammedan Government : but farmers of revenue were also described by the same title. The Permanent Settlement aimed at creating in India a body of land-holders something like the landed gentry of England, and conferred on the zemindār the status of a proprietor holding his lands subject to a fixed amount of quit rent. It was the first of a long series of well-inten-tioned but ill - conceived attempts to transport English institutions into a soil utterly unsuited to them. Sir Henry Maine is not the least weighty among the many weighty authorities who condemn it. "That unlucky experiment, he calls it. "A province like Bengal proper," he adds, "where the village system had fallen to pieces of itself, was the proper field for the creation of a peasant proprietary; but Lord Cornwallis turned it into a country of great estates, and was compelled to take his landlords from the tax-gatherers of his worthless predecessors. The zemindārs of Lower Bengal have the worst reputation as landlords, and appear to have deserved it." It may be noted that by a series of Acts, beginning with Lord Canning's in 1859, the Bengal zemindārs have been restrained from unduly enhancing the rents of their cultivators.

The ryotwāri settlement obtains in four-fifths of the Madras Presidency, the remaining fifth consisting of zemindāri estates. Its introduction there was due to the strong convictions and great influence of Sir Thomas Munro, one of the wisest and most successful of Indian statesmen. Under it the ryot, or actual cultivator, holds direct from the Government, subject to the payment of his assessment, which is fixed for a term of, generally, thirty years. The Bombay ryotwāri system is essentially similar to the Madras, though differing from it in some important details. In Oudh the settlement is with certain territorial magnates called talukdārs, who correspond much more nearly than the Bengal zemindārs with English landlords. Each of them is responsible for a gross sum in respect of the estate which the State recognises as being, in some stronger or weaker sense, his property. This is known as the talukdāri system.

In the North-West and the Punjāb, where the ancient village community has survived more completely than in other parts of India, the mahalwāri system prevails. The mahal, or village, is there the unit of land administration. And so it is in the Central Provinces, where the leading man in each village or estate is recognised as proprietor under the title of malguzār, and the settlement is made with him. But over a large proportion of his tenants he has no power of enhancement or interference. This is a distinctive feature of the malguzāri settlement. There are also in the Central Provinces a number of feudatory chiefs who pay a light tribute.

The tax next in importance to the land tax is the salt tax, which falls, though lightly, upon every inhabitant of India, and yields on an average about six millions sterling annually. Customs and excise yield each between three and four millions, and the stamp duty about the same. The amount of opium duty varies a great deal : it has sometimes reached as much as ten millions sterling. The municipalities have a certain power of taxation on houses, rents, and carriages : they also levy water and conservancy rates, and in some parts, octroi duties. Besides those of Calcutta, Madras, Bombay, and Rangoon, there are close upon eight hundred of them, which manage, or rather, more or less grossly mismanage, at an annual cost of nearly three millions sterling, the affairs of the urban districts entrusted to them by British doctrinaires. Concerning them more will be said hereafter.

I shall have to speak, in some detail, later on, of the material progress of India under the British Rāj. But it may not be amiss to quote here a few words from Sir Mountstuart Grant Duff which admirably summarise it: "Settled government, great supplies of capital and trained scientific ability, have turned the deltas of great rivers from deserts into gardens. . . . Forest legislation and management have been put upon a scientific footing"—the forests of India, I may observe parenthetically, are computed to cover $70\frac{1}{2}$ million acres, or 110,000 square miles.* "The creation of roads and railways all over the land has provided for an immense number of people. The manufacture of cotton fabrics now carried on upon a great scale has provided for many others, as has that of jute. The winning of coal gives employment to thousands. . . . Vast tracts which were considered perfectly useless and were abandoned to the wild beasts, now produce tea and coffee. The man is still alive and well who was the principal agent in introducing cinchona, which, to say nothing of its immense direct effects in saving life and health, has brought ample wages to thousands of labourers employed in its cultivation and to hundreds employed in the working up and the distribution of its alkaloids." To

---

* Such is the Forest Department return of the reserved and protected forests, but much of this area is rather grazing land dotted with scattered trees than forest land in the ordinary acceptation of the term. The "reserved" forests extend to some 50 millions of acres—80,000 square miles—which are being gradually devoted to growing trees, and are under fairly strict conservancy. The "protected" forests are much less strictly preserved.

which we may add, that during the reign of Her late
Majesty the exports and imports of India increased
a thousand per cent. It is perfectly true that the
annual exports of merchandise and treasure exceed
the annual imports by over £20,000,000. We are
sometimes told that this excess of exports over
imports is a steady drain upon the resources of the
country which receives no equivalent for it. And,
no doubt, this is so. But a great part of this
overflow is in payment of interest on money invested by Englishmen in Indian railways, on which
a low rate of interest is guaranteed by Government,
and which involve a loss of £2,000,000 a year.

At the same time it must be confessed that some
charges on the Indian revenues seem utterly indefensible. Such, for example, was the debiting to
India of a part of the cost of the Abyssinian War
of 1867. I do not know who has expressed better
than Sir Henry Brackenbury the true principle
which should regulate the financial relations of the
United Kingdom and the Indian Empire. " The
foreign policy of India is directed entirely by Her
Majesty's Government, and it is the part of British
foreign policy, generally, to secure Great Britain's
rule over her Empire. If we desire to maintain
British rule in India only for India's sake, then I
think it would be fair to make India pay, to the
uttermost farthing, everything that it could be
shown was due to Britain's rule over India. But I
cannot but feel that England's interest, or Britain's
interest, in keeping India under British rule
is enormous. India affords employment to thousands of Britons ; India employs millions of Eng-

lish capital; and Indian commerce has been of immense value to Great Britain. Therefore, it seems to me that India, being held by Great Britain not only for India's sake but for Great Britain's sake, the latter should pay a share of the expenditure for this purpose."

"There has never been," wrote De Tocqueville, "anything so extraordinary under the sun as the conquest, and still more the government, of India by the English ; nothing which, from all points of the globe, so much attracts the eyes of mankind to that little island whose very name was to the Greeks unknown. . . . I think that the English are obeying an instinct which is not only heroical, but true, and a real motive of conservation, in their resolution to keep India at any cost." With this I fully agree. "To keep India at any cost" is most assuredly a duty laid upon this nation. And certain it is that to fail in that duty would be to bring unnumbered woes upon India : to abandon her to the confusion and misery which preceded the rise of the British Rāj. The peace and order which we have introduced into India are a most legitimate ground for self-satisfaction. We may with ample warrant apply to ourselves the fine verses in which Claudian celebrates the beneficent work of imperial Rome, and claim that England is to her great Dependency rather a mother than a sovereign, and has bound to herself those far-off regions by ties of affection.

"Hæc est in gremium victos quæ sola recepit,
    Matris non dominæ ritu, civesque vocavit
    Quos domuit, nexuque pio longinqua revinxit."

Still I must own that there are grave blemishes
on the British Rāj. One of them is that it does
not appeal to the imagination of the people of India.
"The Government" with which they have to do is
an abstraction, and leaves them cold. The Emperor
—a great name and a name to conjure with—
might as well be living in cloudland, among the
Himālayan gods. Better, indeed, for so he would be
nearer to them. Certain it is that here the British
Rāj is at a disadvantage compared with the native
princes, whose yoke is far heavier upon their subjects. *They* are real present deities to their people
—even although they should more resemble devils,
as, to be sure, the Hindu gods for the most part do.
And alien as they sometimes are from the great
mass of their subjects in race, religion, and
language, the mere sight of them seldom fails to
evoke expressions of loyalty, which are as sincere
as enthusiastic. But the Government is a mere
machine, and who can be loyal to a machine—
especially a taxing machine? The Collector, who
is its visible embodiment, is not, as a rule, a
picturesque person, and does not fire the vivid
Oriental imagination. We must say the same of
the Commissioner. Even the Governor, nay, the
Viceroy himself, is a poor pageant compared with
the native prince, who, resplendent with gold
and precious stones, appears on his elephant,
bedecked with gorgeous trimmings, in his silver
howdah, and, escorted by his kinsmen and retainers
on their gaily caparisoned horses, rides through the
narrow streets of his capital, while women and
children rush forth to gaze, delighted, upon the brave

show, and every man, putting one hand on the
ground in token of fealty, shouts, "Maharāja,
Rām, Rām."/

This is, I think, a more serious matter than
Englishmen, in general, realise. "You can govern
men only through the imagination," said the first
Napoleon : and this dictum, true generally in
greater or less degree, is especially true of the
people of India, who are in many respects mere
grown-up children.   But Englishmen are, as a
rule, lacking in imagination : and when it is manifested by them, it is as likely as not to play strange
vagaries — Lord Ellenborough may serve as an
example.   Unquestionably, a serious defect of the
British Rāj is that it is too mechanic, and it ever
tends to become more so.   Eighty, fifty, nay thirty
years ago, the District Officer had a large initiative.   It has been gradually pared away, as the
Secretariat, greedy of reports, and full of faith in
statistics and averages, has carried on a central-
ising work.   The virtual rulers of the country
have become less men and more machines for
grinding out documents, not, as a rule, of very
much practical value when you get them.

Again, I was very much struck, while in India,
with the absence, in most English officials, of any
real knowledge of the daily lives and wants of the
people.   They did not know, and they did not seem
to want to know.   They were hard-working, just,
nay benevolent, but unsympathetic, and in many
cases more than unsympathetic, contemptuous. | I
suppose we English are, in fact, the least adaptable,
the least flexible of races : the most persistent in

type and in personality. No doubt this means moral energy and force of will. But it also means narrowness of intelligence and shortness of vision. We have the defects of our qualities. We carry with us our institutions, our customs, our prejudices—nay, as far as possible, our environment. And we suppose these things to constitute the proper norm for the whole human race. Our chief aspiration—conscious or unconscious—is to Anglicise. We build railways, make canals, and construct harbours in India: we develop its commercial and industrial resources: we endow it, as far as we can, with rational laws and just administration. To what end? To transform it, as far as possible, into our own image and likeness: to suppress its castes, to throw open its zenānas, to teach it English literature, cricket, and football, to put its men into trousers, and its women into petticoats, and, perhaps, to convert it to some form or forms of British Christianity.

CHAPTER XV

CASTE

WE now come to what I suppose is the most distinctive feature of the civilisation of the Hindus. They are divided into a vast number of independent, self-acting, organised groups, which are called castes ; and their whole social framework rests upon this division. There are those who admire it, as a consummate work of social wisdom. Among these is found the Abbé Dubois, who writes, " I believe caste division to be in many respects the *chef d'œuvre*, the happiest effort, of Hindu legislation. I am persuaded that it is simply and solely due to the distribution of the people into castes that India did not lapse into a state of barbarism, and that she preserved and perfected the arts and sciences of civilisation whilst most other nations of the earth remained in a state of barbarism. I do not consider caste to be free from many great drawbacks ; but I believe that the resulting advantages, in the case of a nation constituted like the Hindus, more than outweigh the resulting evils." Europeans in general, and Protestant missionaries in particular, now take a very different view. They would rather agree with the opinion

forcibly expressed by Mr Sherring, in his well-
known work, that caste is "a monstrous engine
of pride, dissension, and shame"; and to this
many cultivated and thoughtful Hindus at the
present day would assent. Thus Babu Hem
Chandra Banerji, who has attained considerable
reputation among his countrymen as a poet, is
stated to have said, "Caste is the real obstacle
to progress in India;" and Mr Shoshee Chunder
Dutt declares, in his *India, Past and Present*,
"The sum total of the effects of caste is, that
civilisation has been brought to a standstill in the
country by its mischievous restrictions, and that
there is no hope of this being remedied till these
restrictions are removed." Of course Brahmins,
for the most part, dissent, as is natural, from
this judgment, and insist on the necessity "of
maintaining the several divisions in Hindu society
as essential parts of its mechanism."

Let us consider a little the origin of caste—
the word we may note, in passing, is not Hindu
at all, but Portuguese. Now beyond question is
it that though the pre-eminence of the Brahmins
over the rest of the people dates as far back as
there are historical memorials of India, the present
fourfold caste system is much less ancient. We
may say with certainty that it did not exist in
that phase of Aryan civilisation—the earliest of
which we have knowledge—revealed to us by the
hymns of the *Rig-Veda*. The sacerdotal and
warrior orders, the Brahmins and Kshatriyas, are
recognised there: but in the genuine hymns we
find no mention of Vaisyas and Sūdras.

"And so," writes Mr Growse in a very learned dissertation on the subject, buried in his Mathura District Memoir, "it appears to have been all along. In the great epic poems, in the dramas, and the whole range of miscellaneous literature, the sacerdotal and military classes are everywhere recognised, and mention of them crops up involuntarily in every familiar narrative. But with Vaisya and Sūdra it is far different. These words (I speak under correction) never occur as caste names, except with deliberate reference to the Manava Code. They might be expunged both from the Rāmāyana and the Māhabhārata without impairing the integrity of either composition. Only a few moral discourses, which are unquestionably late Brahmanical interpolations, and one entire episodical narrative, would have to be sacrificed; the poem in all essentials would be left intact. But should we proceed in the same way to strike out the Brahman and the Kshatriya, the whole framework of the poem would immediately collapse. There is abundant mention of Dhivaras and Napitas, Sūtradhāras and Kumbhakāras, Mahājanas and Banijes, but no comprehension of them all under two heads in the same familiar way that all chieftains are Kshatriyas, and all priests and *littérateurs* Brahmans."

The hypothesis which Mr Growse favours is, "that the institution of caste was the simple result of residence in a conquered country."

"This," he proceeds, "is confirmed by observing that in Kashmir, which was one of the original homes of the Aryan race, and also for many ages secured by its position from foreign aggression, there is to the present day no distinction of caste, but all Hindus are Brahmans. Thus, too, the following remarkable lines from the Māhabhārat, which distinctly declare that in the beginning there was no caste division, but all men, as created by God, were Brahmans: 'There is no distinction of castes; the whole of this world is Brahmanical, as originally created by Brahma; it is only in consequence of men's actions that it has come into a state of caste divisions.' At the time when the older Vedic hymns were written, the

Aryan was still in his primeval home and had not descended upon the plains of Hindustān. After the invasion the conquerors naturally resigned all menial occupations to the aborigines, whom they had vanquished and partially dispossessed, and enjoyed the fruits of victory while prosecuting the congenial pursuits of arms or letters. For several years, or possibly generations, the invaders formed only a small garrison in a hostile country, and constant warfare necessitated the formation of a permanent military body, the ancestors of the modern Kshatriyas and Thākurs. The other part devoted themselves to the maintenance of the religious rites, which they brought with them from their trans-Himālayan home, and the preservation of the sacred hymns and formulæ used in the celebration of public worship. Of this mystic and unwritten lore, once familiar to all, but now, through the exigency of circumstances retained in the memory of only a few, these special families would soon become the sole depositories. The interval between the two classes gradually widened, till the full-blown Brahman was developed, conscious of his superior and exclusive knowledge, and bent upon asserting its prerogatives. The conquered aborigines were known by the name of Nagas or Mlechhas, or other contemptuous terms, and formed the nucleus of all the low castes, whom Manu subsequently grouped together as Sūdras, esteeming them little, if at all, higher than the brute creation. But a society, consisting only of priests, warriors and slaves, could not long exist. Hence the gradual formation of a middle class, consisting of the offspring of mixed marriages, enterprising natives, and such unaspiring members of the dominant race as found trade more profitable or congenial to their tastes than either arms or letters. Last of all, and by no means simultaneously with the other three, as represented in the legends, the Vaisya order was produced."

Such appears to be the most probable account of the fourfold division of Hindu society. The legendary account, of course, is different. Thus is it given in Manu's *Dharma Shastra:* " For the sake of preserving the universe the Being supremely glorious allotted separate duties to those who sprang respectively from his mouth, his arm, his thigh, and his foot. To Brahmans he assigned the duties of reading (the *Veda*), and teaching, of sacrificing, of assisting others to sacrifice, of giving alms, and of receiving gifts. To defend the people, to give alms, to sacrifice, to read (the *Veda*), to shun the allurements of sexual gratification, are in a few words the duties of a Kshatriya. To keep herds of cattle, to bestow largesses, to sacrifice, to read the Scriptures, to carry on trade, to lend at interest, are the duties of a Vaishya. One principal duty the Supreme Ruler assigns to a Sūdra, viz., to serve the before-mentioned classes, without depreciating their work."

This legend of the origin of the four castes "is true so far," Sir William Hunter observes, "that the Brahmins were really the brain power of the Indian people, the Kshatriyas its armed bands, the Vaishyas its food growers, and the Sūdras its downtrodden serfs." Anyhow, whatever may have been the process, the various elements of the Indian people were welded together into castes by the Brahminical legislation, of which the *Code of Manu* (its probable date is B.C. 500) is the earliest and most authoritative record. And as Mr J. N. Bhattachārya observes in his learned work on *Hindu Castes and Sects* :—

"The sentiments which Brahminical legislation engendered and fostered have led to the formation or recognition of a vast number of extra castes and sub-castes. In all probability the laws of the Shastras failed to bring about a complete fusion of all the clans and races that had been intended to be included within the same group, and their recognition as distinct sub-

divisions have also been formed in later times by the operation
of one or more of the following causes :—

1. By migration to different parts of the country.
2. By different sections being devoted to the practice of
   distinct professions.
3. By any section being elevated above or degraded below
   the level of the others.
4. By quarrels between the different sections of the same
   caste as to their relative status.
5. By becoming the followers of one of the modern religious
   teachers.
6. By the multiplication of the illegitimate progeny of
   religious mendicants.

" The Hindu legislators made the castes exclusive, not so
much by prescribing particular professions for each, as by
prohibiting intermarriage and interchange of hospitality on a
footing of equality. In the beginning intermarriage was allowed
so far that a man of a superior caste could lawfully take in
marriage a girl of an inferior caste. But by what may be called
the Hindu New Testaments, intermarriage between the different
castes is prohibited altogether. As to interchange of hospitality, the Shastras lay down that a Brahmin must avoid, if
possible, the eating of any kind of food in the house of a Sūdra,
and that under no circumstances is he to eat any food cooked
with water and salt by a Sūdra, or touched by a Sūdra after
being so cooked. In practice, the lower classes of Brahmins are
sometimes compelled by indigence to honour the Sūdras by
accepting their hospitality—of course eating only uncooked
food or such food as is cooked by Brahmins with materials
supplied by the host. The prejudice against eating cooked
food that has been touched by a man of inferior caste is so
strong, that although the Shastras do not prohibit the eating of
food cooked by a Kshatriya or Vaishya, yet the Brahmins in
most parts of the country would not eat such food. For these
reasons every Hindu household—that can afford to keep a paid
cook—generally entertains the services of a Brahmin for the
performance of its *cuisine*, the result being that, in the larger
towns, the very name of Brahmin has suffered a strange
degradation of late, so as to mean only a cook.

" The most important regulations by which the castes have been made exclusive are those which relate to marriage. In fact, as Mr Risley in his valuable work on the *Castes and Tribes of Bengal* rightly observes, 'caste is a matter mainly relating to marriage.' Matrimonial alliance out of caste is prevented by the seclusion of females, their early marriage, and the social etiquette which requires that even the marriages of boys should be arranged for them by their parents or guardians."

For more than two thousand years the Brahmins have maintained, unchallenged, their position at the apex of Hindu civilisation, and this, not merely in virtue of the supernatural endowments attributed to them, but by force of intellectual superiority. They have been the priests, the philosophers, the physicists, the poets, the legislators of their race. Yes : and we may say the rulers, too. The Abbé Dubois is strictly accurate when he tells us that "the rule of all the Hindu princes, and often that of the Mahomedans, was, properly speaking, Brahminical rule, since all posts of confidence were held by Brahmins." Even at the present time, they take by far the greatest share in the administration of the country, and their ascendancy, though merited by intelligence and culture, is not without its drawbacks. "They swarm in our public offices ; and rightly too," Sir Mountstuart Grant Duff has remarked, "because they can do the work very much better than any of the other castes. At the same time, they *are* a caste, or rather a *congeries* of sub-castes, and they hold together like a vast Trades Union combined with a cousinhood." The Kshatriyas are now represented by the valiant and high-spirited Rājputs. Many claim the name of Vaisyas. The Sūdras are, of course, the most numerous. But the sub-castes—to use Sir Mount-stuart Grant Duff's phrase—have been exceedingly multiplied; and the lines of demarcation between them are strict. Thus ten great septs are reckoned of the Brahmins : five on the north, and five on the south, of the Vindhya range. And these are split up into a vast variety of divisions, the members of which cannot intermarry or eat together. Among the Mahrattas alone there are over two hundred castes.

Caste regulations are extremely arbitrary. Thus, in most parts of India the Kuman, or potters, are held to be a clean caste : in Guzarat they are regarded as exceptionally clean ; but in the Central Provinces and Orissa they are considered unclean. There are various classes of Brahmins who, for one reason or another, are regarded as degraded, and who form, practically, castes apart. The "good Brahmin" will not intermarry with them, or even take a drink of water from their hands. It is notable that connection with the great Hindu temples involves this degradation: nay, even residence at a place of pilgrimage for a few generations tends to lower the status of a Brahminical family. But the Sompara Brahmins, who minister at the shrine of Somnath, appear to have escaped that social ostracism.

The principal rules of caste observed by Hindus at the present moment, Mr Dutt tells us, in his work before quoted, are as follows : "(1) That individuals cannot be married who do not belong to the same caste ; (2) that a man may not sit down to eat with another who is not of his own caste ;

(3) that his meals must not be cooked, except either
by persons of his own caste, or by a Brahmin; (4)
that no man of an inferior caste is to touch his
cooked rations, or even to enter his cook-room; (5)
that no water or other liquor, contaminated by the
touch of a man of inferior caste, can be made use of
—rivers, tanks, and other large sheets of water
being, however, held to be incapable of defilement;
(6) that articles of dry food, such as rice, wheat,
grains, etc., do not become impure by passing
through the hands of a man of inferior caste, so long
as they remain dry, but cannot be taken if they get
wetted or greased; (7) that certain prohibited
articles, such as cow's flesh, pork, fowls, etc., are
not to be taken; and (8) that the ocean is not to be
crossed, nor any of the boundaries of India passed
over."

To this let me add some weighty observations
of Mr Bhattachārya :—

"The main agency by which caste discipline is still maintained
to some extent is the religious sentimentalism of the Hindus
as a nation. But in this respect there is no consistency to be
found in them. For instance, there are lots of men who almost
openly eat forbidden food, and drink forbidden liquors, and yet
their fellow-castemen do not usually hesitate to dine in their
houses, or to have connections with them by marriage. But
if a man goes to Europe he loses his caste, even though he be
a strict vegetarian and teetotaller. Then, again, if a man
marry a widow he loses caste, though such marriage is not in
any way against Shastric injunctions, while the keeping of a
Mohammedan mistress, which is a serious and almost inexpi-
able offence, is not visited with any kind of punishment by
castemen. Similarly, a man may become a Brahmo, or
Agnostic, and yet remain in caste; but if he espouse Christianity or Mohammedanism, his own parents would exclude

him from their house, and disallow every kind of intercourse, except on the most distant terms : he cannot have even a drink of water under his parental roof, except in an earthen pot, which would not be touched afterwards by even the servants of the house, and which he would have to throw away with his own hands, if no scavenger be available.

" The only acts which now lead to exclusion from caste are the following :

1. Embracing Christianity or Mohammedanism.
2. Going to Europe or America.
3. Marrying a widow.
4. Publicly throwing away the sacred thread.
5. Publicly eating beef, pork, or fowl.
6. Publicly eating *kachi* food cooked by a Mohammedan, Christian, or low caste Hindu.
7. Officiating as a priest in the house of a low class Sūdra.
8. By a female going away from home for an immoral purpose.
9. By a widow becoming pregnant.

When a Hindu is excluded from caste :

1. His friends, relatives, and fellow-townsmen refuse to partake of his hospitality.
2. He is not invited to entertainments in their houses.
3. He cannot obtain brides or bridegrooms for his children.
4. Even his own married daughters cannot visit him without running the risk of being excluded from caste.
5. His priest, and even his barber and washerman, refuse to serve him.
6. His fellow-castemen sever their connection with him so completely, that they refuse to assist him even at the funeral of a member of his household.
7. In some cases, the man excluded from caste is debarred access to the public temples.

" To deprive a man of the services of his barber and washerman is becoming more and more difficult in these days. But the other penalties are enforced on excluded persons with more or less rigour, according to circumstances.

"In the mofussil the penalties are most severely felt. Even in the towns such persons find great difficulty in marrying their children, and are, therefore, sometimes obliged to go through very humiliating expiatory ceremonies, and to pay heavy fees to the learned Pundits for winning their good graces."

So much as to caste. There can be no doubt that the vast majority of Hindus tenaciously cling to it, and resent, as one of the worst of outrages, any interference with it. Some of the best authorities are of opinion that a widespread rumour of the Government's intention to abolish caste was largely the cause of the Indian Mutiny in 1857. Of course the exigencies of modern life war against its strict observance. Railway travelling has been a great leveller. We may say the same of most European institutions. But a little judicious casuistry often serves to obviate the difficulties thus caused to the orthodox Hindu. For example, when the water supply was introduced into Calcutta the problem arose, How could the native public generally avail themselves of it in the face of the prohibition in the *Shastras* against drinking water from a vessel which has been touched by people of another caste? For all sorts and conditions of men resorted promiscuously to the standposts whence the water was obtained. The Pundits, after much reflection and discussion, determined that, although it was contrary to the teaching of Hinduism for men of different castes to drink water which came from the same vessel, yet as the people had to pay taxes to meet the expense of bringing this water, such money payment should be considered a sufficient atonement for violating the ordinances of religion by using the water.

That in the event the caste system will either disappear altogether, or be greatly modified, seems certain. But Mr Dutt is doubtless well warranted in thinking that this change "will probably take a long time yet to come." He adds that at present the great majority of "those who kick against caste" are such as "it has virtually repudiated. This," he continues, "is the case throughout the peninsula, barring its metropolitan towns, where the advance of liberalism has been greater, and where the caste system has necessarily outgrown itself. Unfortunately, however, this, as a rule, has not been the work of the schoolmaster. A love of food and drink proscribed by the *Shastras*, and a morbid craving for promiscuous intercourse with females of all orders, have been the chief accelerators of improvement." There can be no question that Mr Dutt has ample warrant for thus writing. As unquestionable seems his conclusion, "For amelioration thus inaugurated, further progression will not be easy to achieve."

CHAPTER XVI

THE HINDU AT HOME

THE people of India are "a dense population of husbandmen." Only one - twentieth part of them live in towns, most of which are overgrown villages : and of cities there are very few. Their lives are guided chiefly by customs which are of much complexity and of extreme antiquity. The social, economical, and religious institutions of an Indian village are substantially now what they were when the *Laws of Manu* were compiled in the fifth or sixth century before Christ ; and these laws, we must always remember, are merely the systematic arrangement of the usages which then existed, and had long existed ; usages having for their object to secure a self-acting organisation, not only for the village community as a whole, but for the various trades and callings of those who dwelt in it. The account given in the seventh Chapter of the *Laws of Manu* is applicable, with very few modifications, to the village system as it now exists. Under this system every village is a sort of tiny republic, administering its own municipal affairs by means of rude but perfectly effective institutions. In its external relations, whether with other villages or the central government, it is represented by a headman. The daily wants of its members are provided for by a set of functionaries whose office is hereditary : a barber, an accountant, a watcher, a money-changer, a smith, a potter, a carpenter, a shoemaker, an astrologer, and in the larger villages, a poet or genealogist, and a few dancing-girls.

I have had occasion to speak in a former Chapter of the importance of the barber among the Hindus. It may surprise those who are not conversant with Indian life to learn that the astrologer, too, is a very considerable person. He it is who casts the horoscope of the newly-born child in a document recognised by the Law Courts as of great authority for determining age. He it is who fixes the hours for weddings, religious festivals, and, indeed, for the initiation and completion of any business of importance.

The astrologer is also, generally, the purohit, or family priest ; and his aid is indispensable to enable the Hindu to go comfortably through life. He is able to avert by the proper precatory formulas (*mantras*), the evil influences of the planets and the bad effects of curses or spells. He purifies the ceremonially unclean, blesses houses, tanks, and wells, consecrates new idols and invokes the deity into them, and performs the sacred ceremonies at weddings and funerals. His aid is highly esteemed by Hindu husbands during their wives' pregnancy. Daughters are much dreaded ; they are, spiritually, useless, as they cannot perform the funeral ceremonies necessary to a man's deliverance from the hell called *put*. And, economically, they are a burden, especially in the higher castes, for their marriage is a costly affair. Hence, when a Hindu wife is *enceinte*, the purohit, or some other holy man, is required to be constant in prayer that the coming child may be of the male sex. I should here note that if this recourse to supernatural help is ineffectual, there is a considerable chance of the newly born daughter's painless extinction—which, considering what her future life would be, may well appear no injury to her. Infanticide is, naturally, little talked of. But, unquestionably, it is largely practised. There are 6,000,000 fewer women than men in India.

But far more important than the purohit is the guru, of whom it may be well to quote the following graphic account from a work by an Indian gentleman of liberal opinions, entitled, *The Hindu Family in Bengal.*

"Akin to the priest is the guru. The guru is the medium of salvation, and therefore his position is higher than that of the priest. Woe to the Hindu whose body and soul have not been purified by the spiritual counsels of the guru! He lives and dies a veritable beast on earth, with no hope of immortal bliss. However charitable may be his gifts, however spotless his character, be his faith in the gods ever so strong, his salvation is impossible without the guru. Both the guru and the priest vie with each other in ignorance and conceit. Both are covetous, unprincipled, and up to every vice ; but the guru is much more revered than his adversary, owing to the former being a less frequent visitor, and to the speculative and mysterious nature of his avocations. The guru's sway over the family is complete. His visits are generally annual, unless he be in a fix for money on account of an impending matrimonial or funeral ceremony in his house, when he certainly comes to you for his ghostly fee. There are many who simply pass their time in the disciples' houses, going from one to another, and remaining as long as they wish, imposing on the hospitality and trading on the superstitious fears of their hosts.

"At one time these visits were regarded as auspicious events. Paterfamilias would consider the morn to have auspiciously dawned which brought with it the radiant face of his guru. . . . Dame Nature has selected him for his precious physiological and anatomical gifts. Picture to yourself a fat, short man, having what the doctors call 'an apoplectic make,' of pretty fair complexion, round face, short nose, long ears, and eyes protruding from their sockets. Picture that face as sleek and soft, shorn of hairy vegetation, and the crown of the head perpetually kept in artificial baldness save a long tuft of hair in the centre. . . . His countenance does not show the least sign of worldly care ; plenty and ease have always been his environment. . . . He comes with half-a-dozen famished beggars, each of whom has an important part to play in his lord's drama. One prepares his food, another his hemp and opium smoking pills, a third looks after his treasure, a fourth shaves him and anoints his body, whilst the sixth helps him in his amatory transactions. These are not paid servants, but mere hirelings who follow him through fire and through water for anything 'that hath a stomach in it.'

"At the sight of the guru and his crew the whole house is thrown into commotion, and even the inmates of the zenāna for the nonce lose their equanimity. 'The lord has come ! ' is the alarm given by the karta, and it is echoed and re-echoed in the whole household. Preparations for his entertainment on an extensive scale are immediately ordered ; all the while the wily guru laughs in his sleeve with the thought that so long as there are cunning men in the world there must be fools. The karta is seen to reach the doorpost of his house and fall prostrate before the guru, who compliments him by coolly putting his foot on the devotee's head as if it was a stepping stone to the attainment of higher honours in store for him. It is habitual with the guru to enter the house with a sorry face and cold demeanour. There is a vein of policy in it—viz. : to terrify the karta, and extort from him a higher fee. This attempt sometimes causes unpleasantness. We have seen gurus

O

insulting their spiritual disciples, cursing and swearing, and exhibiting such conduct as would, under any other circumstances, justify his immediate expulsion from the house.

"On entering the house the guru is escorted to a sitting-chamber, furnished with new carpets (for it is sacrilegious to make him sit on used ones), and is requested to be seated. He will not sit at first till the fascination of large promises becomes irresistible, and he yields. Large demands are sometimes made, which are generally acceded to by the terrified disciples. After this the members of the family are enquired after, and are dismissed with the touch of the holy man's foot. After his bath the guru is regaled with the choicest food, and the whole family and neighbours esteem it a great privilege to partake of what he may leave."

The karta mentioned in the foregoing extract is the head of the Hindu family, which in its normal state is undivided. But of late years partition has become common in those districts where schools of Hindu law are followed which allow any member of a family to demand it and to acquire the portion that falleth to him. In the undivided family the authority of its head, or karta, is very great; and the following account of him by Mr B. Mulleck may be read with interest.

"In his habiliments he is all simplicity. An ordinary cloth of five yards in length constitutes his usual costume. When he goes out he takes an additional piece of cloth to wrap his trunk with. To wear heeled shoes or boots is inconsistent with his venerable position, and he prefers loose slippers. It is his habit to shave his head and face clean, leaving only a tuft of hair about the centre of his head unshaved. This and a bead necklace mark him as a Hindu, and are prized by him as Hindu distinctions. The only perfumery he uses is mustard oil. . . . His education is not of a high order. He can read and write. At all times he is a lover of learning, and such of his children as are mindful of their studies are his especial favourites. Devoid of a liberal education himself, he is possessed of strong common-sense, and his judgments generally smack of practical wisdom. . . . The authors of the Rāmāyana and Māhabhārata are his great pets, and the stories contained in those works delight his imagination.

" For literary and philosophical culture he greatly depends on the priest versed in ancient lore. He accepts the truths enunciated by him without question or cavil, and stores them up in his mind. . . . The only science he cares for is arithmetic, in the knowledge of which he is generally profound. . . . In book-keeping, too, he has some experience.

"In regard to morals, the karta knows that falsehood is a sin. Evasion and equivocation are sometimes his practices when direct falsehood is impossible. To avert loss or injury he may tell an untruth. His self-love verges on selfishness, though he is just and fair in his dealings. . . . Servile obedience is constitutional with him when he has to deal with superiors in office. Flattery is the oil he uses to soften their minds. He is possessed of plenty of gratitude to those who have benefited him ; but his hatred towards his enemies is implacable."

This picture belongs to the past rather than the present. It is of the "fine old Hindu gentleman" of Bengal, who, unquestionably, is fast disappearing. When a karta dies his place is taken by the principal elder of the family, his brother, or it may be his son, provided the son is of mature years. His wife, or it may be his mother, exercises over the women of the family, as grihin, an authority akin to his over its male members.

It will be proper here to say something about the shrādha, or ceremonies for the benefit of the dead, which are regarded by Hindus as being of such great importance. They include the feeding of Brahmins, and the offering of food, sweetmeats, and other delicacies to the spirit of the departed, and his or her ancestors. I take the following account from a highly-esteemed work, *Modern Hinduism*, by Mr Wilkins, who has abridged it from Mr Bose's book, *The Hindus as They Are.*

" About a fortnight after his father's decease, the son goes into a calculation of the amount he ought to spend in the proper performance of the funeral rites. Some of the richer families are said to have expended as much as £20,000 over a funeral in gifts to Brahmins, schools, charitable institutions, and the poor ; but, as it is stated, in the Sāstras, that Rāma-chandra, one of the incarnations of Vishnu, satisfied his ancestors by offering to them balls of sand for funeral cakes, it is taught that the poor can obtain equal benefit to them-selves and ancestors without going to any very great expense. A poor man in these days is held to have performed a proper Shrādha by making an offering of rice, tila seed, and a little fruit, and by feeding one Brahmin only—a ceremony that costs him only about four rupees.

" When twenty days have passed, the son, accompanied by a Brahmin, walks barefooted to invite his friends and others whom he wishes to be present at the ceremony. On the thirtieth day, he and the near relatives, who have been regarded as ceremonially unclean, owing to the death of the deceased, now are shaved, have their nails cut, and put on clean clothes. On the thirty-first day, he goes to the river to bathe, and as religious mendicants are ever on the watch for such people, they clamour for presents, declaring that unless their demands are satisfied, the departed cannot enter heaven. In a well-conducted Shrādha, the son has to provide silver plates and drinking vessels, also a bed and clothing to be given away as presents to the Brahmins who may honour him with their presence.

" When the guests have assembled, amongst the Brahmins will be a number of men who possess some knowledge of Sanskrit. A Shrādha is one of the field days for these gentle-men, who beguile the weary hours before the feast takes place with argumentation on some knotty point in Sanskrit grammar or Hindu philosophy.

" From eight o'clock in the morning to two in the afternoon, the house where a Shrādha is going on is crammed to suffocation. A large awning covers the open courtyard, preventing the free access of air ; carpets are spread on the ground for the Kāyasthas and other castes, whilst the Brahmins, by way of precedence, take their seats on the raised Thākurdālan, or place of worship (*i.e.* the place where the images made for special religious festivals are set up). The presents, with a salver of silver, are arranged in front of the audience, leaving a little space for the musicians, male and female, which form the necessary accompaniment of a Shrādha, for the purpose of imparting solemnity to the scene. . . . The guests begin to come in at eight o'clock, and are courteously asked to take their appropriate seats—Brahmins with Brahmins, Kāyasthas with Kāyasthas, etc. ; the servants supplying them with *hukhas* (pipe) and tobacco. . . . The current topics of the day form the subject of conversation, while the bukha goes round the assembly with great precision and peculiarity." (For each caste a special hukha is preserved, all of the same caste using the same.) " The female relatives are brought in covered palanquins by a separate entrance, shut out from the gaze of the males.

" About ten o'clock the ceremony commences, the priest reading the texts, the son repeating them after him. This occupies about an hour, after which many take their leave, whilst others remain for a share in the gifts to be distributed. And often most unseemly disputes arise amongst these learned men in the division of the spoil. As some of the Brahmins, though present at the Shrādha, will not eat in the house of a Sūdra, they carry home with them uncooked food and other presents.

" On the following day the Brahmins and others are fed. It is this feast that is supposed to restore the son and other relatives of the dead person to ceremonial purity. Besides those specially invited, it is no uncommon thing for as many more to come uninvited to partake of the good things. The food that is provided for these feasts is composed of what is regarded as sweetmeats, and not rice, the ordinary food of the people. To eat rice with a man is to acknowledge equality of caste ; but these sweetmeats may be eaten without the ordinary caste restrictions being broken.

"On the next day the Kāyasthas and other castes are fed, and, if possible, on this day there is a greater crush and confusion than on the Brahmin's day. On the morning of the next day the mourning for the deceased is considered over. After some hours of music in the house by professional singers, the son and nearest relatives, having anointed their bodies with oil and turmeric, remove from the house what is called a brisakat, and fix it on the ground near the house. The brisakat is a painted log of wood about six feet long, on which the figure of an ox is rudely cut. This is a sort of monument to the memory of the deceased. After this they bathe, return home, put on their ordinary dress, and sit down to an ordinary meal."

The vast majority of the Hindus live in a state of great poverty. Their houses are small huts of only one room, without windows to admit the light. The walls consist of coarse straw mats fastened to a framework of bamboos, or of reeds, or of alternate rows of straw and reeds, plastered with mud. But both floor and walls are strewn over with cow-dung, which, unquestionably, has a cleansing effect, and emits a perfume like that of a Tonquin bean. The dwelling-houses of the richer, whether Mohammedans or Hindus, consist of two parts, the zenāna and the boytakhāna. "The boytakhāna," writes Mr J. N. Bhattachārya, "is the outer part of the house where visitors are received. The Mussulmans do sometimes entertain their co-religionists in the boytakhāna, but no orthodox Hindu would enter such a place while the plates are in it, or would remain there a moment after any sign of preparation for introducing any kind of cooked eatables. Hindus and Mohammedans very often exchange visits for ceremonial and official purposes. But even when they are on the most friendly terms, a man professing the one religion will not ask a votary of the other to sit by his table while he is at dinner. The orthodox Hindu's prejudices are such that after sitting on the same carpet with a Mohammedan or a Christian friend, or shaking hands with such a person, he has to put off his clothes, and to bathe or sprinkle his person with the holy water of the Ganges. The Mohammedan gentlemen of the country who know well of these prejudices on the part of their Hindu fellow-countrymen, therefore, never ask them to mix too familiarly, and the Hindus also keep themselves at a sufficient distance to avoid what they must regard as contaminations."

I will conclude the Chapter by putting before my readers the picturesque account of the house of a wealthy Hindu gentleman of Bombay, given by Sir George Birdwood in his admirable work, *The Industrial Arts in India.*

" If we may judge from the example of India, the great art in furniture is to do without it. Except where the social life of the people has been influenced by European ideas, furniture in India is conspicuous chiefly by its absence. In Bombay the wealthy native gentlemen have their houses furnished in the European style, but only the reception rooms, from which they themselves live quite apart, often in a distinct house, connected with the larger mansion by a covered bridge or arcade. Europeans, as a rule, and all strangers, are seen in the public rooms ; and only intimate friends in the private apartments. Passing through the open porch, guarded on either side by a room or recess for attendants, you at once enter a sort of ante-chamber, in which a jeweller is always at work making or repairing the family jewels. Through the windows, across the court, the Brahmin cook is seen among the silver drinking vessels and dishes, preparing for the mid-day meal. In the opposite verandah, into which you next pass, some young girls are engaged under a matron embroidering silk and satin robes ; and at the end of it a door opens and your host welcomes you heartily into his private parlour. He has sent for a chair for you, but sits on the ground himself, on a grass mat, or cotton satrangi, or Kashmir rug, with a round pillow at his back ; and that is all the furniture in the room. Up-country you may pass through a whole palace, and the only furniture in it will be rugs and pillows, and of course the cooking pots and pans, and gold and silver vessels for eating and drinking, and the wardrobes and caskets, and graven images of the gods. But you are simply entranced by the perfect proportions of the rooms, the polish of the ivory-white walls, the gay fresco round the dado, and the beautiful shapes of the niches in the walls, and of the windows ; and by the richness and vigour of the carved work of the doors and projecting beams and pillars of the verandah. You feel that the people of ancient Greece must have lived in something of this way ; and the houses of the rich in the old streets of Bombay, built before the domestic architecture of the people was affected by Portuguese influences, constantly remind you, especially in their wood-work, of the houses of the Ionian Greeks, as the learned have reconstructed them from their remains ; and the woodwork is the essential framework, the solid skeleton, of native houses in Bombay, and is put up complete before a stone or brick is placed on it. The strict rectangular ground plan also of Bombay gardens, and the orderly and symmetrical method in which they are planted, the different species of trees, it may be the cocoanut palm and mango, or the cocoanut palm and areca-nut palm, being planted alternately all round the boundary, with other trees, pomegranates, oranges, jasmines, guavas, roses, cypresses, oleanders, and custard-apples, in regular rows and sections, is identical with the ground plan of the ancient Egyptian and Assyrian gardens. Your host has nothing on but a muslin wrapper, for he is about to have prayers performed, and, as he throws the wrapper off his shoulders and head, and girds it round his waist and sits down, a Brahmin enters and places the gods and sacred vessels before him, burning incense, and going through the customary forms and ceremonies ; while your friend, if you are interested, explains them in their order. So an hour has passed, when a frugal meal, chiefly of unleavened bread and milk, is taken, and then, it being nearly two in the afternoon, an attendant comes in and dresses his master for the Legislative Council, of which he is a member. First he puts on him a soft, close-fitting jacket, and over it a long, white cotton robe : then his stockings, of the finest lisle thread, are drawn on, and his feet placed in a pair of elegant French pumps ; after which the turban is placed on his head, and a long waistband wound round his waist ; and thus arrayed, with a heavily gold-mounted cane in hand, he at last issues forth, clothed and altogether in another mind, into the outer world of English ideas and fashioning."

CHAPTER XVII

WOMAN IN INDIA

WE may confidently assert that a chief test of a
social order, and a sure index to its character, are
afforded by the position which it assigns to woman.
Here is a principal difference between the civilisation
of modern Europe and all other civilisations. And the
difference is unquestionably the outcome of Christianity. We should be strictly accurate in saying
that this religion introduced among mankind a new
conception of the relations of the sexes ; a conception grounded upon its doctrine as to the virtue of
purity. The great moralists of the antique world
had barely suspected the existence of that virtue.
We should hardly exaggerate in speaking of it as
unknown to ancient Rome and Hellas. A wife was,
indeed, expected to be faithful to her husband. But
the duty was derived from the fact that she was his
property ; that her office was to bear his children.
No similar duty was regarded as incumbent upon a
man. The Greek orator, in a well-known passage,
says : "We have courtesans for pleasure, female
house-slaves (παλλακὰς) for daily physical service, and
wives for the procreation of legitimate children, and

for faithfully watching over our domestic concerns."
And a man's intercourse with all these classes of
women was regarded as equally lawful. The new
view which Christianity introduced, rests upon its
teaching concerning the espousal of human nature by
the Incarnate God : "We are members of His body,
of His flesh, and of His bones." And the "we"
includes women as well as men : "in Jesus Christ
there is neither male nor female." Woman, though
the physical inferior, is the spiritual equal of man.
"Sanctification and honour" are the new law of the
relations of the sexes, in virtue of their new creation
in Christ. It has been well observed by a learned
writer : "This is the ever-abiding source of Christian
purity, and the fixing of this doctrine, with all its
consequences, in the minds of men was, of itself, a
moral revolution."

Nowhere, perhaps, is the triumph achieved by
Christianity more remarkable than in this domain
of sexual morality. That its severe discipline of
restraint should have succeeded in bringing into the
obedience of Christ the most imperious and indomi-
table of human appetites, is assuredly, in the strictest
sense of the word, miraculous. But it did more than
this. It exhibited the total denial of that appetite
from religious motives, as a far more excellent thing
than its gratification even within the limits of holy
matrimony. The life of Christ was the type which
His members set before them ; and the following
Him in His virginal purity was recognised as a way
to perfection. It was the supreme consecration of
the virtue of chastity ; and all that was greatest and
noblest during those centuries when the civilisation

of Europe was distinctively Christian grew out of
this root.	One of the profoundest students of
human nature the world has ever seen—for as such
we must assuredly account Balzac—has admirably
said, "La Virginité, mère des grandes choses—
magna parens rerum—tient dans ses belles mains
blanches la clef des mondes supérieures.	Enfin,
cette grandiose et terrible exception mérite tous les
honneurs que lui décerne l'Église Catholique."

The vast majority of mankind ever have dwelt,
and ever will dwell, upon the lower levels of humanity.
Those elect souls who "scorn men's common lure,
life's pleasant things," are always few.	But it makes
all the difference, in any age, of what kind men's
ideals are.	If they are high, severe—yes, let me
venture upon the word—ascetic, a civilisation will be
marked by dignity, magnanimity, virility, however
grave and numerous the derelictions from the stan-
dard commonly recognised.	And herein appears to
me to lie the incontestable greatness of the Middle
Ages.	Chivalry and romance were the true ex-
pressions—fantastic and extravagant, no doubt, at
times—of that teaching of the Church concerning
the virtue of purity which hallowed the graces of
feminine nature with a species of religious venera-
tion.	No one—with the inconsiderable exceptions
offered by sporadic heretical sects—then doubted
the truth of that teaching, whatever his own practice
might be in respect of it.

And even in these very unmedieval ages that
teaching survives in its effects upon the structure
of European society, though the old religious sanc-
tions upon which it rested are widely rejected.	The

elevated position of woman in the Western world is directly due to it. How far woman will retain this elevated position should Christianity become generally discredited, is a question which cannot be pursued here.

It is notable that in India the one faith whose *ethos* has most in common with the Christian, has been the most favourable to woman. The religion of the Buddha, like the religion of Christ, gives her a place beside man as "a helpmeet for him," or, in the phrase of the Vulgate, "like unto him": *adjutorium simile sibi.* It is a very different position from her subjection in Islām, and from her degradation in modern Hinduism. Nothing strikes the visitor to Burmah more forcibly than this. The liberty of the Burmese woman—liberty in the choice of a husband, liberty in the ordering of their lives—presents a singular contrast to the semislavery of their Mohammedan and Hindu sisters. The reader who cares to see more on this subject will find it in the fascinating work to which I have referred in a previous Chapter, *The Soul of a People.*

Concerning the place of woman among Moslems, very few words will suffice. Unquestionably, Mohammed's reform did something for her. He curbed the unrestrained sexual license which he found among his Arab kinsmen. To a certain extent he shielded and protected woman. From the first he prohibited the custom of conditional wedlock, and in the third year of the Hijra he abolished temporary marriage. A well-known passage in the *Qu'rān* allows only four contempor-

aneous wives.   And even this permission is subject
to the proviso, "If you cannot deal fairly and
equitably with all, you shall marry only one."
Perhaps the Qu'rānic legislation deserves the praise
of going as far on behalf of the weaker sex as was
possible in the state of society for which it was
originally promulgated.   It would be absurd to
blame Mohammed for not making monogamy part
of his system, even if he had discerned its superior
excellence as a form of marriage.   But he did not.
Polygamy appeared to him, as to the ancient Hebrew
patriarchs and kings, whose environment much
resembled his, to be the dictate of nature : a dictate
which he himself followed with no sort of misgiving.
But while not denying—as how can we?—that
polygamy may be suitable to certain stages of social
evolution, we must not shut our eyes to the fact
that the Prophet of Islām by—so to speak—stereo-
typing it in his law, unwittingly placed there a
grave obstacle to the progress of Moslem communities.   Mr Justice Amir Ali, indeed, in his learned
and interesting work on the *Life and Teaching of
Mohammed*, tells us that a plurality of wives is
growing rare among Indian Mussulmans.   "The
feeling against it," he writes, "is becoming a strong
social, if not a moral, conviction, and many extraneous circumstances, in combination with this growing feeling, are tending to root out the custom from
among the Indian Mussulmans.   It has become
customary among all classes of the community to
insert in the marriage-deed a clause, by which the
intending husband formally renounces his supposed
right to contract a second union during the continu-

ance of the first marriage. Among the Indian Mussulmans ninety-five men out of every hundred are at the present moment, either by conviction or necessity, monogamists. Among the educated classes versed in the history of their ancestors, and able to compare it with the records of other nations, the custom is regarded with disapprobation. In Persia, only a small fraction of the population enjoy the questionable luxury of plurality of wives. It is earnestly to be hoped that before long a general synod of Moslem doctors will authoritatively declare that polygamy, like slavery, is abhorrent to the laws of Islām." The hope expressed by the learned Judge assuredly merits all sympathy. But its fulfilment does not seem probable in the face of the express teaching of the *Qu'rān* and the undoubted practice of the Prophet.

The position which woman holds in modern Hinduism may serve to show how vastly that system has degenerated from the ancient Vedic religion. Husband and wife were the joint rulers of the old Aryan household. The great Aryan epic poems exhibit the maiden as choosing her own spouse. Very different is the Brahminical conception, as formulated by Manu, of the wifely status: "Let the husband keep his wife employed in the collection and expenditure of wealth, in purification, and in female duty; in the preparation of daily food, and in the superintendence of household utensils. The production of children, the nurture of them when produced, and the daily superintendence of domestic affairs, are the province of the wife." "For women," he says elsewhere, "there are no separate holy rites, fasts, or ceremonies ; all she has to do is to worship her husband, and thus will she become famous in heaven." And again, "Whether a woman be a child, or young, or old, she must ever be dependent. In her childhood she must be in subjection to her parents, in her youth to her husband, and in her old age to her children.". A Hindu woman must not eat with her husband, but must sit at a respectful distance from him. Nor may she walk by his side : she must walk behind him. She must not accost him in the presence of others, nor can he notice her. "A man makes himself ridiculous," writes Mr Dutt, "if he speaks to his wife affectionately before a third person ; and the wife is considered shameless who responds to such familiarity. Young married people are brought together only at night, and parted again in the morning, as if their meeting were a clandestine one. The only male relatives whom the Hindu wife ever notices openly, and at all times, are her husband's younger brothers and all children." She lives in the portion of the house set apart for her—the zenāna—and never leaves it except when invited, on festive or other special occasions, to the houses of relatives, whither she is carried in a close *palki*. I am writing of the women of the upper classes ᐧ *purdah* women, as they are called. Those of the lower classes, of course, are not secluded, but go about freely, taking their share, and often more than their fair share, of the labour of men.

Such is the condition of Hindu wives. Should they become widows their lot is hard indeed. They are to dress in perpetual mourning. They are to wear no ornaments. They are to appear on no festive occasions. They are to display no emblem, and to enjoy no privilege of matrimony. " Let the widow emaciate her body by living on roots, fruits, and flowers," Manu enjoins : "let her not even pronounce the name of another man after her lord is deceased : let her continue till death forgiving injuries, performing harsh duties, avoiding sensual pleasure, and practising virtue." This is by no means an empty precept. The vast majority of Hindu widows live, more or less, up to it. The recent Act which sanctions their re-marriage is, practically, inoperative. The institution of sutti —a comparatively late Brahminical development— has disappeared under British rule. The Hindu widow no longer ascends her husband's funeral pile. But her life is little better than a living death. Of course a Hindu woman has no voice in the choice of her husband. A man's marriage is arranged for him, when he is a mere boy, by his parents or guardians, and is strictly regulated by considerations of caste. He is not consulted in the matter, and has to maintain an attitude of utter indifference regarding it. Girls are accounted by law marriageable at the age of eight : they are, however, given in marriage at the age of two and upwards, till they attain their maturity at about their twelfth year, remaining till then with their own family. " To a Hindu," as the Abbé Dubois remarks, " marriage is the most important and most engrossing event of his life. It is also the most expensive one, and brings many a Hindu to ruin. Some spend on it all that they possess, and a great deal more

P

besides : while others, in order to fulfil what is expected of them, contract debts which they are never able to repay." The expenditure is on feastings and rejoicings, which go on for weeks. Only a son, born in wedlock or adopted in default of male issue, can perform the exequial rites necessary to deliver a man from the hell called *put.* And Manu insists that this is the reason why a son is in the Sanskrit tongue designated *putra.* The right of inheritance and the right of performing funeral obsequies are correlative.

The rules regarding marriage, and consequently regarding inheritance and the family tie, vary greatly among Hindus in the different districts. The Nairs, one of the foremost races in South India, are polyandric ; and a very curious form of polyandry it is. They are married, nominally, to girls of their own caste, with whom they never have any intercourse, and who select vice-husbands (if the phrase may be allowed) at discretion from among other Nairs or Brahmins. And in certain castes in Madura a wife's intercourse with her husband's brothers and near kinsmen is recognised as legitimate, or, at all events, is tolerated. A plurality of wives is regarded among Hindus generally as a luxury for those who can afford it, although their sacred writers teach that a man should not take additional spouses without justifying circumstances. But in the case of the rich or powerful their own *sic volo, sic jubeo,* is accounted, practically, a sufficient justification. Indeed, among princes and great chiefs, sexual relations prevail which recall the practice of the patriarchs and monarchs of the ancient Hebrews. Take, for example, the following interesting picture of the domesticities of the Rājah of Kulu, given by Mr F. St John Gore in his *Lights and Shades of Indian Hill Life* :—

"The Rai of Kulu, though not a ruler, holds a sort of hereditary dukedom, and with it as much of a court and appanage as his somewhat slender means will allow. He can only marry a girl with 'royal' blood in her veins, and should he wish to do so, he receives a proposal from the girl's father offering his daughter in marriage. In the case of a rich girl, the father can command the Rai to come to his house with as many followers and attendants as he considers due to his daughter's position. On the Rai's approach with some two or three hundred followers, he is received in great state, presents are exchanged, and the marriage is completed by a curious cere-mony, in which the bridegroom walks seven times round the bride.

"It is the custom then for the Rani to be accompanied to her new home by a suite of several girls, the daughters of any villagers whom her father has influence enough to impress, though in some instances, if they are beautiful, he has to pay for them. These girls become a part of the Rai's household, and are from time to time supplemented by new purchases of the Rani's, whom she presents to her lord and master.

"The late Rai had two Ranis, the elder and the younger, and some sixteen of these girls, and being a most kind and enlightened man, they were very well treated by him, often accompanying their lord (in closed conveyances) on the occasions of his visits to the Ganges, to bathe in the sacred water.

"The Rani has a room of her own, and her food is cooked for her by a Brahmin, while the girls all live happily together in a big upper room with glass windows on all sides, where they sleep at night on mattresses placed in rows along the wall, each being covered with a clean white durri, on which the occupant's name is carefully embroidered. In the daytime the mattresses are rolled up and put away, and each girl cooks her own food, in little rooms set aside for the purpose. The Rai's bed stands in the middle of the room, and he spends his time partly here and partly with the Ranis, without apparently exciting any jealousy in this well-ordered household.

"The simplicity of the whole arrangement may be gathered from the fact that these 'ladies-in-waiting' receive as pay each eighty pounds of grain a month, two pieces of homespun and two pairs of shoes a year, while one anna (about a penny) is given her a month as pocket money. The girls always dress in the homespun cloth of the country, the Ranis alone wearing the richer coloured muslins.

"No doubt some people will urge that the position of these girls is nothing more nor less than slavery ; but slavery is such a wide word and covers so many varied conditions of life, that it may be said to include almost every phase, since no one is quite his own master. In spite of the horror this name implies to the average Briton, as a matter of fact in the East domestic slavery only becomes an evil when those in subjection begin to desire to change their life, which they very rarely wish to do, for they accept dependence and subjection with no different feelings from those of a Western girl in a humble state of life, who is obliged to earn her living by service.

"In considering the position of these girls who belong to the household of a Raja, it must be remembered that they acquire a status that has been held in honour ever since the days of Solomon. Their life of ease and comfort, with ample provision of food and clothing, their freedom from all care under the protection of an indulgent master, must be con-trasted with the alternative offered to them by remaining at home. In the latter case they would make a *mariage de convenance*—in other words, be sold by their father for a few rupees to some young peasant. A life of toil and drudgery would then commence, in which 'home life,' as we know it, would most probably be embittered by the infidelity of the husband and by her own intrigues, with an old age of neglect and want as a consummation. Of the two the latter picture presents quite as many features of slavery as the former, with the addition also of hard labour for life."

We saw just now from Manu that the special functions of woman are the production and nurture

of children and the superintendence of domestic
affairs. But of these, owing to the transcendant
importance attached among Hindus to offspring,
maternity is regarded as by far the greatest. It is
fenced round with minute regulations, which are
imposed upon the wife for months before the
child is born. They are much too numerous to
be detailed here: I can cite only a few of
them. "The pregnant wife must not wear any
clothes over which birds have flown: she must
always wear a knot in her dress (sāri) where it
is fastened round her waist: in order to avoid the
contact of evil spirits, she must not walk or sit in
the open courtyard of her house, and must wear a
thin reed, five inches long, tied in the knot of her
hair: as a means of easily getting through her
trouble, she has to wear an amulet round her neck,
containing flowers consecrated to Baba Thākur, a
deity worshipped chiefly by the lower orders of the
people; and she must daily drink a few drops of
water that have been touched by this amulet."

After the child has been born, the new mother
has to undergo the ceremony of purification, which
is of as much importance among the Hindus as it
was among the ancient Hebrews, and is much more
inconvenient. Miss Leslie thus describes it in her
work, *The Dawn of Light*:—"Her nails were cut,
her hair tied up; she was put in a palanquin, the
bedding having been taken out, and carried to the
river, a distance of six miles. The bearers waded
into the stream with their burden as far as they
could go, and the sacred waters gushed in, around,
and upon her, shut up in her dark box. She was

then carried back all those six miles in her wet
clothes, and such was the efficacy of the bath, that
from that time she was reckoned ceremonially clean.
The neighbours were feasted with sweetmeats,
and puja (worship) was offered to the goddess
Sāsthi."

It should be noted that Hindu wives are, with
very rare exceptions, unswervingly faithful to their
husbands. "Among good castes," says the Abbé
Dubois, "females in general, and married women in
particular, are worthy to be set forth as patterns of
chastity and conjugal fidelity to individuals of their
sex in more enlightened countries." This is the
more meritorious, as only in the rarest of cases are
Hindu wives companions to their husbands. How
can they be? "The conversation of Hindu women,"
Mr Dutt avers, "is for the most part inane and
frivolous, which affords a correct proof of the
emptiness of their minds. . . . The husband, when
talking to his wife, carefully avoids every discourse
that might require the exercise of reason. He dis-
cusses with her domestic matters only. . . . Every
question that requires a careful mind to appreciate,
he carefully and habitually eschews. A supine
vacuity of thought is the necessary result." No
doubt children in India, as everywhere else, constitute a strong tie between husband and wife: no
doubt in India, as elsewhere, conjugal relations
produce what Lord Bacon calls "a kind of fondness
which use engendereth." Still, though a husband
may be affectionately disposed, though a mother-in-
law may be good-natured, the position of a Hindu
wife is, at the best, deplorable. Of the sweetness

of love's young dream she has had no experience. The element of romance which in European countries may idealise the nuptials of the humblest, does not enter into her life. Mere legal coupling is all that is permitted to her. With extremely few exceptions, Hindu wives are, to quote Mr Dutt again, "household drudges merely."

This very intelligent and highly educated Indian gentleman wishes that they should be something more: and is not without a word of sympathy for the plan of zenāna teaching, initiated by certain benevolent Europeans; though he considers—and I believe with good warrant—that "it has achieved nothing to speak of up to this time." Personally, Mr Dutt, while desiring education of a sort for his countrywomen, does "not think the European model the best to imitate, or wish that they should possess the accomplishments of an English miss." He tells us he would not have them "dance, or sing, or do the pretty." In fact, Mr Dutt must be well aware—though he does not go on to say so—that a Hindu gentleman who desires a *companion* of the other sex, will not seek her in wedlock, but will turn for her to a class of women whose business it is "to dance, or sing, and do the pretty"; a class whose position in Hindu society it is necessary to understand, if we would properly estimate the character of Hindu civilisation. I shall, therefore, say a few words regarding it, the more especially as it is grossly misconceived by the great majority of European writers on India. Mr Crook, the author of a very meritorious work on *The Tribes and Castes of the North-West Provinces, and Oudh,* tells us: "One curious point as regards Indian prostitutes is the tolerance with which they are received into even respectable houses, and the absence of the strong social disfavour in which the class is held in European countries." This is true, as far as it goes; but it does not go far enough. To say that Indian dancing-girls "are received with tolerance into even respectable houses" is a most inadequate statement. They are invited, as a matter of course, to the homes of native gentlemen on all great occasions, such as thread or marriage ceremonies, birthdays, or house-warmings (as we should say). It is a proverbial saying, that without the jingling of their feet-bells, a dwelling-place does not become pure. And they are treated by all castes with the utmost deference, being even allowed to sit in the assemblies of great persons, who would not accord such an honour to their own wives and daughters. To call them "prostitutes" is, of course, quite accurate. But it is quite misleading, also, to ordinary English readers. Dancing-girls (*dāsis*) are prostitutes indeed. But their profession is a recognised and respected one; and many of them (*dēvidāsis*) exercise a religious ministry, and bear their appointed part in the worship offered in the temples. These occupy in Hinduism a place corresponding to that which nuns hold in Christianity. Just as nuns are consecrated to the God of Purity whom Christians adore, so dancing-girls are consecrated to one or another of the impure deities of the Hindu Pantheon. As nuns are termed the brides of Christ, so are dancing-girls termed the brides of the idol, or of the deity represented by the idol, in whose temple they perform their function. They dance before him several times daily, and sing hymns, generally of what we should deem an obscene character, in his honour; and they receive stipends from the temple endowments, varying in amount according to the income, sanctity, or popularity of the fane. " Their ranks are recruited," writes Mr Sherring, in his work, *Hindu Tribes and Castes*, " by the purchase of female children of any caste, and also by members of certain Hindu castes vowing to present daughters to the temple on recovering from illness, or relief from other mis- fortune. The female children of the dancing-women are always brought up to their mother's profession, and so are the children purchased by them, or assigned to the temple service by the free-will of their parents." They are carefully educated in the arts of music and dancing, and are also taught to write and read : some of them not only sing, but compose songs. They have their own peculiar customs of adoption and inheritance, which the Courts uphold—it is a wonder that no fanatic has raised an outcry against this State recognition of vice—their property, which is often considerable, descending in the female line first, and then in the male, and going on failure of issue, to their temple, should they belong to one. No discredit attaches to their calling. They are " under the impression that they have taken to a most honourable profession, by following which they are honouring the gods, and are appreciated both by gods and men." And a man's intercourse with them, so far from being regarded as flagitious, is considered an act of faith and worship, and, according to some religious writers, effaces all sins.

Such are the dancing-girls of India; and such they have been for more than two thousand years, a distinctive and most significant feature of Hindu civilisation. Readers of Sir Edwin Arnold's *Light of Asia*, which represents, with much fidelity, the manners and customs of the country six centuries before the Christian era, will remember his description of these women :

> " And on another day there passed that road
> A band of tinselled girls, the nautch dancers
> Of Indra's temple in the town, with those
> Who made their music—one that beat a drum
> Set round with peacock feathers, one that blew
> The piping bansuli, and one that twitched
> A three-stringed sitar. Lightly tripped they down
> From ledge to ledge, and through the chequered paths,
> To some gay festival, the silver bells
> Chiming soft peals about the small brown feet,
> Armlets and wrist-rings tattling answer shrill;
> While he that bore the sitar thrummed and twanged
> His threads of brass, and she beside him sang :—
>
> > " *Fair goes the dancing when the sitar's tuned ;*
> > *Tune us the sitar neither low nor high,*
> > *And we will dance away the hearts of men.*
> > *The string o'erstretched breaks, and the music flies ;*
> > *The string o'er slack is dumb, and music dies ;*
> > *Tune us the sitar neither low nor high.*"

We may take exception, indeed, to the very Tennysonian ditty which Sir Edwin Arnold puts into the mouth of his nautch - girl. The song which fell on Gotama Buddha's ears was assuredly

not of that character. But the rest of the picture
is accurate enough, as far as it goes. To complete it, I may add that the physical charms of
these women are often considerable, especially in
Northern India. Their figures are almost always
naturally good. Their limbs are finely moulded,
their arms, and hands, and feet delicately shaped.
Their complexions are usually of an olive tint:
dark brunette, we may say. Their eyes are large
and languishing; and are made to look more
lustrous than they really are, by a line of pencilled
black drawn on the edges of the eyelids. Their
eyebrows are greatly cared for, and are of a regu-
larity seldom seen in European women. Their
faces are oval, their foreheads high and smooth.
Their pose and general attitude are graceful and
natural. Their dress is both modest and, in the
highest degree, picturesque, consisting of pyjamas,
bodice, skirt, and cloak or wrap. Their attire on
ceremonial occasions differs from their ordinary
raiment only in its profuse ornamentation with
gold, silver, and pearls, lace, or velvet. They are
fond of ornaments—some thirty different varieties
are reckoned of the jewellery they wear—and of
perfumes, and they decorate their heads with sweet-
smelling flowers. Their manners are refined and
gentle, and perfectly unembarrassed.

It is to these women that the Hindu gentleman
turns for the companionship which his home does
not supply. No doubt this situation is lamentably
common among ourselves. But—for that is the
point which I wish to emphasise—it is generally
condemned by European public opinion as irregular

and improper, whereas it appears to the natives of
India natural and normal. Sometimes the young
Hindu is fired by it into enthusiasm, which finds out-
let in verse—even English verse, if he happens to
be of the Anglicised type. I have before me a
monograph on the dancing-women of Bombay by
an accomplished gentleman, Mr K. Raghunathji,
which seems to have been much appreciated by a
judicious public, for it has gone through many
editions. It is prefaced by a poetical dedication to
a nautch-girl, of the name of Roshun, which I am
tempted to quote, both as an illustration of what I
am writing, and as a specimen of the Anglicised
Hindu muse.

"Smiling songstress, wouldst thou hear me
   Plead successful love to thee?
Wouldst thou, faithful, ever near me
   Grateful yield thy love to me?

Every other tie forsaken,
   Every other chain unknown,
In this bosom should there waken
   Not a feeling but thine own?

What are all fantastic notions,
   In a world unfeeling bred,
Deadening all the heart's emotions,
   By the dulness of the head?

What are learnings?—Vaunted pages.
   Wearying tales and dreams at best :
What the wisdom of the sages
   Who forbid us to be blest?

Worldly toil and vain repining,
   Pride, ambition, henceforth cease :
Form and folly hence resigning,
   All my future thought be peace!

Peace that dwells in love's embraces,
Joy that sports in Roshun's arms,
In those accents, in those graces
Dearer far than prouder charms!"

I must refer the reader desirous of further information regarding dancing-girls to Mr Raghunathji's work. I will merely observe that in this, as in some other matters, the Mohammedan invaders of India adopted the institutions which they found in the country. Mr Justice Amir Ali tells us, " By their intermixture with the Brahminical races, among whom prostitution was a legalised custom, their moral ideas have become lax; the conception of human dignity and spiritual purity has become degraded; the class of *hetairai* has become as popular among them as among their Pagan neighbours." Whether or no this is an exact account of the matter, certain it is that there exists a class of dancing-girls professing the faith of Islām. And if Mr Raghunathji is well-informed, an attempt was made to provide a Christian variety of them, but without success. " The Portuguese," he asserts, " when they took possession of Goa, laid their hands on some of these women, and forcibly converted them to Christianity, and not content with such conversion, they kept them as their mistresses. Their descendants have ever since been free from caste prejudices in respect to carnal intercourse with people of other than their own caste. They do not, however, observe Christian rites, but Hinduism in all its details."

CHAPTER XVIII

SELF-GOVERNMENT IN INDIA

SELF-GOVERNMENT is a phrase very grateful to English ears. And there is good reason why it should be so. Whether all that bears the name of self-government among us is really such, is an interesting and important question, the discussion of which would be out of place here. This blessing of self-government, which is our joy and our crown in the political order, ought, we are told, in certain quarters, to be conferred in all its fullness upon India. The so-called National Congresses which, from time to time, assemble there in their thousands, are fond of harping on this theme, and play some very surprising variations thereon. And a great deal has been done by British administrators of a certain school, in the way of concession of the desired boon. Some eight hundred odd municipalities have been created in India, the election of the municipal commissioners being vested in all who have property within the happy areas. Women, as well as men, enjoy the privilege. But, as a matter of fact, none of the fair sex, except dancing-girls,

238

appear to have availed themselves of it. These municipalities, in greater or less numbers, and in one form or another, have existed in India for several decades. More recently a further instalment of self-government has been conferred upon the country by the institution of Local and District Boards. Of the Local Boards, two-thirds are elected by what is supposed to be the people. And they, in their turn, elect a certain number of the members of the District Boards.

The results of these essays in self-government in India are such—to quote the words of a well-known French publicist, M. Filon—as to give rise to sad reflections. The two most considerable of the municipalities, those of Calcutta and Bombay, have been fruitful in tall talk and in jobbery, but so unfruitful in good work as to require drastic remodelling by recent legislation. And they are fair types of the municipalities generally. The Local and District Boards have been tolerable precisely in proportion to their inactivity. I add that their so-called representative character is the emptiest of pretences. The people whom they are supposed to represent know nothing and care nothing about them. The astute Hindus who get themselves elected—a large proportion of them are *vakils*, that is lawyers—represent their own personal interests, and their strong desire to gratify those interests by such means as their official position offers. And they represent nothing else.

Such is the result of the attempt to introduce representative government into India, a result foreseen by the wisest Englishmen when the movement

for endowing that country with them was in progress.
Thus, Sir Henry Maine said it would be matter of
surprise to him " that municipal institutions should
flourish at all " there : and that it would be "still
more wonderful that they should, in any case, be
based upon a system of popular representation."
Municipal institutions, he remarked, had had in
Europe "an almost unbroken career of two thousand
years," and in India it was proposed to "create"
them.   Surely, he added, "this might be asserted,
on the strength of English experience, that it was a
most difficult, if not insoluble, problem, to create a
constituency, or set of constituencies, in which one
class should not have the power to oppress the
others or to protect itself at their expense.   And
considering how native society is divided into castes,
and sects, and religions, and races, it would be surprising that there should be practicable, anywhere, a
system of municipal election at once fair and free."

As a matter of fact, the pretence at representative government which we find in India is neither
fair nor free.   It is a fraud and a folly.   You cannot
manufacture a fair and free system of representative
government merely by publishing a "list of registered
voters" and gazetting a man as "a returned representative."   Your registered voters do not vote
fairly or freely.   They vote as machines.   How
should it be otherwise when they have no notion of
communal advantage or municipal issues?   And the
interests which the returned representative represents—his own—are, as a rule, diametrically opposed
to the true interests of those whose suffrages he
procures by a well-devised mixture of flattery and

fiction. If he represents anything else, it is race feeling : the hatred of Islām is potent among the Hindu majorities of the larger towns. Complaints of unfair treatment by the municipalities are rife among the Mohammedan section of the community, and there can be no question that, in most instances, they are too well founded. Local self-government as exhibited by the municipalities and boards, district and local, in India, is a fraud ; an even grosser fraud than local self-government in New York as manipulated by Tammany Hall—which is saying a great deal. For the longeval traditions and inbred sentiments which more or less check jobbery, corruption, oppression among people of the Anglo-Saxon race, are not operative among the people of India.

' But local self-government in India is even more a folly than a fraud. It is the outcome of that insane sophism which, brought into fashion by the Jacobins of the last century, still dominates the minds of Radical politicians, that the world is peopled by a multitude of unrelated human units, all alike and all equivalent. It is of no use to point these faddists and fanatics to the most patent facts of human nature and of human life. The vast variety of the phenomena of civilised society is hidden from their eyes. And they endeavour, with no shadow of misgiving, to shape the government of Asiatic populations by à priori theories long fallen into discredit among scientific students of politics in Europe. |

| The population of India consists of a vast and most mixed multitude in various stages of civilisation, of whom not one man in ten and one woman

Q

in one hundred and sixty is able to read : a multitude belonging to at least fourteen distinct races, speaking some seventy-eight different languages, and divided from each other by customs and creeds, as much as by huge mountain ranges, vast forests, trackless deserts, and great rivers. As much as?—Nay, more than. But the word "divided" is far too weak. Bitterly hostile, we should rather say. There can be no question at all—to give merely one instance — that the deep-seated hatred between Hindus and Mohammedans, a hatred which the vernacular newspapers are ever fomenting, would deluge the cities of India with blood, but for the Pax Britannica, and the bayonets which maintain it. There are no political ties among the inhabitants of that country. There is no national feeling. They care, as a rule, for nothing outside their own family or caste. "India for the Indians!" What Indians? Pathans or Tamulians? Sikhs or Burmese? Rājputs or Mahrattas? Bengalis or Jāts? To treat the population of India as though they were a homogeneous people—like the Chinese—is an absurdity which it might seem difficult to surpass. Yet it is surpassed when the "Congresses," which from time to time assemble to discuss Indian affairs, pretend to be representative of races existing in such great variety and in such different psychological and moral conditions.

The pretence is utterly hollow. These Congresses are the most impudent of impostures. The sixty millions of Mohammedans stand contemptuously aloof from them. The great Hindu nobles take no part in them. The tillers of the

soil do not so much as know of their existence.⟨
Even those vernacular newspapers which trade on
disaffection to the British Rāj, cannot refrain from
flouts and gibes at them. Thus the *Bangobāsi*, which
I understand to be the most influential and the
most widely circulated of Bengali journals, describes
them as "annual merry-makings, extending over
three days : periodical merry-makings of English
educated baboos, bent on enjoying a holiday. For
three days," continues this candid friend, "they
amuse themselves, emit cut-and-dried speeches,
form foolish resolutions and gather materials for a
year's equally foolish writing, and then depart
home, and then—what then? All this ranting, and
blustering, and speech-making, all this waste of money
ends, as it must, like a dream—in nothingness"!

⟨ The truth is, that what these Congresses do really
represent is the stucco civilisation of the baboo :
the conceit and cupidity of the Anglicised Hindu,
of whom perhaps the worst variety is the " Europe-
returned." The "educated" native, as the phrase
goes, is in no sense a representative of the great
mass of the inhabitants of India, and has no
sort of influence with them. The vast bulk of
the population, the cultivators of the land, know
and care nothing about him. The hardy, warlike races who furnish our best soldiers, utterly
despise him. The writer in the Hindu newspapers, the orator at Indian Congresses, has,
really, no more claim to speak for the natives of
India than the three tailors of Tooley Street
had to speak for the people of England. He
is not, ordinarily, a product of our rule of

whom we should be proud. Hindu gentlemen
there are—it has been my privilege to count
such among my personal friends — who have
thoroughly assimilated the intellectual culture of
the Western world, without losing their hereditary manners and traditions.   But the average
young Hindu, turned out by our Anglo-Indian
colleges, is a very different manner of man.   He
is the product of an elaborate system of cramming, and is stuffed—for examination purposes—
with knowledge which he cannot digest.   He
repeats, glibly enough, the words of the great
and wise of our race, as they have come before
him in his text-books.   But to repeat their words is
one thing : to think their thoughts is quite another.
M. Filon has remarked, with equal quaintness
and truth, " The mass of facts, sentiments, and
ideas, which constitute Western civilisation, forms
for him a second soul, altogether external, which
is superimposed on his first soul, and conceals
and envelopes it.   But no fusion is possible."
The Indian Universities send forth every year
some five thousand graduates, of the vast
majority of whom this is the true account.
Their aim, in most cases, is to get Government
employment.   Naturally, the greater number fail
in this aim, as the supply of places in the public
service falls very far short of the demand.   On
their inevitable disappointment, they, as often as
not, turn demagogues, and become writers in those
vernacular newspapers, the existence of which is
much vaunted, in certain quarters, as a triumph
of Western civilisation in India. | As a matter

of fact, these prints appear to be an unmixed evil. At all events, after careful and prolonged inquiry, I have never been able to ascertain that they do any good whatever. The chief object of those who write in them appears to be to minister to the rancorous feeling already existing between Hindus and Mohammedans, and to preach disaffection to the British Rāj. If the ability and influence of this spuriously educated proletariat were in proportion to their cupidity and conceit, they would doubtless form a grave political danger. Anyhow, they have a just cause of complaint against us. For are not we the authors of their aspirations and disappointment?

These are the Indians who complain of their practical exclusion from the Covenanted Civil Service, and who demand, as a remedy for their grievance, the simultaneous holding in India of the examinations by which admission to it is gained. And, as we all know, their complaint is echoed by a certain number of Radical doctrinaires in England, and finds utterance from time to time in the House of Commons. We are told—I summarise the arguments from a debate on the subject—that the Proclamation of 1858 promised admission into the public service to all qualified persons, irrespective of race and creed: that the necessity under which candidates for the Covenanted Service at present lie of presenting themselves for examination in London, practically invalidates this promise, so far as the vast majority of the natives of India are concerned: that the natives are naturally studious, and very zealous in the pursuit of an object, and intellectually not at all inferior to the English: that they are as good men of business as the English (and even better), and more fitted to fill public offices in the country, because of their intimate acquaintance with the manners and customs of their fellow-countrymen: that to promote them to positions of authority and trust is the only way of raising their moral tone: and that under the present system the advantages are reaped by one class, while the work is done by another. The answer to this is that for the great administrative offices in India other qualities are absolutely necessary besides industry and zeal in the pursuit of an object, intellectual suppleness, business capacity, and knowledge of Indian manners and customs. The quality wanted above all is virility, physical and mental; and that is a quality lacking to many quick-witted but utterly effeminate Indians who would gain admittance to the Civil Service if the proposed change were made. You cannot, by any amount of cramming, recreate character, and impart to the crammed the veracity, the self-sacrifice, the self-respect, which Englishmen instinctively associate with the manly idea. "I am afraid," the late Lord Iddesleigh very sensibly said, "that the effect of the change proposed would be to bring in a large number of individuals of intellectual ability who would not have the strength required for administration. When we talk of ruling for the benefit of the people of India, we must think not only of those likely to carry off these appointments, but of the 150,000,000, of whom only a small proportion belong to the intellectual class; we must consider whether we should provide the best machinery for Government by choosing successful competitors. They would be, to a great extent, Bengalese and others of the less vigorous but more advanced and educated races; and although they would carry off prizes of a purely intellectual character, they would probably fail most conspicuously in positions of difficulty. They would be employed without the advantages of Englishmen, without the prestige of the English race, and without the energy of the English character, and we could not rely upon their being treated with that esteem which in the East is attached to persons distinguished by birth and family connection. Under these circumstances we ought to be cautious how we throw open the door by competitive examinations." We certainly ought. It cannot be said that, even as at present worked, the system of selecting the administrators of the Indian Empire by competitive examination, is an unmixed success. It is very far indeed from being that. How should it be? You may test by examination papers a young man's power of cram, and cleverness in veiling superficiality and inaccuracy. You may test by a *viva voce* examination, properly conducted,* his real knowledge and mental qualities.

* I speak from some experience as an examiner: and I should like to instance as perfect models of the *viva voce* examiner's art—for it is an art—the specimens given by Cardinal Newman in his paper on *Elementary Studies*, which will be found in his volume entitled *The Idea of a University*, p. 331. (Third Ed.)

But you cannot test, by any application of questions and answers, his possession of the virile qualities needed in a ruler of men. The present system of bestowing appointments in the Covenanted Civil Service of India is, on the face of it, ill adapted to its proper end, and the wonder is that it has not worked more badly in practice. But the change in it desired by Indian agitators and English doctrinaires would reduce it to an absurdity—which, perhaps, is the weightiest argument in favour of that change.

Are we then, it may be asked, to make no provision for admitting the natives of India to a larger share in the administration of the country? As a matter of fact, at the present time 2500 natives of India are employed in important judicial and administrative posts as against 750 Europeans. Still, it must be confessed, that under the British Rāj, the native leaders of Indian society have largely been effaced. I believe Lord Lytton was well advised when he wrote: " The fundamental political mistake of able and experienced Indian officials is a belief that we can hold India securely by what they call good government ; that is to say, by improving the condition of the ryot, strictly administering justice, spending immense sums on irrigation works, etc. Politically speaking, the Indian peasantry is an inert mass. If it ever moves at all, it will move in obedience, not to its British benefactors, but to its native chiefs and princes, however tyrannical they may be. . . . The Indian chiefs and princes are not a mere *noblesse.* They are a powerful aristocracy. To secure completely and efficiently utilise the Indian aristocracy is, I am convinced, the most important problem now before us." It appears to me that we should sedulously seek for those among them most fitted socially, morally, and intellectually to rule, and associate them with Englishmen, freely and liberally, even in the highest offices. Such are the Mahommedans of Northern India — one of the noblest races in the country. Such are the chivalrous and truth-loving Rājputs : men far better qualified by innate character to exercise authority than the natives who become proficient in the art of cram, and glibly answer examination papers. I mention these two classes merely as striking examples of virile races. But I am far from asserting that manliness is their special monopoly among the people of India. It is to be found—I myself have found it—among all classes and all creeds in that country. And the door for admitting into the higher branches of the service of Government those possessing it, should be selection, examination being employed, when employed at all, merely as a test of their endowment with the necessary intellectual qualifications. As a matter of fact, the Indian Governments possess this power of selection, under an Act of Parliament passed in 1870, to provide "additional facilities for the employment of natives of proved merit and ability in the Civil Service of Her Majesty in India." Its object was to enable them to bestow upon natives—whether public servants or not—of exceptional merit, important offices usually held by members of the Covenanted Civil Service. For

more than twenty years it remained a dead letter.
Then Regulations were drawn up, as required by
its provisions, for carrying it into effect, and, to
some extent, they have been put in practice.

This is, at all events, a step in the right
direction. It may be well here to quote the
words written so long ago as 1827 by Sir
Thomas Munro, one of the greatest and most
successful of Indian administrators : "We ought,"
Munro wrote, "to look forward to a time when
natives may be employed in almost every office,
however high, and we ought to prepare them
gradually for such a change by entrusting them
with higher duties from time to time, in proportion
as experience may prove their being qualified to
discharge them. The employment," he went on to
say, "of natives in high offices will be as much for
our own advantage as theirs : it will tend both to
the economy and efficiency of the administration of
public affairs. Every time that a native is raised
to a higher office than had before been filled by any
of his countrymen, a new impulse will be given to
the whole establishment : the hope of attaining the
higher office will excite emulation among those who
hold the inferior ones, and improve the whole. But
this improvement will take place in a much greater
degree when the new office is one of a high and
independent nature, like that of a judge. The
person who is appointed to it will be conscious that
he enjoys some share in the administration of the
affairs of his country ; he will feel that his own rank
and character have been elevated by his having
been selected for the high office which he holds ;

and his feelings will pervade every class of the department to which he belongs." And elsewhere we find Munro writing : " Whenever the public business falls into arrears, it is said to be owing to the want of a sufficient number of Europeans : and more European agency is recommended as a cure for every evil. Such agency . . . ought rather to be abridged than enlarged, because it is, in many cases, much less efficient than that of the natives. *For the discharge of all subordinate duties, but especially in the judicial line, the natives are infinitely better qualified than Europeans.* I have never seen any European whom I thought competent, from his knowledge of the language and the people, to ascertain the value of the evidence given before him. . . . But it is said that the natives are too corrupt to be trusted. This is an old objection, and one which is generally applicable, in similar circumstances, to the natives of every country. . . . While we persist in withholding liberal salaries from the natives, we shall have the services of the worst part of them : by making the services adequate to the trust, we shall secure the services of the best. *Natives should be employed in every situation where they are better calculated than the Europeans to discharge the duty required.* In all original suits, they are much fitter to investigate the merits than Europeans." That appears to be the true principle : " Natives should be employed in every situation where they are better calculated than the Europeans to discharge the duty required." And, unquestionably, they are singularly well qualified, in a great many instances, for judicial office. The law is a study extremely congenial to them. And they often attain great distinction in it. Some of the very best Judges in our Indian High Courts have been natives. And I should like to gratify a personal feeling by quoting the well-merited tribute paid to one such by an eminent English lawyer who held the high office of Chief Justice of Madras.

"We are assembled here to express our very great regret at the loss we have sustained by the death of Sir T. Muttuswami Ayar. His death is undoubtedly a loss to the whole country and the crown. A profound Hindu jurist, a man with very excellent knowledge of English law, with very great strength of mind, possessing that most useful quality in a Judge, common sense, he was undoubtedly a great Judge. Very unassuming in manner, he had great strength of mind and independence of character. His judgments were carefully considered, and the decisions he ultimately arrived at were, in a great majority of instances, upheld in the final Court of Appeal. His advice was often asked for by the other Judges of this court, and—I can speak from experience—was always freely given and was most valuable. He was a man who did honour to the great profession of the law, an upright Judge who administered justice without distinction of race or creed ; a well-read scholar, and a gentleman in the best and truest acceptation of the word. The High Court by his death has sustained a heavy loss, a loss which, undoubtedly, it can ill bear."

CHAPTER XIX

CONCERNING two of the fine arts, as they exist in India, a very cursory mention will suffice. Music, of course, flourishes there, as in every nation under heaven, being, I suppose, a universal manifestation of what Schiller calls the *Spieltrieb* in man. But it differs so fundamentally from what we are accustomed to, as to sound simply barbaric to European ears. It produces, Sir William Hunter quaintly says, "the effect of a Scotch ballad, in a minor key, sung intentionally a little out of tune." From the very earliest times it was a favourite pursuit of the Hindus, as the numerous references to it in Vedic literature sufficiently show. And it appears to have been reduced to a methodical system three or four centuries before the Christian era. Weber, in his work on *Indian Literature,* mentions the names of several ancient writers who composed treatises upon it. But only fragments of them remain. He adds, "There are also various modern Indian works on music, but the whole subject has been little investigated." "The art," Sir William Hunter

observes, "still awaits investigation by some
eminent Western Professor ; and the contempt with
which Europeans in India regard it, merely proves
their ignorance of the system on which Hindu
music is built up."

Painting, in India, never passed beyond a rudi-
mentary state. The laws of perspective were
unknown to its artists. They succeeded best
in portraits, where perspective is not required.
They also attained to much excellence in illumina-
tion.

But the art in which the Hindus achieve their
greatest triumphs is their architecture, the varieties
of which have been classified by that great authority
Mr Ferguson, according to the affinities of their
progressive development, from the ancient Buddhist,
"a wooden style painfully struggling into lithic
form" through all its historical and geographical
modifications, to the truly lithic forms known as the
Jaina, the Dravidian, the Chalukyan, and the Indo-
Aryan. The Buddhist sculptures unquestionably
show traces of Greek influences, and in the Kashmīr temples, built between the sixth and twelfth
centuries of our era, that influence is even more
distinctly discernible. The rock-cut assembly halls
of the Buddhists, which are found chiefly in Western
India, have as their most striking feature "the
peaked arch over the façades, and door and window
fronts, which is identical in character with the Ogee
pointed arch of the façade of the Church of St
Mark at Venice." Next in date to the Buddhist
style is the Jaina, specially characterised by the
horizontal archway and the bracket form of capital.

"The northern Jaina style is seen principally in beautiful Jaina cities of temples at Palatina and Girnar, in Gujerat, and at Mount Abū, the chief peak of the Aravalli range, where the sacred Nucki Talao ('pearl lake') is one of the loveliest gems of architecture in all India."

"Of the three varieties of Brahminical architecture," writes Sir George Birdwood, in his *Industrial Arts of India*, "the Dravidian style prevails in the Dakhan, south of the Kistna, the Chalukyan between the Kistna and Mahanuddi, and the Indo-Aryan in Hindustān. The Dravidian temple is distinguished by its rectangular ground-plan and storeyed pyramidal tower; the Chalukyan by its star-like ground-plan, and pyramidal tower; and the Indo-Aryan by its square ground-plan, and curvilinear *sikra* or tower. In the Dravidian style, the temple almost invariably includes, besides the *vimāna* or towered shrine, the *mantapa* or porch leading to the shrine : the *choultri* or pillared hall ; numerous other buildings ; elegant *stambhas* or pillars, bearing the images or flags of the gods, or numberless lamps all connected with the temple worship and service ; tanks and gardens, and avenues of palms and sacred trees ; and all these various portions are surrounded by the temple enclosure, with its grand *gopuras* or gateways. The architectural effect therefore of such temples as those of Tanjore, Tiruvalur, Seringham, Chillambaram, Rameswaram, Madura, Tinnevelly, Conjeveram, Vellore, Perur, and Vijayanagar, is most imposing. There is nothing in Europe that can be compared with their grandeur and solemnity, and for parallels to them we must go back to ancient Egypt and Assyria, and the temple at Jerusalem. The rock-cut kylās at Ellora was executed by southern Dravidians, either the Cheras or Cholas, who had sway there during the eclipse of the Chalukyas between A.D. 750 and 950.

"The noblest example of the Chalukyas style is the great temple of Halabid, the old capital of the Rājput Bellalas of Mysore. Unfortunately, it was never finished, having been stopped by the Mahommedan conquest A.D. 1310. It is a double temple. The building is raised on a terrace from five feet to six feet in height. On this stands a frieze of elephants, 2000 in number, following all the sinuosities of the star-like ground-plan. Above it is a frieze of lions, then a band of scrollwork of infinite beauty and variety of design, over which is a frieze of horsemen ; and then comes another scroll, over which is a frieze representing the conquest of Sanka by Rāma. Then succeed two friezes, one above the other, of celestial beasts and celestial birds ; and above these a cornice of scroll-work, bearing a rail, divided into panels, each containing two figures ; over which are windows of pierced slabs of stone, divided at regular intervals, marked by the abutments of the temple by groups five feet six inches in height, of the gods and heavenly Apsaras of the Hindu pantheon. Above all would have risen, if the temple had been finished, the pyramidal towers of the structure. The Chalukyan style is seen also in the temple of Kait Iswara at Halabīd, and the temples of Somnathpur and Baillur, both in Mysore ; and in those of Buchropully, not far from Hyderabad, and of Hammoncondah or Warangal, also in the Nizam's dominion. . . ."

" There are many splendid structural temples of the so-called Indo-Aryan style in Central or Northern India, at Gwalior, Khajuraho, Udaipur, Benares, and Bindraband ; and one of a remarkable aberrant form at Kandinagar near Dinaj-pur. The peculiar curved arch seen in pavilions connected with temples along the banks of the Ganges, and in the archi-tecture generally of Northern India, is derived from the curvi-linear roof which the Bengalis have learned to give their houses, by bending the bamboos used as a support for the thatch, or tiles. At the South Kensington museum the same curved form is seen in the roof of a shrine of Byzantine work."

I cannot pass away from the subject of these magnificent fanes without an expression of regret at the neglect of them too often observable. Until quite lately the ruling power concerned itself with their preservation. The Hindu Rājahs exercised direct and efficient control over them. And Moham-medan sovereigns, with few exceptions, made some provision against their deterioration and decay. This policy was continued in the early years of the British Rāj; and the Collectors of the several districts were looked upon as churchwardens — they sometimes so described themselves—of the pagodas within their jurisdiction. That gave much umbrage — not unnaturally — to many excellent people, particularly to those specially interested in Christian proselytism. And, in great measure owing to their representations, an Act was passed in 1863 by which the Government divested itself of all connection with Hindu religious institutions, the control and supervision of which was vested in managers or committees, to be appointed in the manner prescribed in the Act. In numerous instances these managers have proved themselves mismanagers, many cases of neglect, and some of peculation, having been brought home to them. It is open under the Act to any temple-worshipper to institute a suit in the Civil Court for the remedy of such malpractices. But the managers are often wealthy, and litigation is costly. As a matter of fact, this provision of the Act has been little resorted to ; and it is felt by many excellent Hindus that some simpler and more expeditious means should be provided for the proper conservation of their grand religious edifices. It cannot be said that the British rulers of India have hitherto shown much solicitude for the architectural monuments of the country. Certainly—unlike the Mohammedan sovereigns whose splendid mosques and tombs rival in beauty the Hindu pagodas—they have erected no public buildings, or hardly any, till quite lately,

which are not of appalling ugliness. The Department of Public Works has aimed at cheap utility—
not always with much success—in its edifices, and
has entirely eschewed æsthetic considerations. Only
the other day I noticed in one of the public prints a
complaint that its myrmidons had painted over
the delicate white chunam of the walls of an Indian
palace with some foul distemper!

But to return to the Hindus and their art. It
may be truly said that the artistic spirit displayed
in the architecture of their temples penetrates the
life of the people. From the earliest times they
have been famous, throughout the world, for their
skill in the production of delicate woven fabrics, in
the blending of colours, in the working of metals
and precious stones. Everything that comes from
the hands of their artisans, down to the cheapest
toy or earthen vessel, is a work of art. On this
subject let us hear Sir George Birdwood, who, I
suppose, is the greatest living authority concerning it.

"Every house in India is likewise a nursery of the
beautiful. In the meanest village hut, the mother of the
family will be found with her daughters engaged in spinning
or weaving; and in the proudest native houses of the great
polytechnical cities, the mistress, with her maid-servants, may
be seen at all hours of the day embroidering cloth in coloured
silks, and silver and gold thread, reminding the visitor of
similar household scenes in ancient Rome before slaves came,
during the pampered period of the Cæsars, to be employed in
such work. There is thus a universally diffused popular
appreciation of technical skill and taste in workmanship,
which must necessarily have had its effect in promoting the
unrivalled excellence of the historical art handicrafts of
India. . . . The people possess the tradition of a system of

decoration founded on perfect principles which they have
learnt, through centuries of practice, to apply with unerring
truth. . . . Apart from the natural beauty of the dyes used,
and the knowledge, taste, and skill of the natives of India in
the harmonious arrangement of colours, the charm of their
textile fabrics lies in the simplicity and treatment of the
decorative details. The knob and flower pattern appears
universally, but infinitely modified, never being seen twice
under the same form ; and the *seventi* and lotus, which have
been reduced through extreme conventionalisation to one
pattern. We have beside the shoe flower, and parrots, and
peacocks, and lions, and tigers, the men on horseback, or on
foot, hunting or fighting. These objects are always represented quite flat as in mosaic work, or in *draps entaillez*, and
generally symmetrically and in alternation. The symmetrical
representation of natural objects in ornamentation, and their
alternation seems through long habit to have become intuitive
in the natives of the East. If you get them to copy a plant,
they will peg it down flat on the ground, laying its leaves, and
buds, and flowers out symmetrically on either side of the
central stem, and then only will they begin to copy it. If the
leaves and flowers of the plant are not naturally opposite but
alternate, they will add others to make it symmetrical, or at
least will make it appear so in the drawing. The intuitive
feeling for alternation is seen in their gardens and heard in
their music, and is as satisfactory in their music as in their
decoration, when heard amid the associations which naturally
call it forth. When the same form is used all over a fabric
the interchange of light and shade, and the effect of alternation, are at once obtained by working the ornament alternately
in two tints of the same colour. Each object, or division of an
object, is painted in its own proper colour, but without shades
of the colour, or light and shade of any kind, so that the
ornamentation looks perfectly flat, and laid like mosaic, on
the ground. It is in this way that the natural surface of any
object decorated is maintained in its integrity. This, added to
the perfect harmony and distribution of the colouring, is the
specific charm of Indian and Oriental decoration generally.
Nothing can be more ignorant or ridiculous than the English
and French methods of representing huge nosegays, or bunches

of fern leaves tied together by flowing pink ribbons, in light and shade, on carpets, with the effect of full relief. One knows not where to walk among them. Continually also are to be seen perfectly shaped vases spoiled by the appearance of flowers in full relief stuck round them, or of birds flying out of them. Such egregious mistakes are never made by the Indian decorative artist. Each ornament, particularly in textile fabrics, is generally traced round also with a line, in colour which harmonises it with the ground on which it is laid. In embroideries with variegated silks, for instance, on cloth, or satin, or velvet, a gold or silver thread is run round the outline of the pattern, defining it, and giving a uniform tone to the whole texture. Gold is generally laid on purple, or in the lighter kincobs, on pink or red. An ornament on a gold ground is generally worked round with a dark thread to soften the glister of the gold. In carpets, however gay in colour, a low tone is secured by a general black outline of the details. All violent contrasts are avoided. The richest colours are used, but are so arranged as to produce the effect of a neutral bloom, which tones down every detail almost to the softness and transparency of atmosphere. The gold-braided snuff-coloured cashmere shawl in the collection of the Prince of Wales presents this ethereal appearance. Light materials are lightly coloured, and ornamented, heavier, more richly, and, in the case of apparel, both the colouring and the ornaments are adapted to the effect which the fabric will produce when worn and in motion. It is only through generations of patient practice that men attain to the mystery of such subtleties. It is difficult to analyse the secret of the harmonious bloom of Indian texture, even with the aid of Chevreul's prismatic scale. When large ornaments are used, they are filled up with the most exquisite details, as in the cone patterns in cashmere shawls. The vice of Indian decoration is its tendency to run riot, as in Indian arms ; but Indian textile fabrics, at least, are singularly free from it, and particularly the carpets."

Next, I will put before my readers Sir George Birdwood's striking account of the way in which the Kuman or potters work,—rude but true artists, of whom there are some three and a half millions throughout India :—

"The Indian potter's wheel is of the simplest and rudest kind. It is a horizontal fly-wheel, two or three feet in diameter, loaded heavily with clay around the rim, and put in motion by the hand : and once set spinning, it revolves for five or seven minutes with a perfectly steady and true motion. The clay to be moulded is heaped on the centre of the wheel, and the potter squats down on the ground before it. A few vigorous turns, and away spins the wheel, round and round, and still and silent as a 'sleeping' top, while at once the shapeless heap of clay begins to grow under the potter's hand into all sorts of faultless forms of archaic fictile art, which are carried off to be dried and baked as fast as they are thrown from the wheel. Any polishing is done by rubbing the baked jars and pots with a pebble. There is an immense demand for these water jars, cooking pots, and earthen frying pans and dishes. The Hindus have a religious prejudice against using an earthen vessel twice, and generally it is broken after the first pollution, and hence the demand for common earthenware in all Hindu families. There is an immense demand also for painted clay idols, which are also thrown away after being worshipped ; and thus the potter, in virtue of his calling, is an hereditary officer in every Indian village. In the Dekhan, the potter's field is just outside the village. Near the wheel is a heap of clay, and before it rise two or three stacks of pots and pans, while the verandah of his hut is filled with the smaller wares and painted images of the gods, and epic heroes of the Rāmāyana and Mahabhārata. He has to supply the entire village community with pitchers and cooking pans, and jars for storing grain and spices and salt, and to furnish travellers with any of these vessels they may require. Also, when the new corn begins to sprout, he has to take a water-jar to each field for the use of those engaged in watching the crop. But he is allowed to make bricks and tiles also, and for these he is paid, exclusively of his fees, which amount to between £4 and £5 a year.

Altogether he earns between £10 and £12 a year, and is passing rich with it. He enjoys beside, the dignity of certain ceremonial and honorific offices. He bangs the big drum, and chants the hymns in honour of Jami, an incarnation of the great goddess Bhavani, at marriages ; and, at the dowra or village harvest home festivals, he prepares the barbat or mutton stew. He is, in truth, one of the most useful and respected members of the community, and in the happy organisation of Hindu village life there is no man happier than the hereditary potter, or Kumbar.

" We cannot overlook this serenity and dignity of his life, if we would rightly understand the Indian handicraftsman's work. He knows nothing of the desperate struggle for existence which oppresses the life and crushes the very soul out of the English working man. He has his assured place, inherited from father to son for a hundred generations, in the national church and state organisation, while nature provides everything to his hand, but the little food and less clothing he needs, and the simple tools of the trade. The English working man must provide for house rent, coals, furniture, warm clothing, animal food, and spirits, and for the education of his children, before he can give a mind free from family anxieties to his work. But the sun is the Indian workman's co-operative landlord, coal merchant, upholsterer, tailor, publican, and butcher ; the head partner, from whom he gets almost everything he wants, and free of all cost but his labour contribution towards the village trade's union corporation, of which he is an indispensable and essential member. This at once relieves him from an incalculable dead weight of cares, and enables him to give to his work, which is also a religious function, that contentment of mind and leisure, and pride and pleasure in it for its own sake, which are essential to all artistic excellence.

" The cause of all his comfort, of his hereditary skill, and of the religious constitution under which his marvellous craftsmanship has been perfected, is the system of landed tenure which has prevailed in India, and stereotyped the social condition and civilisation of the country from the time of the Code of Manu."

Sir George Birdwood's account of the trade guilds of India should also be given :—

"The trade guilds of the great polytechnical cities of India are not, however, always exactly coincident with the sectarian or ethnical caste of a particular class of artizans. Sometimes the same trade is pursued by men of different castes, and its guild generally includes every member of the trade it represents without strict reference to caste. The government of the guilds or unions is analogous to that of the village communities and castes, that is, by hereditary officers. Each separate guild is managed by a court of aldermen or *mahajans* (literally " great gentlemen "). Nominally it is composed of all the freemen of the caste, but a special position is allowed to the *seths*, lords, or chiefs of the guild, who are ordinarily two in number, and hold their position by hereditary right. The only other office-bearer is a salaried clerk or *gumasta*.

"Membership in the guild is also hereditary, but newcomers may be admitted into it on the payment of an entrance fee, which in Ahmedabad amounts to £2 for paper-makers and £50 for tinsmiths. No unqualified person can remain in or enter a guild. It is not the practice to execute indentures of apprenticeship, but every boy born in a working caste of necessity learns his father's handicraft, and when he has mastered it, at once takes his place as an hereditary freeman of his caste or trade guild, his father, or, if he be an orphan, the young man himself, giving a dinner to the guild on the occasion. In large cities the guilds command great influence. The *Nagar-Seth*, or City lord, of Ahmedabad, is the titular head of all the guilds, and the highest personage in the city, and is treated as its representative by the Government. In ordinary times he does not interfere in the internal affairs of the guilds, their management being left to the chief alderman of each separate guild, called the *Chautana Seth*, or 'lord of the market.'

"Under British rule, which secures the freest exercise of individual energy and initiative, the authority of the trade guilds in India has necessarily been relaxed, to the marked detriment of those handicrafts, the perfection of which depends

on hereditary processes and skill. The overwhelming importa-
tions of British manufactures also is even more detrimental to
their prosperity and influence, for it has in many places brought
wholesale ruin on the hereditary native craftsmen, and forced
them into agriculture and even domestic service. But the
guilds, by the stubborn resistance, further stimulated by caste
prejudice, which they oppose to all innovations, still continue,
in this forlorn way, to serve a beneficial end, in maintaining
for probably another generation, the traditional excellence of
the sumptuary arts of India, against the fierce and merciless
competition of the English manufacturers. The guilds are
condemned by many for fixing the hours of labour and the
amount of work to be done in them by strict by-laws, the
slightest infringement of which is punished by severe fines,
which are the chief source of their income. But the object of
these rules is to give the weak and unfortunate the same
chance in life as others more favoured by nature. These rules
naturally follow from the theocratic conceptions which have
governed the whole organisation of social life in India, and it is
incontrovertible that the unrestricted development of the
competitive impulse in European life, particularly in the
pursuit of personal gain, is absolutely antagonistic to the
growth of the sentiment of humanity and of real religious
convictions among men."

I will end my citations from Sir George
Birdwood's most interesting volume with a
warning which has received only too ample justification since it was written some twenty years
ago.

"What is chiefly to be dreaded is the general introduction
of machinery into India. We are just beginning in Europe to
understand what things may be done by machinery, and
what must be done by hand-work, if art is of the slightest
consideration in the matter. But if, owing to the operation
of certain economic causes, machinery were to be gradually
introduced into India for the manufacture of its great traditional handicrafts, there would ensue an industrial revolution

which, if not directed by an intelligent and instructed public opinion and the general prevalence of refined taste, would inevitably throw the traditional arts of the country into the same confusion of principles, and of their practical application to the objects of daily necessity, which has for three generations been the destruction of decorative art and of middle-class taste in England and North-Western Europe, and the United States of America.

"The social and moral evils of the introduction of machinery into India are likely to be still greater. At present the industries of India are carried on all over the country, although hand-weaving is everywhere languishing in the unequal competition with Manchester and the Presidency mills. But in every Indian village all the traditional handicrafts are still to be found at work.

"Outside the entrance of the single village street, on an exposed rise of ground, the hereditary potter sits by his wheel moulding the swift revolving clay by the natural curves of his hands. At the back of the houses, which form the low irregular street, there are two or three looms at work in blue, and scarlet, and gold, the frames hanging between the acacia trees, the yellow flowers of which drop fast on the webs as they are being woven. In the street, the brass and coppersmiths are hammering away at their pots and pans, and further down, in the verandah of the rich man's house, is the jeweller working rupees and gold mohrs into fair jewellery, gold and silver earrings, and round tires like the moon, bracelets, and tablets, and nose-rings, and tinkling ornaments for the feet, taking his designs from the fruits and flowers around him, or from the traditional forms represented in the paintings and carvings of the great temple, which rises over the groves of mangoes and palms at the end of the street above the lotus-covered village tank. At half-past three or four in the afternoon the whole street is lighted up by the moving robes of the women going down to draw water from the tank, each with two or three water jars on her head ; and so, while they are going and returning in single file, the scene glows like Titian's canvas, and moves like the stately procession of the Panathenaic frieze. Later, the men drive in the mild grey kine from the moaning plain, the looms are folded up, the coppersmiths are silent, the elders gather in the gate, the lights begin to glimmer in the fast-falling darkness, the feasting and the music are heard on every side, and late into the night the songs are sung from the Ramayānā or Māhabhārata.   The next morning with sunrise, after the simple ablutions and adorations performed in the open air before the houses, the same day begins again.   This is the daily life going on all over Western India in the village communities of the Dekhan, among a people happy in their simple manners and frugal way of life, and in the culture derived from the grand epics of a religion in which they live and move, and have their daily being, and in which the highest expression of their literature, art, and civilisation has been stereotyped for 3000 years.

" But of late years these handicraftsmen, for the sake of whose works the whole world has been ceaselessly pouring its bullion for 3000 years into India, and who, for all the marvellous tissue and embroidery they have wrought, have polluted no rivers, deformed no pleasing prospects, nor poisoned any air ; whose skill and individuality the training of countless generations has developed to the highest perfection, these hereditary handi-craftsmen are being everywhere gathered from their democratic village communities in hundreds and thousands into the colossal mills of Bombay, to drudge in gangs for tempting wages, at manufacturing piece goods, in competition with Manchester, in the production of which they are no more intellectually and morally concerned than the grinder of a barrel organ in the tunes turned out from it.

"I do not mean to depreciate the proper functions of machines in modern civilisation, but machinery should be the servant and never the master of men.   It cannot minister to the beauty and pleasure of life, it can only be the slave of life's drudgery ; and it should be kept rigorously in its place, in India as well as England.   When in England machinery is, by the force of cultivated taste and opinion, no longer allowed to intrude into the domain of art manufactures, which belongs exclusively to the trained mind and hand of individual workmen, wealth will become more equally diffused throughout society, and the working classes, through the elevating influence of their daily work, and the growing respect for their talent, and skill, and culture, will rise at once in social, civil, and political position, raising the whole country to the highest classes, with them ; and Europe will learn to taste of some of that content and happiness in life which is to be still found in the Pagan East, as it was once found in Pagan Greece and Rome."

CHAPTER XX

WE are accustomed to think of the Government of India as essentially conservative. It is a bureaucracy. And dislike of change is a leading characteristic of bureaucracies. But in truth the policy of the Government of India is, in some respects, most unstable and uncertain. It has been notably so as to the Frontier Question. Thus, Lord Auckland, so long ago as 1837-38, began by a policy of conquest towards Afghānistān. Probably he had not reflected upon its difficulties. Certainly he was ill-informed as to the nature and condition of the country. He ended by a policy of alliance, which can hardly be said to have been crowned with success. The shame of the disaster and retreat of 1842 was wiped out, doubtless, by the expedition of Generals Pollock and Nott in the autumn of that year. It is not unlikely that the conviction of our strength brought home to the Afghan by the triumph of their arms restrained Dost Mohammed Ali from attacking us during the period of the Indian Mutiny. And subsequently to that event the buffer state theory, and the "masterly inaction" doctrine prevailed. When Lord Lytton held the Viceroyalty, this policy fell into discredit. The two points deemed essential by that statesman—and the wisest of Indian administrators have agreed with him—were that British agents should reside at Herat, or elsewhere on the Northern Frontier of Afghānistān, and that Kandahār should be retained in British hands. Both have been abandoned. The victorious campaign of Lord Roberts, after the murder of Cavagnari, practically placed the country at the disposal of the Government of India. "Afghanistan might have been declared a British possession, and might, without disproportionate effort, have been transformed into such a bulwark for India, as the Punjāb has been since the second Sikh war." But a change of Government at home raised politicians to power who had a morbid dread of increasing the Empire, and a love for sentimental phraseology. The splendid opportunity was lost; and the old policy of alliance was resorted to once more. The Government of India has, however, thought itself bound to supplement that policy by the establishment and multiplication of posts in the tribal territories adjoining the Kabul kingdom. "Gilgit and Hunza have been annexed; Chitral has received a British garrison; relations have been opened with Kaffirstan." And "the possession of the passes through the Sulimans, between Quetta and Peshāwar, makes it possible to move forces into Afghānistān when they may be required."

The preceding quotations are taken from the Chapter on India in Mr Spenser Wilkinson's book,

The Great Alternative, one of the weightiest political works, in my judgment, published during the last half century. I shall have occasion again to refer to it later on. Of course the importance of the north-west frontier lies in this, that it has been the recognised road for the invaders of India during well-nigh three thousand years. The masters of Central Asia, whether Scythians, Greeks, Persians, Afghans or Turkomans, have made their way through the Khyber pass to the plains of Hindustān. Central Asia has now fallen under the domination of Russia. Her lines of railway, constructed, assuredly, not for commercial but for political and military purposes, traverse that vast region, and run almost to the gates of Herāt. Now Herāt is the key to Afghānistān, and Afghānistān is the key to India. At the present moment Russia is formally established close to Herāt, while the nearest British troops are at Chaman, 500 miles distant. That Russia has in view the occupation of Herāt and of Western Afghānistān, and eventually of Kandahār, and the gradual absorption of the whole country, who can doubt? And who can doubt her object? But on this subject let me quote the words of one who speaks regarding it with an authority to which I cannot pretend. "That the ablest soldiers of Russia," writes Colonel Durand in his fascinating book *The Making of a Frontier*, "believe in the possibility of conquering India, no one who has had the chance of studying the question can doubt. Her diplomatists may not consider the task one to be undertaken; they are fairly busy elsewhere. None the less do her tentacles creep cautiously forward toward our

Indian frontier. To-day, it is the Pamirs; to-morrow, it will be Chinese Turkestan or part of Persia which is quietly swallowed. For every point of possible attack gained is to her advantage ; and every man of ours who can be locked up in India, or guarding its frontiers when the Battle of Armageddon does come, must be withdrawn from the real chessboard, wherever that may be. This is the crucial point."

We were told by an eminent person, a few years ago, that Russophobia is "an antiquated superstition." That is a convenient way of labelling facts inconvenient to a party politician. For myself, I adopt the words of Earl Roberts in his masterly speech in the House of Lords on the 7th of March 1892. "I do not object to the appellation of Russophobe, if Russophobe means one who is convinced that the forces of civilisation will compel Great Britain and Russia to eventually meet in Asia, and who is equally convinced that, if Russia is ever allowed to cross the great Hindu Kush barrier, and possess herself of Afghānistān and the Borderland, an attack on India will be merely a matter of time. *This barrier Russia must never cross.*" Those last half dozen words contain the real solution of the frontier question. And here I shall return to the work of Mr Spenser Wilkinson, from which I quoted in an earlier part of this Chapter, and shall present the outlines of a masterly argument, occupying several pages, which the reader specially interested in the present subject will do well to peruse at large. The fundamental question, he observes, is whether for the purpose of resisting an army advancing from Central Asia towards India the most favourable battlefield is to be sought in the mountainous country of Afghānistān, or on the Indian, or on the Central Asian side of the mountains. There are those who tell us that the South African War has demonstrated the physical impossibility of a Russian conquest of India against a Great Power holding the passes and menacing from various points the invader's communications. But Mr Spenser Wilkinson is surely well warranted when he remarks, "A mountainous country lends itself conveniently to a resistance of which the purpose is delay, but when a decisive victory is necessary, a mountainous country is advantageous not to the defence but to the attack." Again, "To await attack on the Indian side of the mountains is objectionable, partly on the ground that it would enable the enemy, by choosing his own time for attack, to neutralise all the military disadvantages to which in theory it would expose him, and partly for the grave political reason that to permit an invading army to reach the valley of the Indus would be to put a premium upon every form of sedition." It follows "that the best form of defence is to meet the attack upon the side of the mountains remote from the Indus, Afghānistān being conquered and made into a British province, or such an alliance being secured with the rulers of the country as would ensure not only their resistance to Russia, but their readiness to receive and faithfully support a British army temporarily sent into the country, to aid in its defence." It must be confessed that the past does not afford much reason for

anticipating these good dispositions in the Afghan
rulers. Few thoughtful people can doubt that
one of the gravest of our many grave mistakes in
India, is our failure to occupy and hold Kandahār
years ago, as a safeguard against Russian advance
and aggression to our detriment in Afghānistān.
Even as I write, the death of Abdur Rahman opens
a prospect of disturbances in the fretful realm which
his iron hand held in awe : disturbances which may
give Russia her opportunity. Anyhow, sooner or
later, it is sure to come. And can any man of even
moderate intelligence doubt that she will seize it?
And then? Well, then, the Afghan question will
be re-opened in earnest. And England, as usual,
will pay the price—a deservedly heavy one—for
allowing the gravest interests of her empire to be
made the shuttlecock of politicians playing " the
party game."

CHAPTER XXI

THE CONDITION OF INDIA

NOTHING is commoner than to hear pæans of jubilation over the progress of India under British rule. Nor is there .any difficulty in finding grounds to justify such proud boasting. I touched upon this subject in a previous Chapter. Here let me return to it for a moment, and exhibit, more in detail, India's debt to British enterprise and British capital. First, then, India owes to England the greatest irrigation works which the world has ever seen—works upon which, from first to last, over £30,000,000 have been spent. In Hindustān, there are those on the Ganges, opened by Lord Dalhousie in 1854, and since vastly enlarged and improved : the total length of the main channels and branches of the two canals fed by this great river—I have before me the official returns for the year 1899—is 1096 miles, and the area irrigated by them is 1,605,740 acres. There is the Bari Doāb canal, 353 miles long, and irrigating 771,451 acres. There are the East and West Jumna canals, 488 miles long, and

274

irrigating 946,220 acres. There is the Sirhind canal, 319 miles long, and irrigating 782,730 acres. There is the Sone project, the portion of which already constructed extends to 367 miles, and irrigates 440,796 acres. There is the Chenab canal, opened in the spring of 1887, when it irrigated only 10,854 acres; and now, through a succession of extensions, irrigating a million and a half: in the near future it will irrigate two millions: the total length of its main channel and branches is 429 miles. A scheme of almost equal magnitude, from which, when completed, as great results may be expected, is the Jhelum canal, designed to irrigate the large tract of arid country lying between the town of that name and the Indus, to the south of the Salt Range mountains. Besides these vast undertakings there are many smaller works of a like kind which need not be enumerated here.

In the Bombay Presidency there are no irrigation canals, except in the subject province of Sind, where the waters of the Indus are brought upon its burnt-up soil by a number of canals all of much less magnitude than those just spoken of. But in the Madras Presidency, the works due, directly or indirectly, to the late Sir Arthur Cotton, one of the greatest hydraulic engineers that ever lived—if not the greatest—are upon a colossal scale and are of singular interest. His gigantic project for covering the whole face of India with a system of canals, which should serve both for irrigation and navigation, if it had been carried out—and many considerable authorities think that it could and should have been — would simply have transformed the material condition of the country. As it is, the achievements which he was permitted to accomplish are a splendid monument of his skill and patience, and an unending gain to the land where he spent the best years of his long and laborious life. And since I possess some personal acquaintance with them, I shall speak of them a little in detail.

The earliest of them are the works on the Cauvery and Coleroon Rivers, in the districts of Trichinopoly, Tanjore, and South Arcot, built by Cotton in 1835-36. They embraced the construction of two dams, or anicuts, the first at the head of the Coleroon, which had the effect of turning a portion of its waters into the Cauvery on the right, at the same time securing an abundant supply for the land in the Trichinopoly district on the left; the second, a still larger work, 70 miles lower down the Coleroon, which intercepted the water still flowing down that river, mainly through the deep sands in its bed, and provided an adequate supply for the Southern Taluks of South Arcot. The financial success of these Cauvery Delta works, which irrigate 954,123 acres, has been such as has seldom resulted from any public undertaking. The last official returns (1899-1900) give the percentage of net revenue on capital at 33.33 per cent. The increased value of private property, due to them, has been equally large, while in seasons of scarcity, these districts have not only been preserved from the horrors of famine, but have been able to pour large supplies of food into the adjoining regions.

Sir Arthur Cotton's next great work was the

Godavery anicut. In 1845 he laid before the Indian Government a project for building a dam across the river which flows through that district: a magnificent stream having its source in the Western Ghāts, fed by the almost unfailing south-west monsoon, and only needing the exercise of the genius which had brought prosperity to Tanjore and Trichinopoly, to convey its waters over the land on either side of it. The work was of greater magnitude, and presented more serious difficulties, than those on the Cauvery and Coleroon. The total breadth of the river at the point where it was decided to build the anicut was rather more than three miles and a half. But the stream was divided by three islands or *lankas*, and so the length of those portions of the dams whose foundations were in its bed was $2\frac{1}{4}$ miles. Even so, it was a stupendous work — the Dowlaishwaram branch of the anicut alone being of greater length than the two Coleroon anicuts put together. Moreover, unlike Tanjore and Trichinopoly, the Godavery district was comparatively destitute of irrigation channels, while in high freshes the river overflowed its banks, and flooded the surrounding country. The financial returns of these works are less than those of the Cauvery works, as the cost of keeping them up is greater. Still they yield over 15 per cent. They irrigate 749,612 acres: and they have converted a region once among the poorest in India into one of the most prosperous.

The Kistna anicut, built a few years later, though actually planned by Sir Atwell Lake, and carried out by Major-General Orr, was originally

projected by Sir Arthur Cotton, and was eventually
undertaken chiefly in consequence of his enthusiastic
advocacy.   It irrigates 589,354 acres, and yields
an interest of over 15 per cent. on the capital
expended.   The name of Cotton is still gratefully
cherished by the people of the district, as appears
from an address presented by the inhabitants of
Bezwada to Sir Mountstuart Grant Duff, when
Governor of Madras.   I give an extract from it :—

"As the huge volumes of water flowed gradually on, laden
with rich, fertilising yellow silt, gathered by the river in
its course through the Deccan, the enthusiastic General, Sir
Arthur Cotton, called it liquid gold! The anicut, with its
ramified canals, has certainly turned it into solid gold.
At one stroke the mouths of a hungry and dying people
have been filled with bread, and the coffers of the Government with money.   In place of dashing madly on to be
lost in the sea, the Kistna now spreads fertility and beauty
on all sides, and had your Excellency come at a later period
of the year, the extensive tracts of flat country between this
and the coast would present you with a sight worth seeing.   No
longer struggling for a bare existence, or held in the grasp
of money-lenders, the people rejoice among their smiling
crops, and the money-lenders have become almost extinct.
Even in famine years the Kistna never fails to do its duty,
and the dire poverty that existed during the childhood of
middle-aged men is almost forgotten in the general prosperity ; and it is meet that we should express gratitude to the
good Government that has done these great things for us."

But these works, great and important as they
are, do not by any means constitute the whole of
the boon conferred upon Southern India by Sir
Arthur Cotton.   He founded a school of hydraulic
engineering, which is still developing the resources
of other Indian rivers, and converting the "liquid
gold" which they contain into the "solid gold"

of the Bezwada address. On the Pennar river, in the Nellore district, on the Cortiliar, on the Palār, Cheyair and Vellār, in the districts of North and South Arcot and Chingleput, works have been carried out, which, though necessarily less productive than those on the three larger rivers, still considerably increase the food supply of the country. Further south, on the borders of the Madura district and of the native state of Travancore, there has lately been constructed an irrigation work, commonly known as the Periyār project, even more ambitious in design, and presenting greater difficulties of execution, than any as yet undertaken in India. It was grandly conceived, and has been perfectly executed. It consists in turning from west to east the course of the river Periyār, a large stream rising in the Travancore hills, which, flowing northward, has hitherto fruitlessly poured its fertilising treasure into the Arabian Sea. Now, by means of a great dam—the second greatest in the world—and of a tunnel, through the Ghāts, a mile and a half in length, it has been compelled to mingle with the Vaigai river, and the vast volume of water spreads plenty through the land as far as the Bay of Bengal. When fully completed, it will irrigate at least 150,000 acres for rice cultivation, and will feed half a million of people. Surely we may say, "These are imperial works, and worthy kings"; fit memorials of the ruling race.

Some of the canals * designed primarily for irri-

* Namely, the Orissa, Sone, and Midnapur canals in Bengal; the Ganges, Lower Ganges, and Agra canals in the North-West Provinces and Oude; the Western Jumna and Sirhind canals

gation serve also, more or less, for navigation. They constitute part of the work done by the British Rāj for opening up communication throughout the country. A great work it has been, covering India not only with metalled roads, but also with a system of railways, of which 23,763 miles were open for traffic on 31st March 1900.

Another result of British rule in India has been the initiation of mining industry. Coal is found principally, but by no means exclusively, in Bengal, where there are over 200 mines. The total output of coal in 1899 was nearly 5,000,000 tons. The outturn of Indian gold mines in the same year was 448,071 ounces.

Let us pass on to manufactures. India has taken rank as a manufacturing country, in virtue of the cotton industry, introduced in 1851 —"the most striking," according to Sir William Lee Warner, in his *Citizen of India*, "of all the benefits which British capital and British experience have conferred upon the labour of India." Thacker's *Directory* gives a list of one hundred and fifty-eight cotton mills. More than a hundred are in Bombay, many of them being owned by Hindus and Parsis. It appears from the official returns that there are in India 773 cotton ginning factories and cotton presses. The export of cotton is about 11,000,000 hundredweight.

in the Punjāb ; and the Godavery, Kistna, and Kurnool canals in Madras. Of the merely navigation canals the most important are the Calcutta and Eastern, 737 miles long, the Orissa canal, 102 miles long, and the Buckingham canal in the Madras Presidency, 262 miles long.

India also owes to the British connection the introduction and development of the tea industry. There are 735 tea gardens in the country: 211 being in Assam and 105 at Darjeeling. The average annual export of tea is not far short of 200,000,000 pounds. There are in the Madras Presidency and in Mysore 360 coffee estates, and these export annually some 32,000,000 pounds of coffee. There are 276 indigo concerns, and these export, annually, in good years, nearly 200,000 hundredweight of that commodity. There is an annual export of about 1,000,000 tons of jute—29 jute mills are in existence—and there is a like export of wheat.*

* The following tabulated statement, compiled from the official returns of the chief Indian exports, in the last five years, may be of interest :

		1895-6	1896-7 *	1897-8 *	1898-9	1899-1900
Rice	cwts.	31,152,000	28,274,000	26,747,000	37,942,000	32,271,000
Wheat & Flour	,,	10,665,000	2,510,000	2,898,000	20,203,000	10,262,000
Oilseeds	,,	13,672,000	11,398,000	12,553,000	19,280,000	15,775,000
Raw Cotton	,,	5,248,000	5,216,000	3,723,000	5,411,000	4,373,000
Raw Jute	,,	12,267,000	11,464,000	15,023,000	9,865,000	9,725,000
Hides & Skins	,,	1,114,000	996,000	1,275,000	1,110,000	1,735,000
Coffee	,,	291,000	211,000	225,000	270,000	281,000
Indigo	,,	187,000	170,000	134,000	135,000	111,000
Opium	,,	84,000	86,000	78,000	93,000	93,000
Tea	millions of lbs.	137.7	148.9	151.5	157.5	175.0
Raw Wool	millions of lbs.	31.0	28.4	30.9	28.0	31.9
Gold	value in lakhs of rupees	250	220	237	234	201

* Years affected by famine.

It should be noted that the export of indigo is falling off owing to the invention in Germany of a chemical dye stated to be quite equal to the vegetable extract. And the export of coffee is pretty certain to fall off, if France applies the maximum tariff against it.

There are also 160 rice cleansing mills, 85 saw mills, 9 paper factories, 135 tanneries, 106 iron foundries, 103 flour mills, 195 oil factories, and 26 tobacco factories; and all these industries sprang up during the reign of Her late Majesty. In short, as Sir William Lee Warner enthusiastically declares : " There is no direction in which British enterprise and capital are not pushing their way in order to extend the manufactures of India, and thus to open up to its vast population new trades and industries. The trade returns of Indian commerce, as well as the census figures of 'occupations or means of subsistence,' show plainly the magnitude of the revolution in the industrial life of India which is taking place. All this activity means new sources of income to the working men of India and profitable openings for its tradesmen and capitalists. The fact is too easily forgotten, and for centuries the country has had at its command coal, gold, petroleum, tea, coffee, and cotton, and yet it was unable to turn its wealth to account. Why was this the case? The country needed peace, enterprise, and capital, which it never secured until it fell under British administration."

To complete this pleasing picture, a few words must be said as to the great cities which British rule has called into existence in India. First in order comes Calcutta, in 1700 a mere collection of huts : now a city of palaces, with 850,000 inhabitants ; its rivers and docks crowded with craft of all nations ; its broad streets and spacious squares full of busy crowds, hurrying to and from its offices and shops, as it lies in the bright sunlight, white and radiant— one of the great markets of the world. Truly, indeed, it is but a whited sepulchre, standing, as it does, in a pestiferous marsh, and enveloped by an atmosphere like a perpetual vapour bath, fatal both to mental and physical vigour. All the greater, perhaps we may say, should be our admiration of the courage and enterprise which have made it what it is.

But, though the normal seat of the Government of India, Calcutta is outshone by that other great city which has grown up in the West under the British Rāj. Bombay, with its huge docks, its splendid, if incongruous buildings, its vast public works, is a magnificent memorial of English rule. In the commercial advantages of its position, as in beauty of scenery, it is unsurpassed by any of the cities of the East. It serves as a splendid gate of entrance to India. It is the most cosmopolitan of cities. Some forty odd languages may be heard in its bazaars, where Europeans, Arabs, Persians, Afghans, Negroes, Parsis, Jews, and Chinese jostle one another. It is a medley of all the religions, all the races, all the architectures, all the industries of the world. Its inhabitants amount to 770,000 : so that in population it ranks third among the cities of the whole British Empire, Calcutta ranking second.

The other great city of the Indian Empire, Madras, if it cannot rival the splendour of Calcutta and Bombay — which it certainly cannot—at all events greatly excels them in comfort as a residence for Europeans. Its roomy houses, surrounded by spacious lawns (compounds, as they are called) in its suburbs of Numgumbaukum and the Adyar, provide the space and air so grateful to Western

dwellers in the tropics; while the heat of its days—
a dry heat for the most part, which is much less
trying than a moist—is tempered by the perennial
sea breeze of the evening. It has grown up slowly
around the Fort or Factory of St George, established in 1639. Its population at the present time
is just over half a million.

Such are some of the more striking items of the
progress achieved by India under British rule. Unquestionably they are tokens of prosperity. But of
whose prosperity? Of the prosperity of the people of
India? The test of a people's prosperity is not the
extension of exports, the multiplication of manufactures or other industries, the construction of cities.
No. A prosperous country is one in which the
great mass of the inhabitants are able to procure,
with moderate toil, what is necessary for living
human lives, lives of frugal and assured comfort.
Judged by this criterion, can India be called prosperous?

Comfort, of course, is a relative term. It cannot
be measured by an absolute standard. In a tropical
country, like India, the standard is very low. Little
clothing is required there. Simple diet suffices.
Artificial wants are very few, and, for the most part,
are not costly. The Indian Empire is a peasant
empire. Ninety per cent. of the people live by the
land. It has been happily said that the aspiration
of Horace is pretty much that of the Indian ryot :—

> "Hoc erat in votis ; modus agri non ita magnus,
> Hortus ubi et tecto vicinus jugis aquæ fons,
> Et paulum silvæ super his foret."

An unfailing well of water, a plot of land and a bit

of orchard—that will satisfy his heart's desire, if, indeed, you add the cattle needful to him : "the ryot's children," as they are called in many parts. Such is the ryot's ideal. Very few realise it. An acre may stand for the *modus agri*, the necessary plot of land. A man to an acre, or 640 men to the square mile, is the utmost density of population which India can comfortably support, except near towns or in irrigated districts. But millions of peasants in India are struggling to live on half an acre. Their existence is a constant battle with starvation, ending, too often, in defeat. Their difficulty is not to live *human* lives—lives up to the level of their poor standard of comfort—but to live at all and not die. People in England very generally talk of rice as the staple food of the natives of India. But in truth rice is the staple food of only one-third of the population. The rest live on a coarse kind of pulse and millet. And the water drunk by them is, as a rule, detestable, and is the fruitful source of disease. There is, I suppose, no country in the world where the live stock is so wretched. Speaking generally, it may be said that during two-thirds of the year the cattle are kept just above starvation point—not, let me add, through the fault of the owner, who, as a rule, is merciful to his beasts. The native plough is of the roughest description and penetrates but a little way into the soil. It costs the ryot two or three rupees. He could not afford anything better, and probably would not buy it if he could. For his habit of mind is intensely conservative.

Such is rural life in India for vast numbers.

And it is by no means superfluous to insist on this truth. The popular conception of the wealth of the "gorgeous East" is singularly deep-rooted, nor are there wanting grave authors whose authority seems to have sanctioned the common misconception regarding the riches of India. Thus, so careful and exact a writer as Elphinstone remarks that "the fertile soil and rich productions of India have been long proverbial," without any indication of the great limitations which should be placed upon the proverb to which he refers. It is true, indeed, that the productions of India are "rich," but it is only a small portion of the total area of her soil which can be pronounced to be fertile. Taking the country as a whole, we find vast tracts of dry and poor land, producing either nothing, or the most scanty crops, while the luxuriant vegetation popularly associated with the tropics is met with only in "the flowery lap of some irriguous valley." The greater part of the agriculture of the country is dependent upon the periodical rains, and their failure for even one year is enough for widespread misery; while a recurrence of the misfortune in the next, raises the popular suffering to the most frightful pitch.

We may truly say that in India, except in the irrigated tracts, famine is chronic—endemic. It always has been. A Mohammedan historian, describing the drought which ravaged the Deccan 250 years ago, tells us, "Thousands of people emigrated and many perished before they reached more favoured provinces; vast numbers died at home, whole districts were depopulated, and some

had not recovered at the end of forty years." Such
events are constantly recurring in the annals of the
country.

During the first eighty years of the nineteenth
century, 18,000,000 of people perished of famine.
In one year alone—the year in which Her late
Majesty assumed the title of Empress—5,000,000
of the people in Southern India were starved to
death. In the district of Bellary, with which I
am personally well acquainted — a region twice
the size of Wales—one-fourth of the population
perished in the famine of 1876-1877. I never shall
forget my own famine experiences ; how, as I rode
out on horseback, morning after morning, I passed
crowds of wandering skeletons, and saw human
corpses lying by the roadside, unburied, uncared
for, and half devoured by dogs and vultures : how,
sadder sight still, children, "the joy of the world,"
as the old Greeks deemed, had become its ineffable
sorrow, and were forsaken by the very women who
had borne them, wolfish hunger killing even the
maternal instinct. Those children, their bright
eyes shining from hollow sockets, their flesh
utterly wasted away, and only gristle, and sinew,
and cold shrivelled skin remaining, their heads
mere skulls, their puny frames full of loathsome
diseases, engendered by the starvation in which
they had been conceived, and born, and nurtured—
they haunt me still. Famine relief is organised
now—at all events in the territories directly under
British rule—in a way undreamt of then. The
Government does not now allow its subjects to
starve. Yet famine still slays its thousands and

hundreds of thousands in British India. The Government cannot interfere to prevent mortality caused by disease, springing from, or greatly helped by inanition. And here I should like to quote an extract from Lord Curzon's letter to the Lord Mayor of London concerning the recent famine. The letter is dated 23rd May 1900.

"We are struggling with a famine greater in its intensity over the areas afflicted than any previously recorded visitation. I say greater, because, though fewer persons will, as I hope, die in this famine than in any previous droughts, yet incomparably more persons are suffering, and are only being saved from death by the combined exertions of Government and of private effort, and because the loss of crops and cattle, amounting to an almost complete denudation of the stricken area, are immeasurably greater in the present instance than in any previously recorded affliction. . . . In the middle of May 1897, an area of 205,000 square miles, with a population of 40,000,000 persons, was affected. In the middle of May 1900, the figures are 417,000 square miles (or nearly one-fourth of the entire extent of the Indian Empire), and 54,000,000 persons. In May 1897, 3,811,000 persons were in receipt of Government relief; in May 1900, the total relieved is 5,607,000. At the present moment, if we take the whole of the afflicted regions in British India, 15 per cent. of the entire population are being supported by Government (in many parts the proportion is nearly double)."

Is this the picture of a prosperous country? Is there, then, any remedy for this widespread and ever-recurring suffering, arising from the abject poverty of a vast proportion of the population of India? The first step towards answering the question is to ascertain the causes of that poverty.* The

* I have at p. 183 called attention to the constant depletion of India by the withdrawal of a third of her net revenue as one cause of her impoverishment.

most obvious cause is, of course, the failure of the crops when the periodical rains on which they depend do not fall. Another is the great pressure of the population on the soil *in certain districts.* I would call special attention to these last words : for as Sir William Hunter has pointed out, "there is plenty of land in India for the whole population : what is required is not the diminution of the people, but their more equal distribution." India is not over-populated. Nor is it true that the population is largely or rapidly increasing. That is evident from the recent census. During the ten years ending on the first of March 1901, the addition to the population in the whole of India was under 7,000,000. There seems to be no sort of warrant for the assertion sometimes made, that the day is not far distant when the 287,000,000 in India will be doubled, nay, trebled, quadrupled.

A third cause of the ryot's penury is his perpetual indebtedness to the usurer. Custom—the great guide of his life—demands lavish expenditure at marriages and funerals. To obtain the means for it he borrows, in utter heedlessness of consequences, the requisite money. And debts of that sort are viewed by him as something more than mere legal obligations—concerning which he is not always very scrupulous. They are debts of honour, secured by a sentiment of piety, a sanction of religion. Under native rule, they were seldom enforced by process of law. Under British administration, the usurer resorts freely to the courts, the result being that the ryot is often mercilessly stripped of all his property, real and personal. The picture which Sir

George Wingate has painted is too true : " This miserable struggle between the debtor and creditor is thoroughly debasing to both. The creditor is made by it a grasping, hard-hearted oppressor ; the debtor, a crouching, false-hearted slave. It is dis-heartening to contemplate, and yet it would be a weakness to conceal the fact, that this antagonism of classes and degradation of the people which is fast spreading over the land is the work of our laws and our rule." The usurer, in fact, appropriates the unearned increment. It appears from an official return now before me, that in Assam nearly 68 per cent., in the North-West Provinces nearly 47 per cent., in the Central Provinces nearly 37 per cent., and in Madras nearly 18 per cent. of the landlords are of the money-lending class. Under the British Rāj the land has, to a large extent, passed away from the hereditary cultivators. And this change is fraught with grave political danger in some parts of India : for example, in the Punjāb. I may note, in passing, that next to the usurer as a cause of impoverishment, comes the lawyer. The natives of all parts of India are not only intensely but reck-lessly litigious. They love the jangle of a lawsuit, and do not stop to count its cost. I suppose it was the consideration of these things which caused Sir Madhava Rao to write, " The longer one lives, observes, and thinks, the more does one feel that there is no community on the face of the earth, which suffers less from political evils, and more from self-inflicted, or self-accepted, or self-created, and there-fore avoidable evils, than the Hindu community."

I should judge from this that an unduly high

assessment of the land-tax—which certainly would be a political evil—was not regarded by Sir Madhava Rao as one of the causes of India's poverty. There are, however, some weighty, and many noisy publicists, who take a different view.

Such, then, are the causes of the ryot's penury : the occasional failure of the crops from want of water ; the too great pressure of the almost entirely agricultural population on the soil in certain districts; the ryot's own improvidence ; and, in the judgment of some, as we have just now seen, the unduly high assessment of the land-tax. Let us inquire how far the first three of these evils are remediable, and whether the fourth does, in fact, exist.

First, as to the deficiency of the water required by the cultivator. Now it is certain that there is, as a rule, no want of moisture in India. The average rainfall there is considerably in excess of the rainfall in this island. But instead of being spread all over the year, as with us, it is confined to a few months.* The south-west monsoon, which

* Nor does it descend upon the tracts where it is most wanted. There can be no question that the reckless and wholesale destruction, during long centuries, of the wood which covered the mountain slopes has injuriously affected the rainfall. Humboldt remarks, "Indirectly the want of rain and the absence of vegetation act and react upon each other. It does not rain because the naked sandy surface, having no vegetable covering, becomes more powerfully heated by the solar rays, and thus radiates more heat, and the absence of rain forbids the desert being converted into a steppe or grassy plain, because without water no such organic development is possible." I should observe that the work of the Forest Department has hitherto been rather to protect such forests as still remain than to replace those which have disappeared.

brings the water supply to the more northerly and westerly parts of India, begins early in June and ends in September. The north-east monsoon, which supplies the greater part of the Madras Presidency, prevails from the middle of October to the middle of December. The problem is to store the water thus brought to the country. When it is most wanted, Indian rivers are comparatively dry. The very nature of the climate and the inequality of the rainfall of India, have led to the practice of irrigation from time immemorial. It is absolutely necessary in Sind and the Punjāb. It is hardly less necessary in the region about Delhi and Agra, and in the tract lying between the Aravalli and Chittur hills, in the eastern part of the Bombay Presidency, in the greater part of the Nizam's territory, and in the ceded districts of Madras, in Mysore, and the Carnatic. It is so far necessary in the Eastern Provinces of Madras, as well as in Central India, that without it a failure of the periodical rains must produce a most serious dearth. It is unnecessary in the rest of India—which " rest," it will be seen, includes a comparatively small portion of the area of the country.

I have in an earlier page touched upon the work done by the British Rāj for irrigation. But I should here note that many of the systems now administered by the Department of Public Works are an inheritance from previous rulers of India who, some in greater and others in less measure, made provision for this great need. The net result of their labours is very considerable. Indeed, it has been said—and there is no exaggeration in the saying —that the works executed by them for the storage

of water "surpass in immensity what are conven-
tionally esteemed the wonders of the world." Many
of their anicuts still hold in check the fertilising
streams for the thirsty lands. And the districts
comprehended in the Madras Presidency owe to
them 60,000 tanks, with about 35,000 miles of embankment, and 350,000 masonry works. Some of
the vastest of these tanks are of unknown antiquity;
for example, the Virānum tank, with its area of 35
square miles, and its embankment of 12 miles; the
Cauverypauk tank, with its embankment of 4 miles
"rivetted along its entire length with stone"; the
Chembrumbaukum tank, looking like a picturesque
inland sea. But of these 60,000 tanks, some 10,000
have been allowed to fall out of working order. I am,
of course, well aware that it does not always pay to
repair a tank. But it is a patent fact that many
have been allowed to go to ruin through the persistent neglect of petty works, which would have
been in the highest degree remunerative if executed
in time. There can be no doubt, as it seems to me,
that the Government is bound to keep in good
order existing irrigation works, not only for the
sake of the revenue, nor even for the higher motive
of increasing the provision of food for the country,
but also because of the capital which on the faith of
its virtual engagement to supply water, has been
invested by the holders of the contiguous lands.

No doubt a great deal more may and should be
done in India, for irrigation on a large scale, by the
construction both of tanks and of river dams. Vast
volumes of water—the country's most precious
possession—now steadily running to waste, might

be retained and utilised, to the incalculable relief of human suffering and the vast increase of the Empire's wealth. There is a considerable volume of water in every large Indian river, even during the driest season ; and during the monsoon freshes there is an enormous quantity. And here I will quote some weighty words from a valuable paper recently contributed by General Frederick Cotton to *Blackwood's Magazine*.

" We have an example set us by some engineer of former ages, which is much to the point, of what is wanted at the present day. Quite in the south of the peninsula there is a river—the Viga, if I remember right—the water of which was so admirably utilised that only in exceptional years did a drop of it reach the sea. The river was dammed here and there, and the channels leading the water off for irrigation had tanks to store water for the perfecting of the crop after the freshes ended—which is exactly the principle on which the great rivers should be treated as far as possible. There has been an idea of late that if water is to be stored it will be necessary to find sites for enormous lakes in which to collect it. It is true that the larger the reservoirs are, the cheaper the cost of storing water will be. But if the value of the water is what I hope I have proved it to be, that is not the first consideration. To explain how sites may be found everywhere, I would ask my readers to look at the Trigonometrical Survey map of the peninsula of India, where they will find that almost any shallow valley is made by an embankment across it into a retaining reservoir. These tanks, so-called, being dependent upon the local rains, are valueless in seasons of drought, and in consequence do nothing to secure the peninsula from famine. This would not be the case if a stream, led from a never-failing river, ran through the country to supply them. Indeed our great hydraulic engineer, Sir Arthur Cotton, had a scheme for making such an artificial river to secure the supply of these tanks. But I only call attention to the possibility to show that, as every part of India has its valleys, there is no good reason why water should not be stored on the old native river Viga system in all parts of the country."

But there is one more, and a less costly means of storing water, as to which I will cite another professional writer, who appears to me well to merit serious attention. In a very striking article in *The Indian Review* of June 1900, Mr Alfred Chatterton writes as follows :—

"The storage of water is likely to become the great Indian engineering problem, and attention will doubtless be paid to that portion of the rainfall which is absorbed by the earth and disappears from sight, to find its way by deep and tortuous subterranean passages to the sea. Two and one-half million wells irrigating fully ten million acres of land attest the importance of the underground storage of water, and indicate that in this direction there are immense possibilities. Underground water has never, in India, been studied properly by engineers or geologists, and wells are sunk in a happy-go-lucky manner to a hap-hazard depth. They are constructed with primitive appliances and at small cost. Expectations are not usually great, and as they are generally realised the people are content. Some wells dry up in the hot weather, some wells always respond to the demands that are made upon them, and nothing is really *known* about their capacity to supply water. A few elementary calculations, however, will show that the quantity of water drawn from most wells is but an insignificant fraction of the stores that must be below, and which are continuously passing away through permeable strata till they ultimately reach the sea. . . . Very few wells exist which are known to yield enough water to offer any inducement to employ mechanical arrangements for pumping water from them. It is easy to see why this is so. The depth of the well is limited by the fact that the primitive methods of sinking in vogue among the ryots prevent them going more than a few feet below the hot weather level of the water. With an engine and pump to keep the well dry much greater depths might be attained, and possibly the supply of water enormously increased. . . . It is sufficiently demonstrated that the employment of oil engines for pumping water is a perfectly practical method, and can be employed with advantage whenever the quantity of water to be dealt with amounts to half a cubic per second. The initial capital outlay is beyond the means of the ordinary ryot, but it is not beyond those of many landowners, and if only sufficient interest could be aroused among them in the improvement of their estates, the ultimate benefit to the country at large would be incalculable.

" The two and one-half million wells in India represent a capital outlay not far short of forty crores of rupees, and what is wanted almost as much as new wells is the systematic improvement of those already in existence. Many are probably far too shallow and others are too small and do not present a sufficient area for percolation. To jump holes from 10 to 30 feet in depth and a few inches in diameter at the bottom of some wells is not a very difficult matter, and the value of the tube would probably be greatly enhanced if the rock at the bottom were loosened by the explosion of two or three small charges of dynamite. To run short adits in the hot weather from the bottoms of many wells is perfectly feasible, and both methods if tried would yield results far in excess of the cost. Yet these things are not done because the ryots do not know of their value ; and even if they did, they would regard them with suspicion as innovations to be classed with many other attempts, by Europeans, at agricultural improvements. These are suggestions which have been tried in other places with success ; but so little do we know about this subject, that I put them forward with diffidence, and simply with a view to drawing attention to the urgent necessity for a systematic attempt to investigate the conditions under which the stores of subterranean water exist."

This must suffice as to the means of improving the water supply of India, and so, of increasing the production of food stuffs in that country. The next question is how to remedy those evils tending to the ryot's penury, which Sir Madhava Rao describes as " self-inflicted, self-accepted, and self-created " evils

arising from the Hindu's blind improvidence, reckless expenditure, unwillingness to shake off im-
poverishing customs and ingrained litigiousness.
I suppose a radical reform of them could be effected
only by a complete transformation of character.
Legislation can do little. What it can do, and
ought to have done long ago, and of late years has
done, to some extent, is to protect the ryot against
the usurer, who is ever ready to eat him up. "To
some extent," I say: a beginning has been made.
But it is only a beginning. I am well aware of the
difficulties by which the subject is surrounded; of
the danger that measures intended to repress and
punish the mischievous usurer may hamper the
perfectly legitimate operations of the useful banker.
But the nefariousness of turning the misery, folly,
or ignorance of the borrower to the enrichment of
the lender is unquestionable. As unquestionable
is it that more stringent measures in restraint of
this crime of usury are wanted in India. They will,
I trust, commend themselves to the Indian legis-
latures as sounder views prevail than those now
generally current on the subject. And in order to
indicate what those sounder views are, I will here
quote a page, in which I have endeavoured to
expound them, from my *First Principles in
Politics*.

"Conspicuous among agreements against public
policy should be reckoned those tainted by usury;
although in these, for the most part, there is not that
free consent which is of the essence of a contract,
overmastering distress having fettered the borrower's
volition. Assuredly, it is the function of the State

to repress such pacts, not only through its civil courts, but, in gross cases, through its criminal tribunals. The essence of usury is extortion. It is extortion under colour of law, which is, from an ethical point of view, more heinous, in itself, than extortion by threats or by physical violence. We are sometimes told—we are often told—that the reprobation of usury as wrong, is an exploded medieval superstition. It appears to me that the principle which guided the philosophers and legislators of former ages in this matter is valid for all time, and that Shylock is quite as noxious in the twentieth century as he was in the sixteenth ; nay, more noxious, for his abominable operations are conducted upon a much wider scale. True it is that the function of money in this modern world is other than it was in the Middle Ages, where other economical conditions prevailed. In those ages almost all farming or producing had for its object direct use, not sale ; rent, in the sense of a competition price paid for the occupation of land, was unknown ; the vast developments of commerce and industry now surrounding us, would have appeared the wildest and most fantastic dreams. Money is not now, as it was in earlier periods of civilisation, a mere medium of *private* exchange for the purposes of housekeeping. It is a medium of *commercial* exchange and fruitful lending; it is no longer barren, a thing to be hoarded in cellars and chests. In the mercantile society of modern life, commercial credit is an essential factor ; and to put money out to interest, in genuine business adventures, is, in itself, not immoral because, in itself, not unfruitful. For

what usury really means—this is the definition of
the Fourth Lateran Council—is 'the attempt to
draw profit and increment, without labour, without
cost, and without risk, from the use of a thing that
does not fructify.' And in spite of the change of
circumstances, there can be no question of the vast
prevalence of usury, thus understood, in our own
day; and as little of its malignancy. Here,
assuredly, it is the function of the State to inter-
vene, for the protection of individual rights and of
its own supreme right."

Something, I am convinced, may be done, and
ought to be done, in mitigation of the ryot's penury,
by further well-considered legislation for delivering
him, as completely as possible, from the toils of the
usurer, who—this must never be forgotten—should
be carefully distinguished from the harmless necessary money-lender. Something may be done, too,
to relieve the too great pressure on the soil of
the population in certain districts. No doubt Sir
William Hunter is well warranted in writing, "in
proportion as we can enforce good government
under the native chiefs of India, we must expect to
see a gradual movement of the people into the feudatory States." Moreover, wise measures might, and
should be, adopted and encouraged, for the diversion
of a portion of the population now engaged in
agriculture, to other means of subsistence. And it
is cheering to find that the better educated and
more influential natives are alive to the necessity of
working for this end. Thus the Punjāb Zemindāry
Association, in the prospectus of its proposed weekly
Journal, *Indian Wealth*, expresses its desire " to

cure the growing poverty of India by pressing the claims of the development of the material resources of the country, by reviving the old arts and industries of India, encouraging her trade and commerce to be undertaken by educated classes, and teaching the people of India the advantages and principles of co-operation and self-help, by advancing the cause of agriculture and agricultural education, and also by providing the most useful information on political, moral, social, and educational subjects."

The right lines upon which to work are here clearly, if rather broadly indicated. As we have seen, something considerable has been accomplished under the British Rāj for the development of the material resources of India. Her trade and commerce have greatly increased. But is it possible to revive her old arts and industries? There are men still alive who can remember the days when weaving was a prosperous occupation in the country, and millions lived on it. That industry has been destroyed by the deluging of the country with cheap Manchester goods made by machinery, and by the refusal of protection to Indian weavers. But on this subject let us hear Mr J. N. Battachārya, who writes thus in his work on *Hindu Castes and Sects* :—

"The weavers of India were, until recently, a very pros-perous class, but the importation of machine-made piece goods from Manchester has, of late, thrown many thousands of them out of employ. These dragged on a life of poverty for some years, and at last either died of semi-starvation, or were forced by necessity to become menial servants or tillers of the soil. As the hand-looms of India are now constructed, the best weaver, with the assistance of his whole family to dress and card the yarn, cannot turn out more than five yards of cloth a day, but the motive power required to work such a loom is very slight, and the machinery might certainly be so improved as to enable one man to work at least half-a-dozen similar looms. It is said by some, that if the weaving industry of India has ceased to be paying in consequence of the competition of foreign piece goods, the Indian weavers should, despite their caste prejudices, take up some other line of business. The principle of Free Trade has been invoked in order to justify our indifference, and that of our Government, to the sufferings brought on the millions of our weavers by the import of Manchester piece goods. But neither the science of Political Economy, nor the principle of Free Trade, requires that when foreign goods make their way into the markets of a country, the people of it should make no efforts to save the sinking vessel of their own industries. The principle of Free Trade insists only upon absolute freedom being left to the consumer to buy his goods from the cheapest and best market according to his own judgment.

"In this country domestic industry alone suits the genius of the people, and, so far as the weaving industry is concerned, it is certainly not desirable, even from the point of view of political economy, that the hand-looms should be superseded by steam-power looms. Domestic industry does not involve any expenditure on account of supervision, mill buildings, or brokerage to company promoters. Domestic industry cannot render it necessary to collect raw materials or manufactured goods in one place to such an extent as to involve the risk of any heavy loss by fire, shipwreck, or damp. The skill possessed by a people of a country in any art being, according to the science of political economy, an important part of its capital, India is at present suffering a prodigious loss, through allowing the skill acquired by her weavers by generations of practice to remain unemployed and become deteriorated. A very little improvement in the hand-looms might not only enable them yet to hold their own against foreign competition, but save the heavy loss to the Indian people and to the world which now takes place in freight, insurance, warehousing, and other charges incurred unnecessarily for the benefit of Manchester. The weavers of India are themselves too ignorant of the mechanical sciences, and too poor, at present, to make the necessary improvements in their looms, by their own capital and exertions. The matter is one which deserves the earnest attention of our publicists."

I fully agree with Mr Battachārya that this matter well deserves the earnest attention of our publicists. Again, in many parts of India, excellent sources of iron ores are found. But they are absolutely neglected except in Chutia Nagpore and the Central Provinces, on account of the importation of hardware from Europe. It is much to be regretted that Indian cutlery, padlocks, swords, nails, and hooks are superseded by the far inferior work of English factories. And I must commend to my readers Mr Battachārya's weighty remarks on the position of the Indian Kamars, or workers in iron :—

"If, in spite of their skill, the Indian Kamars are not able to hold their own in the local markets, their failure is not to be attributed to any fault on their part. The products of a domestic industry must necessarily be more costly than machine-made wares. Then, again, the out-turn of the small manufactories to be found in the remote villages cannot be so easily collected together, in a commercial focus, for distribution and exchange, as the produce of large foundries. The result of these causes is very strikingly illustrated by the fact that while the worthless padlocks turned out by the factories in Birmingham are to be had in every hardware shop in India, and sell in millions, the Kamars padlocks of the ancient types, which are considered by all to be the best and safest mechanisms of the kind, cannot generally be had either for love or money, and can be procured only by special order to some workmen whose very names are generally unknown—the advantages of the modern art of advertisement being as yet quite unknown to them. Circumstanced as India now is, the revival and improvement of the iron industry of the country seems to be well-nigh beyond the bounds of immediate possibility. It is only the patronage of the railways that can render large foundries pecuniarily successful. But the Indian railways are all practically in the hands of the Indian Government, and knowing well how our rulers are handicapped by the party politics of the Home Government, no reasonable man can expect them to deny their patronage to the English manufacturers for the sake of benefiting an Indian industry." *

There can be no question whatever that the great development of machinery in England, in the early decades of the present century, was a terrible blow to the prosperity of India. Free Trade was a second. The native handicrafts, sustained by no capital, relying merely on traditional skill and personal initiative, perished, and hideous manufactured wares took the place of their beautiful products. And the Government, fast bound in the sophisms of the old "orthodox" political economy, with its gospel of *Laissez-faire*, did nothing to remedy the evil. It is certain that the neglect of Indian industries is one of the causes of the present distressed condition of India. The raw products of the country are exported, manufactured, and sent back to be sold in the Indian market. Foreign workmen thus take the bread out of the mouths of starving millions in India. Sir M. M. Bhownaggree very justly remarks, " When it is remembered that most of the articles that form the export trade leave the country devoid of any native skilled manipulation, they ought to cease to mislead one into the

* I quote Mr Battachārya's words as I find them ; but it is right to add that the State railways are now encouraging local iron manufactures with the approval of the Secretary of State.

belief that the industrial capacity of India is at all commensurate with her natural wealth of produce, or that the value of her exports of raw material can be at all an index of her inherent capacity for increased industrial production, if scientifically and technically trained, as it is too often mistakenly supposed to be the case."

There would seem to be two remedies for these evils. The first is, the introduction and maintenance by the Government of industrial and technical education. The fostering of the aluminium industry in the Madras School of Arts is a specimen of what might be done, and ought to be done, on a large scale; although we can hardly hope that it will result in the productions of such fabrics as the muslin of Dacca, the pottery of Sind, or the silk brocade of Ahmedabad. The second is the protection of Indian industries in respect of foreign competition. Surely it is high time that the stupid old shibboleths of Free Trade were discarded. Surely the wonderful progress made by the nascent industries of America, Germany, and Japan, under a protective tariff, should open the eyes of the most theory blind.

Lastly, it is said that the ryot is overtaxed; that the Government takes more than its fair share of the produce of the land. This is not the spontaneous cry of the ryots themselves. They are largely inarticulate—"theirs but to do and die," we may say. Besides, the natives of India have been accustomed, for countless generations, to the most enormous and oppressive taxation—taxation often extending to half the produce of their fields. They have been accustomed to see its proceeds lavished on dancing-girls, devotees, beggars, and all manner of superstitions, filthy and fantastic. And they have made no complaint. It has all seemed to them in accordance with the fitness of things. Even the Emperor Akbar, the best of Indian rulers, is said to have laid it down : " Enough shall be left to the cultivator for the keep of himself and his family till next season, and for the seed for sowing. The rest is the land-tax." A very considerable authority, Mr O'Dwyer, tells us : " The native system in practice limited its demand only to the ability of the landowner to pay. The British Government abandoned the rights it inherited, placed itself in the position of a rent-charger in place of that of a proprietor, and left a margin of profit—the difference between a rent and a rack rent—in the hands of the actual tillers of the soil."

Of course, this does not prove that the cry as to over assessment, raised on behalf of the ryot by Anglicised Hindus and their English sympathisers, is unfounded. In some parts of India—the Central Provinces, for example—there seem to be good grounds for it : the incidence of the land-tax is curiously unequal. The question, which certainly deserves the fullest inquiry, can only be glanced at here. Personally, I incline to think that the rigid inflexibility of the land-tax is a greater evil than its weight. Under native rule the Government took a certain share of the gross produce ; or rather, in most cases, an uncertain share ; for whatever the theory as to its amount, in practice as much was usually taken as could be got without breaking the

ryot's back. But then, the claim of the Government did not arise till the crop was reaped. Under
the present system—I am of course speaking of the
districts where there is no permanent settlement—
there is a rigid cash assessment on each field, pay-
able before the crop is marketed, nay, possibly while
it is still unripe. And to obtain it, the ryot goes
off to the village Shylock. No doubt the intention
of the British Rāj in making this change was excellent. It was the result of a zeal for ordered government and systematised administration. But, unfortunately, the zeal was not according to knowledge.

And—to return to a thought on which I touched
in a previous Chapter—it is perhaps to this want
of knowledge, or of insight, let me rather say, that
we should attribute the chief errors which have
marred our rule in India. To grasp the secrets
of a civilisation such as that which we found
there, is no easy task; a civilisation which has
grown up amid influences, and under conditions,
utterly alien from us. The four great agents
which have shaped the morals and manners, the
creeds and customs, of the Western World are:
Greek philosophy, Roman jurisprudence, Christianity and Teutonic traditions: of these the
existing European order is made and moulded.
In India we have the outcome of the very
different forces which have been glanced at in
the preceding pages. Hence the great gulf
which is fixed between its civilisation and ours.
The average middle-class Englishman does not

in the least realise how great that gulf is. He
thinks it can be bridged over by a few Acts of
the legislature, and a system of public instruction.
| If I wanted to point to a type of him, I do not
know where to find a better than Lord Macaulay.
The ideals, beliefs, aspirations of Macaulay, were
those of the middle-class Englishman. And they
were adorned by the great rhetorical gift, due to
his Celtic blood, I suppose, which he employed,
so successfully, to recommend them to the admiration of mankind. Of English narrowness, insu-
larity, self-sufficiency, he is an almost perfect
specimen. Contempt for Oriental literature, philosophy, art, could hardly be carried further than
he carried it. " Not English," he said, of these
things ; and in that he found their sufficient
condemnation. He laboured with all his might
to substitute things English for them. And he
easily carried his countrymen with him.

But he was also a typical Englishman in other,
and more precious, qualities — in rectitude of
intention, in love of justice, in devotion to duty.
And it is precisely because of these qualities that
the English, in spite of defects of character and
temperament, have accomplished the great things
in India, which only eyes blinded by hatred can
fail to discern, and which only minds warped by
prejudice can undervalue. They are the qualities out
of which sprang the greatness of that older imperial
race whose traditions and methods England has
largely inherited. | They were the dominant qualities
of that great Moslem ruler, who, as a poet of our
own has admirably fabled, wrapt with future times,

beheld the far-off accomplishment of the work for which he lived.

"I dream'd
That stone by stone, I rear'd a sacred fane,
A temple, neither Pagod, Mosque, nor Church,
But loftier, simpler, always open-doored
To every breath from heaven.   .   .
.   .   .   .   I watch'd my son,
And those that followed, loosen stone from stone
All my fair work ; and from the ruin arose
The shriek and curse of trampled millions, even
As in the time before : but while I groan'd,
From out the sunset pour'd an alien race,
Who fitted stone to stone again, and Truth,
Peace, Love, and Justice, came and dwelt therein :
Nor in the fields without were seen or heard
Fires of Suttee, nor wail of baby-wife
Or Indian widow : and in sleep I said,
' All praise to Alla by whatever hands
My mission be accomplish'd.' "

Yes, that is the task lying before England in India—few nobler have been set before any nation —to accomplish the mission of Akbar.

APPENDICES

APPENDIX A

The following Proclamation, creating a new frontier province, was issued on the 25th October 1901 :—

WHEREAS the following territories, that is to say, the districts of Peshawar, Kohat, and Hazara (as altered by the Notification of the Punjāb Government, No. 994, dated the 17th October 1901), the Bannu and Marwat Tahsils of the district of Bannu, and the Tank, Dera Ismail Khan and Kulachi Tahsils of the district of Dera Ismail Khan (as altered by the Notifications of the Punjāb Government, Nos. 992 and 993, dated the 17th October 1901), are part of the dominions of His Majesty the King, Emperor of India ;

AND WHEREAS it is expedient that the said territories, which are now under the administration of the Lieutenant-Governor of the Punjāb, should be formed into a separate Province and constituted a Chief Commissionership under the administration of a Chief Commissioner :

KNOW ALL MEN, AND IT IS HEREBY PROCLAIMED, that His Excellency the Viceroy and Governor-General of India in Council, in exercise of the powers conferred by section 3 of the Government of India Act, 1854 (17 and 18 Vict., c. 77), and with the sanction and approbation of the Secretary of State for India, is pleased hereby to take the said territories under his immediate authority and management, on and with effect from the 9th day of November 1901 ; and further to direct that, on and with effect from the said 9th day of November 1901, the said territories shall be formed into a separate Province and constituted a Chief Commissionership, to be called the Chief Commissionership of the North-West Frontier Province, and to be administered by a Chief Commissioner.

By order of His Excellency the Viceroy and Governor-General of India in Council,

J. P. HEWETT,
Secretary to the Government of India.

GOD SAVE THE KING-EMPEROR.

APPENDIX B

STATEMENT OF THE NET REVENUE AND EXPENDITURE OF THE INDIAN EMPIRE, 1899-1900.

NET REVENUE.

LAND REVENUE, ETC.—

Land Revenue, ...	£16,444,825	
Forests, ...	1,232,685	
Tributes from Native States, . . .	586,603	
		£18,264,113
OPIUM—Net Receipts, ...		2,670,589

TAXATION—

Salt, ...	5,573,775	
Stamps, ...	3,225,920	
Excise, ...	3,810,539	
Provincial Rates, ...	2,495,458	
Customs, ...	3,058,795	
Assessed Taxes, ...	1,292,729	
Registration, ...	287,164	
		19,744,380

MISCELLANEOUS RECEIPTS—

Mint, ...	289,183	
Miscellaneous, ...	99,382	
		388,565
EXCHANGE, ...		80,949

TOTAL NET REVENUE, . . .		£40,986,698

NET EXPENDITURE.

DEBT SERVICES—

Interest on Public Debt (other than that charged to Railways and Irrigation) and other Obligations, . . .		£1,342,283

MILITARY SERVICES—

Army, ...	£14,165,743	
Buildings and Roads : Military . . .	801,782	
Special Defence Works, ...	874	
		14,968,399
COLLECTION OF REVENUE, ...		4,448,839

COMMERCIAL SERVICES—

Post Office, ...	– 126,068	
Telegraph, ...	– 105,891	
Railways, ...	– 76,756	
Irrigation, ...	– 136,387	
	– 445,102	
FAMINE RELIEF AND INSURANCE, ...		2,098,848

CIVIL SERVICES—

Civil Departments, ...	9,597,544	
Miscellaneous Civil Charges, ...	3,513,138	
Construction of Railways (charged against Revenue in addition to that under Famine Insurance), ...	2,356	
Buildings and Roads : Civil, ...	2,891,990	
Provincial and Local Surpluses or Deficits, .	– 206,220	
		15,798,808

TOTAL NET EXPENDITURE, . .		£38,212,075

INDEX

ABDUL FAZL, 87
Abdur Rahman, his death, 273
Aborigines of India, the, 31
Adi-Granth, the, 149-150
Administration of India, the British account of, 176-182
Afghānistān, British occupation of, 109
Ahmed Shāh, 97
Ain-y-Akbāri, the, 88
Akacamukhiris, 134
Akbar, 79-89 ; alleged dictum of, on the land-tax, 304
Akbarnāmeh, the, 87, 88
Alā-ud-dīn, 74
Alexander the Great, his Punjāb Campaign, 58
Alps, the, compared with the Himālayas, 8-10
Amir Ali, Mr Justice, on Moslem polygamy, 222-223 ; on Moslem dancing women, 237
Andaman Islands, the, 27
Anquetil Duperron, 151
Aravalli Mountains, the, 18
Arbuthnot, Sir Alexander, on Christian Missionaries in India, 169
Architecture, Indian, 254-258
Aristocracy, the Indian, Lord Lytton on, 248
Arnold, Sir Edwin, his description of dancing girls, 234

Art, penetrates the life of the Hind people, 258, 265-266 ; Moham medan, in India, 88, 93, 258
Arts, the Fine, in India, 253-267
Aryans, the, invade India, 32 occupy Hindustān, 33 ; thei present numbers, 34 ; their lan guage, 37-38
Ascetics, Hindu, 134
Asoka, 59-61
Assam, account of, 15
Assaye, the battle of (1803), 107
Astrologer, the Indian, 207
Auckland, Lord, his Governor Generalship, 109 ; his Afgha policy, 268
Aurungzebe, 93-96
Auvaiyār, her poetry, 41
Avadhutas, 134

BĀBER, 77, 79
Baden-Powell, B. H., his *Lan Systems of British India* quote 17 ; referred to, 185
Baines, Mr, on Christian Mission in India, 163-164
Balance Sheet of the India Empire, 313
Balūchistān, 14
Bangobāsi, the, on Indian Cor gresses, 243

315

Barber, the, his importance in Hinduism, 132, 207

Baroda, account of, 21

Barth, his *Religions of India* quoted, 42, 45, 120-121, 122-123, 137

Battachārya, Mr Jogendra Nath, on caste, 198-200 ; on exclusion from caste, 202-204 ; on Indian dwelling houses, 214 ; on the ruin of the Indian weavers, 300-302 ; on the Indian Kamars, 302-303

Beiram, 79-81

Benares, 135-136

Bengal, account of, 15

Bentinck, Lord William, his Governor-Generalship, 109

Berar, account of, 22

Beschi, Father, 42, 156

Bhagavat-Gīta, the, 45-49, 125

Bhownaggree, Sir M. M., on the industrial capacity of India, 303

Bible Societies, their work in India, 167

Birdwood, Sir George, his *The Industrial Arts in India* quoted, 215-217, 255-256, 258-260, 261-267

Black Hole of Calcutta, the tragedy of, 102

Blandford, Mr, his *India, Burmah, and Ceylon* quoted, 24-25, 27

Bombay, comes into possession of the English, 100 ; account of, 283

Bombay Presidency, the physical characteristics of, 22

Brackenbury, Sir Henry, on the financial relations of India and England, 189

Brāhmanas, the, 44, 121

Brahma, 128

Brahmaputra, the, 7, 11-12, 15

Brahmins, growth of their powei 122 ; religion of the educated 128 ; power attributed to, 132 immemorial pre-eminence of, i India, 195, 200 ; ascendency o at the present day, 200 ; caste and sub-castes of, 201

Buddha, Gotama, *see* Sākya-Muni

Buddhism, account of, 138-144

Bunsen, on the date of Zoroaste 152

Burmah, physical characteristics o 24-27 ; annexation of, 108, 115 condition of women in, 221

Burmese language, the, 80

Burnell, Dr, on early Christianit in India, 154

CALCUTTA, account of, 282-283

Caldwell, Bishop, 170

Canals, Indian, 274-280

Canning, Earl, his Governoi Generalship and Viceroyalt 112-114

Caste in India, 194-205

Casuistry of Hindu Pundits, 204

Catholicism in India, 155-159

Cattle in India, 285

Central Indian Agency, the, 20-21

Central Provinces, the, account o 21

Chandragupta, 59

Chatterton, Mr Alfred, on th underground storage of water ii India, 295-296

Chindwin, the, 25

Christianity in India, 154-170

Cicero, his definition of supersti tion, 131

Civil Service of India, 179-180 complaints as to the exclusion o natives from, 245-248

Clive, Lord, his career, work, an character, 101-103

Coal mines in India, 280
Coffee industry in India, 281
Collector-Magistrate, the, his functions, 177-179
Competitive examinations, 247-248
Condition of India, the, 274-308
Congresses, Indian, 238, 242-243
Cornwallis, the Marquis, his Governor-Generalships, 105, 108
Cotton, Sir Arthur, his work in India, 275-278
Cotton, General Frederick, on storage of water in India, 294-295
Cotton industry in India, the, 280 ; annual export of, from India, 281
Councils, Executive, 176, 177 ; Legislative, 177
Cramming in India, 244, 246
Crook, Mr, on Indian dancing girls, 231
Curzon, Lord, on the Indian Famine of 1900, 288
Custom, the guide of life in India, 289

DALHOUSIE, the Marquis of, his Governor-Generalship, 110-112
Dancing girls, Hindu, are among the endowed ministers of the temples, 131 ; some account of, 231-237 ; Mohammedan, 237 ; attempt to provide a Christian variety of, 237
Darius Hystaspes, his invasion of the Punjáb, 58
Darmestetter, Professor, on the Zend-Avesta, 152
Dāsis, 232
Davids, Mr Rhys, his Buddhism quoted, 124
Deccan, the meaning of the word, 13, 18 ; physical characteristics of, 18-23 ; languages of, 38-39

Defects of the British Government in India, 190-192, 306-307
Demagogues, Indian, 244
Deutsch on Mohammedanism, 145
Dēvidāsis, 232
Dhuleep Singh, 111
Dhya cultivator, the, his method, 22
Diamper, the Synod of, 155
Dravidians, the, 31-34 ; their languages, 38-39 ; their literature, 41-42
Dryden's conception of Aurungzebe, 95
Dubois, the Abbé, on the difficulty of making converts to Christianity in India, 162-163 ; on British rule in India, 173 ; on caste, 192 ; on Brahminical rule in India, 200 ; on marriage among the Hindus, 225 ; on wifely fidelity among the Hindus, 230
Dufferin, the Marquis of, his Viceroyalty, 115
Dupleix, 101
Durand, Col., on the Imperial Service Troops, 175-176 ; on a Russian invasion of India, 270
Dutt, Mr Shoshee Chunder, on caste, 195, 201-202 ; on the prospects of the caste system, 205 ; on Indian wives, 230

EAST INDIA Company, its genesis, 99 ; its suppression as a ruling body, 113
Eggeling, Herr, on the Brāhmanas, 44
Elgin, the Earl of, his Viceroyalty, 114
Ellenborough, the Earl of, his Somnath Proclamation, 69 ; his Governor-Generalship, 107
Elphinstone, his account of Mobammed Cāsim, 66-67 ; on Akbar's

scheme of government, 82 ; on Akbar's religion, 85 ; on Shah Jehān's administration, 92 ; on the fall of the Moghul Empire, 97 ; on the fertility of India, 286

Empress of India, proclamation of the, 114

English, the, their conquest of India, 98-115

Everest, Mount, 10

Exports and imports of India, 188, 281

Exports, Indian, tabulated statement of, 281

FA HIAN, 62

Famine in India, 286-288

Feizi, 86-87

Ferdousi, 72

Ferguson, Mr, on Hindu architecture, 254

Fielding, Mr, his *The Soul of a People* referred to, 139, 221

Filon, M., on attempts at self-government in India, 239 ; on the Anglicised Hindu, 244

Finances of the Indian Empire, 182-187

Fīruz, 76

Forest Department, the Indian, 188

Franciscans, the, their work in India, 156

Francis Xavier, St, his work in India, 156

Freeman, Mr, on Mohammed, 145

Free trade, a terrible blow to the prosperity of India, 303 ; its discredited shibboleths, 304

French, the, struggle of British with, in India, 100-102

Frontier Province, the, creation of, 14, 176, 311

Frontier Question, the, 268-273

GANESA, 126, 135

Ganges, the, 12, 15, 136

Geiger on Zoroastrianism, 151

Ghāts, the Eastern and Wester 19-20

Godavery, the, 19, 20

Golab Singh, sale of Kashmīr t 110, 174

Gold, annual export of, from Indi 281

Gore, Mr F. St John, his accou of the Rājah of Kulu's domestic ties, 227-228

Gough, Lord, 110

Gough, Mr, on the *Upanishads*, 5

Governor, the Indian, 177

Grant Duff, Sir Mountstuart, on th material progress of India und British rule, 187-188 ; on th preponderance of Brahmins i the public offices of India, 200

Grihin, the, 211

Growse, Mr, his view of caste, 19t on the institution of caste, 19 197

Guicowar, his state, 21 ; his impor ance, 175

Guilds, trade, in India, *see* Tra Guilds.

Guptas, 65

Guru, the, 133, 208-210

HARDINGE, Lord, his Governo Generalship, 109-110

Hastings, the Marquis of, h Governor-Generalship, 108

Hastings, Warren, his career, wor and character, 104-105

Heber, Bishop, on Akbar's tomb,

Hides, annual export of, from Indi 281

High Courts in India, 180

Himālayas, the, principal cha acteristics of, 6-12

Hinduism, difficulty of defining, 119; Vedic, 120-121; Brahminical, 121-123; its struggle with Buddhism, 123-125; modern, 125-137
Hindustān, proper sense of the word, 5, 13; divisions of, 13; physical characteristics of, 13-17; irrigation works in, 274-275
Hindustāni language, the, 38
Hiouen Tshang, 63-64
Holkar, his country, 21
Hooker, Sir Joseph, introduces into England a beautiful species of rhododendron, 10
Houses, Indian, 214-217
Humāyon, 79
Humboldt, on the want of rain and the absence of vegetation, 291
Hunter, Sir William, his *Statistical Survey*, 4; on the products of Hindustān, 16-17; on the products of the Deccan, 23; on the products of Burmah, 26; on Catholic Missions in India, 157, 158; on the legend of the origin of castes, 198; on the population of India, 289; on the probable influx of population into the feudatory states of India, 299
Hyderabad, account of, 22

IDDESLEIGH, the first Earl of, on the proposal to admit natives more freely to the Covenanted Civil Service of India, 246-247
Ilbert Bill, the so-called, 114
Imperial Service Troops, the, 175
Impurity, place of, in the Hindu religion, 131, 232, 233-234
India, its vastness and variety, 3-4; divisions of, 5-6; its physical characteristics, 5-27; its races, languages, and literature, 31-51;

its history, 55-115; its religions, 114-117; some principal aspects of to-day, 122; depletion of, 183, 288
Indigo, annual export of, from India, 281
Indus, the, 7, 11, 14
Industries, new, in India, 280-282
Inquisition, the, of Goa, its achievements, 155
Irawadi, the, 24-25
Irrigation works in India, Firūz's, 76; Krishna Rāya's, 78; British, 274-279; need of, 291-292; antique, 292-293; additional required, 293-296

JACOBITE Christians in India, 155
Jainism, 144-145
Jehānghīr, 89-92
Jesuits, their work in India, 156-157
Jizia, the, abolished by Akbar, 82; restored by Aurungzebe, 94
Jumna, the, 12, 15
Justice, administration of, in India, 180-182
Jute industry in India, the, 281

KĀLI, 128, 135
Kālidāsa, 49
Kamars, the Indian, 302
Kanishka, 61
Karma, 123, 141-143, 144
Karāh-prasād, 150
Karta, the, 210-211
Kashmīr, scenery of, 8; area of, 10; sold to Golab Singh, 110, 174
Kāsim, his exploits and fate, 66-67
Kerr, Mr, his *Domestic Life in India* quoted, 161
Kewhom, the, 24, 25
Khāfi Khān, on Shāh Jehān's government, 92; on Aurungzebe's old age, 95

Kolarians, the, 31 ; their dialects, 39

Köppen on the Buddha's teaching, 58

Krishna-Rāya, 78

Kshatriya, theoretical duties of a, 198

Kulu, the Rājah of, his domesticities, 227-228

Kural of Tiruvallular, the, 41

Kush, the Hindu, 6

Kutāb-ud-dīn, 73

LAKE, Lord, 107

Land tenure, systems of, in India, 185-187

Land-tax in India, 183-186, 291, 304-306

Law in India, 180

Lawrence, Lord, his Viceroyalty, 114

Lee Warner, Sir William, on the cotton industry in India, 280 ; on Indian progress, 282

Legislative Councils in India, 177

Leslie, Miss, her *The Dawn of Light* quoted, 229-230

Lingam, the, 126-127, 131, 166

Lorinser, Dr, his view of the *Gita*, 48

Lyall, Sir Alfred, on Mohammedanism, 148

Lytton, Earl, his Viceroyalty, 114 ; on the Indian aristocracy, 248 ; his frontier policy, 269

MACAULAY, Lord, on misgovernment in Bengal, 102 ; on Clive, 103 ; on Warren Hastings, 104 ; on Lord William Bentinck, 109 ; a type of the middle-class Englishman, 306-307

Machinery in India, 264-265, 266, 300, 302-303

Maclean, Dr Charles, his *Madr Manual* referred to, 32

Madhava Rao, Sir, on the evi which afflict the Hindu con munity, 290

Madras, city of, account of, 283

Madras Presidency, the physic characteristics of, 22-23 ; irrig tion works in, 275-279

Mahābhārata, the, 45-49 ; its hi torical value, 49, 56

Mahal Rachtra, 21

Mahalwāri system, the, 187

Maine, Sir Henry, on Englis ignorance of India, 3 ; on Lor Cornwallis's permanent settl ment, 186 ; on municipal instit tions in India, 240

Makti, 161

Malguzāri system, the, 187

Mānasarowar, Lake, 7, 11, 20

Manchester, India's prosperity sacr ficed to, 300-301

Mantras, 132, 133, 207

Manu, the Laws of, quoted referred to, 57, 122, 197-198, 20 223, 225, 226, 228

Marks, frontal, 127, 132

Marriage, Christian conception o 218 - 221 ; among Buddhist 221 ; among Mohammedan 221-223 ; among Hindus, 22 231

Max Müller, his *Lectures on t Science of Language* quoted, 3 39 ; his translation of a Ved hymn quoted, 43 ; debt due t in respect of the *Sacred Books the East*, 51 ; on modern Hind ism, 135

Mayo, the Earl of, his Viceroyalt 114

Megasthenes, his account of Hindu stān, 59

Mendicants, religious, in modern Hinduism, 133-134
Milton on spiritual and civil liberty, 84
Mīrā Bāī, 137
Missionaries in India, Catholic, 155-159; Protestant, 159-162, 165-170
Mlechhas, 65, 127
Mohammed, his character, doctrine, and work, 145-146; his legislation on marriage, 221-224
Mohammed of Ghazni, 68-72
Mohammed Ghorī, 73
Mohammed Tughlak, 74-76
Mohammedanism, 145-148
Moksha, 144
Mongolians in India, 31-33
Monsoon, the Indian, 11, 291-292
Mulleck, Mr B., on the Karta, 210-211
Municipalities in India, 187, 238-241
Munro, Sir Thomas, introduces the ryotwāri settlement in Madras, 186; on the employment of natives in the public service of India, 250-251
Music, Indian, 253
Mussulmans, first appear in India, 66; invasion of India by, 66-67, 96-97; character of Indian, 147; injustice of their exclusion from their fair share of public posts in India, 147
Mutiny, the Indian, causes of, 112, 204
Muttuswami Ayar, Sir T., 252
Mysore, the Maharājah of, his country, 22; his importance, 175

NĀDIR SHĀH, his invasion of India, 96
Nagas, 134

Nairs, the, their polyandry, 226
Nānak Shāh founds the Sikh religion, 96; his teaching, 149-151
Narasimmiyengar, Mr V. H., on Christian missions in India, 164
Nerbudda, the, 18, 19, 20, 21, 22
Newspapers, the Indian vernacular, 244-245
Nicobar Islands, the, 27
Nirvāna, 142, 143
Nizam of Hyderabad, the, his country, 22; his importance, 174
North-West Provinces and Oudh, account of, 15
Northbrook, the Earl of, his Viceroyalty, 114
Nucki Talao, 255
Nūr Jehān, 90-92

O'DWYER, Mr, on the native land-tax system, 305
Oil seeds, annual exportation of, from India, 281
Oudh, account of, 15; annexation of, 111
Opium, duty on, 187; annual export of, from India, 281

PADROADO, the, 158
Painting in India, 254
Pāli language, the, 38
Pānipat, first battle of (1526), 77; second battle of (1556), 79; third battle of (1761), 97
Paramanahavas, 134
Party Game, the, penalty for playing, 273
Parsis, the, their history and number, 35; their religion, 151-153
Permanent settlement, Lord Cornwallis's, 185
Plassy, battle of (1757), 102

Plough, the Indian, 285
Police, the Indian, 181
Polygamy among Mohammedans, 222 ; among Hindus, 226-228
Pondicherry, the settlement of, founded, 100 ; captured, 101
Pope, the Rev. Dr, on the Tirāga Chintāmami, 41
Population of India, constituents of, 34-35, 241-242 ; alleged density of, 285, 289
Potters, Indian, 261-262, 265
Prākrit dialects, the, 37-38
Pratinoksha, the, quoted, 143
Prosperity, true test of a country's, 284
Protestantism in India, 159-160
Provinces of Akbar's dominions, 82 ; of the Indian Empire, 174
Public works in India, 274-280
Punarbhava, 123
Pundits, Hindu, their casuistry, 204
Punjāb, the, account of, 13-14
Purānas, the, 44
Purification after childbirth among the Hindus, 229
Purity, Christian doctrine of, 218-220
Purohit, the, 207-208

RAGHUNATHJI, Mr K., his monograph on the dancing women of Bombay quoted, 236-237
Rainfall in India, 291
Rāj, the British, 173-193
Rājputāna, account of, 14-15
Rājputs, the, establish themselves in Rājputāna, 73 ; their seventeen principalities, 174 ; chivalrous and truth-loving, 249
Rāmāyana, the, 45 ; its historical value, 49, 56
Registered voters in India, 240
Religions of India, 119-170

Representation, popular, in Indi 238-241
Rhys Davis, Mr, on the disappea ance of Buddhism from Indi 64 ; on the Buddha's teachin 124
Rice, cultivation of, in India, 16, 2: 26 ; the universal food of th Burmese, 27 ; annual export o from India, 281
Ripon, the Marquis of, his Vice royalty, 114-115
Risley, Mr, on caste, 200
Roberts, Earl, on the Frontie Question, 271
Runjeet Singh, 110
Ryot, the Indian, 284-285, 304
Ryotwāri system, the, 186

Sacred Books of the East, grea value of the translations from th Sanskrit in, 51
Saktists, 126, 129, 131
Sākya-Muni, his religion, 57-58 123-124, 138-144
Samsāra, 123
Sankarachārya, 125-126
Sanskrit language, the, som account of, 36-37
Sarasvatī, 128
Sātpur Hills, the, 18, 22
Sayce, Professor, on Sanskrit, 36 37 ; on the modern Aryan lan guage of India, 38 ; on the isolat ing languages, 40 ; on the *Veda* 42-43
Scindia, his country, 21
Scythians, the, their inroads int India, 33 ; their invasion o India, 65
Sebektegin, 68
Self-government in India, 236 252
Shāh Jehān, 92-93

Sherring, the Rev. Mr, on caste, 195 ; on dancing girls, 233
Shrāda, a, 211-214
Shaving, Hindu superstition concerning, 132
Sikh religion, the, 149-151
Sīlāditya, 63-64
Sin, conception of, in Hinduism, 120-121, 130, 132, 234
Sind, account of, 14
Siva, 125-127, 130, 135
Sivajī, 96
Smriti, 120
Sobrāon, battle of (1845), 110
Soma, 121
Somnath idol, the, legend of, 69
Sruti, 120
Stephens, Thomas, visits India (1578), 99
Strathnairn, Lord, 112
Sūdra, theoretical duties of a, 198
Sultans, Mohammedan, of the Deccan, 78
Sung Yun, 62
Sutlej, the, 13, 20
Sutti, tolerated by Akbar, 83 ; abolished by the British Government, 109 ; unknown in the Vedic religion, 121

TĀJ MAHĀL, the, 93
Tālikot, the battle of, 78
Talukdāri system, the, 186
Tamerlane, his descent on India, 76-77
Tanhā, 140, 143
Tank, meaning of the word, 17
Tanks in India, 17, 292
Tantras, the, 45, 128
Taylor, the Rev. Isaac, on Islām, 146
Tea industry in India, 281
Telang, Mr K. T., on the date of the Bhagavat Gīta, 48

Temples, Hindu, their grandeur and solemnity, 255-256 ; British neglect of the conservation of, 257
Textile fabrics of India, 259-260, 266, 304
"Thomas," the traditional introducer of Christianity into India : disputes concerning, 154
Thread, the sacred, 132-133
Thugs, 131
Tibeto-Burman languages, 39-40
Tippu Sultan, 105, 106, 157
Tirāga-Chintāmami, the, 41
Tocqueville, M. de, on the British conquest and government of India, 98, 189-190
Trade Guilds of India, 263
Truths, the Four Noble, 141

UNIVERSITIES, the Indian, founded by Lord Dalhousie, 111 ; their work, 244
Upanishads, the, 49-51, 122-123
Urdhvatalines, 134
Usurer, the, in India, 289-290, 297
Usury, the true view of, 297-299

VAISHYAS, 195-198
Varuna, 120
Vedānta philosophy, the, 49-51, 125
Vedas, the, 42-44, 119-121
Viceroy of India, his authority, 176
Vijayanagar, the kingdom of, 77-78
Vikramāditya, 65
Village, the Indian, its immemorial institutions, 206-207, 262, 266
Vindhya Mountains, the savage inhabitants of, 4, 32, 33, 165 ; divide Hindustān from the Deccan, 13, 18 ; account of, 18-19
Virginity, place of, in Christianity, 219-220
Vishnu, 127-128, 129, 130, 135

WANDIWASH, battle of (1760), 101
Warner, Sir William Lee, on pro-
gress in India, 281, 282
Weber, on the religion of the Indo-
Aryans, 121 ; on Indian music,
253
Wellesley, the Marquis, his Gover-
nor-Generalship, 106-108
Wellington, the Duke of, his work
in India, 107
Wells, irrigation, in India, 295
Wheat, where produced in India,
16, 21 ; export of, from India, 281
Wheeler, Mr Talboys, on the pros-
pects of Mohammedanism in
India, 148
Widows, Hindu, 224-225
Wilkins, Mr, his *Modern Hinduism*
quoted, 129, 212 ; on Indian
Mussulmans, 147
Wilkinson, Mr Spenser, on the
Frontier Question, 269, 272-273
Williams, Sir Monier, his transla-
tion of the Bhāgavat-Gīta quoted
40-48 ; on the transfer of th
worship of Brahmā to th
Brahmins, 128 ; on Christianit
in India, 160, 161
Wilson, Mr Andrew, his compariso
between the Himālayas and th
Alps, 7-10 ; on the parallelis
between the Western Ghāts an
the Himālayas, 20
Wingate, Sir George, on debto
and creditor in India, 290
Wool, annual export of, from India
281

YOMA Mountains, the, 25
Yoni, the, 127, 131, 166

ZEMINDĀR, meaning of the word
185
Zemindāri system, the, 185
Zend-Avesta, the, 152-153
Zoroaster, 152

PRINTED BY OLIVER AND BOYD, TWEEDDALE COURT, EDINBURGH

SD - #0047 - 040422 - C0 - 229/152/19 - PB - 9781330026298 - Gloss Lamination